FORCES OF WARMACHINE

PROTECTORATE OF MENOTH

CREDITS

WARMACHINE created by
Matt Wilson

Project Director
Bryan Cutler

Game Design
Matt Wilson

Lead Designer
Jason Soles

Additional Development
David Carl
Brian Putnam

Art Direction
Kris Aubin

Lead Writer
Douglas Seacat

Additional Writing
Simon Berman
David Carl
Matt DiPietro
Jason Soles
Matt Wilson

Continuity
Jason Soles

Editing
Darla Kennerud
Sheelin Arnaud

Cover Illustration
Andrea Uderzo

Illustrations
Daren Bader
Chippy
Eric Deschamps
Ilich Henriquez
Imaginary Friends Studios
Jeremy Jarvis
Mark Gibbons
Marek Okon
Lucio Parillo
Dave Rapoza
Brian Snoddy
Andrea Uderzo
Franz Vohlwinkel
Chris Walton
Eva Widermann
Kieran Yanner

Concept Illustration
Chris Walton
Matt Wilson

Graphic Design/Layout
Kris Aubin
Kim Goddard
Josh Manderville
Stuart Spengler

Studio Director
Ron Kruzie

Miniature Sculpting
Sean Bullough
Gregory Clavilier
Christian Danckworth
Roy Eastland
Chaz Elliot
Pete Flannery
Todd Harris
Bobby Jackson
Werner Klocke
Aragorn Marks
Mike McVey
Ben Misenar
Jerzy Montwill
Paul Muller
Edgar Ramos
Jose Roig
Ben Saunders
Steve Saunders
Jim Warner
Kevin White
Jeff Wilhelm
John Winter

Resin Caster
Sean Bullough

Miniature Painting
Matt DiPietro
Ron Kruzie
Allison McVey
Mike McVey
Quentin Smith
Rob Stoddard

Hobby Manager
Rob Hawkins

Terrain
Rob Hawkins
Alfonzo Falco

Photography
Kris Aubin
Kim Goddard
Rob Hawkins
Stuart Spengler

Development Manager
David Carl

Development
Michael Faciane

Product Line Coordinator
Rob Stoddard

Creative Manager
Ed Bourelle

President
Sherry Yeary

Chief Creative Officer
Matt Wilson

Executive Assistant
Chare Kerzman

Marketing Coordinator
William Shick

Customer Service
Adam Johnson

Convention Coordinator
Dave Dauterive

Community Manager & Staff Writer
Simon Berman

Volunteer Coordinator
Jack Coleman

No Quarter EIC
Eric Cagle

Licensing & Contract Manager
Brent Waldher

Production Director
Mark Christensen

Technical Director
Kelly Yeager

Production Manager
Doug Colton

Production
Trey Alley
Max Barsana
Alex Chobot
Doug Colton
Joel Falkenhagen
Joe Lee
Michael McIntosh
Jacob Stanley
Benjamin Tracy
Clint Whiteside

Sys Admin/Webmaster
Daryl Roberts

Infernals
Jeremy Galeone
Peter Gaublomme
Joachim Molkow
Brian Putnam
Gilles Reynaud
John Simon
Donald Sullivan

Playtest Coordinator
David Carl

Playtesters
Greg Anecito
Kris Aubin
Alex Badion
Simon Berman
Ed Bourelle
Dan Brandt
Erik Breidenstein
David Carl
Kevin Clark
Jack Coleman
Our Player Community
Dave Dauterive
Michael Faciane
Joel Falkenhagen
Rob Hawkins
All Field Test Participants
Adam Poirier
Douglas Seacat
William Shick
Jason Soles
Rob Stoddard
Chris Walton
Erik-Jason Yaple

Proofreading
Ed Bourelle
Dave Dauterive
Darla Kennerud
William Shick
Rob Stoddard
Brent Waldher

THE ROAD TO SALVATION

FACTION BACKGROUND

The Protectorate of Menoth is a nation forged in turmoil and utterly dedicated to the will of an ancient and unforgiving god: Menoth, the Creator of Man. Led by the scrutators, a ruthless priest caste, the Sul-Menites of the Protectorate have initiated a great crusade for the singular purpose of spreading the Creator's dominion across the face of Caen.

Although the faith of the Sul-Menites is ancient, their nation is of more recent origins, having arisen from the Cygnaran Civil War that was sparked to bring Cygnar back to proper worship of the Creator. Following their defeat, the Menites bided their time in the harsh lands east of Caspia; there they built an army in secret, preparing for the day when they could defy those who sought to control them and seize hold of their own destiny.

Now the Protectorate stands as a formidable power, armed with both righteous weapons of war and the resolve of faith. They have amassed a fervent host ready to march forth to enlighten the vast heathen countries for Menoth's greater glory. Their armies sweep across Immoren as a holy tide, darkening the skies with the soot and smoke from the holy flames of their crusade.

PLAYING PROTECTORATE OF MENOTH

The Protectorate army is characterized by an unwavering faith that manifests as layers of protective measures designed to thwart the most determined foes. Spells, feats, and abilities combine to weave an intricate veil of protection over the Menite forces. Even when the faithful inevitably fall in battle, their sacrifice serves only to solidify the army's resolve or bolster its strength. Often, by the time an enemy successfully unravels this puzzle it is too late to turn the tide.

Protectorate warjacks are typically sturdy and economical machines capable of taking a beating and then striking back with powerful maces, flails, and conflagrations. With the proper support, however, these warjacks become unparalleled in both resistance to enemy attacks and the devastation they can cause. The songs of the Choir of Menoth, the divine magic of priests and warcasters, combines with the expertise of the vassals to make even the lowliest instrument of the Creator's wrath into an unstoppable killing machine. With the blessings of the hierarch . . .

**Let Your Righteous Wrath
Burn the Unbelievers!**

TABLE OF CONTENTS

Visit: www.privateerpress.com

Privateer Press, Inc. 13434 NE 16th St. Suite 120 • Bellevue, WA 98005

Tel (425) 643-5900 • Fax (425) 643-5902

For online customer service, email frontdesk@privateerpress.com

First printing: February 2010. Printed in China.

Forces of WARMACHINE: Protectorate of Menoth . . . . ISBN: 978-1-933362-60-1 . . . . . .PIP 1027

Forces of WARMACHINE: Protectorate of Menoth Hardcover . . . ISBN: 978-1-933362-61-8 . . . . . .PIP 1028

KNOWLEDGE IS POWER
PROTECTORATE-OCCUPIED LLAEL

Vice Scrutator Vindictus walked into the audience chamber of the hierarch with the austere confidence that was the hallmark of a man of his caste and station. His mask was burnished to shine like a mirror, his robes pristine, his warcaster armor immaculate. He showed no discomfort at having been summoned, though he knew Severius had gained information on matters he had hoped to keep quiet a little longer.

He passed the vigilant ranks of Knights Exemplar and Flameguard as well as clusters of priests to stand in the open floor of the chamber. Ahead of him light streamed through high stained-glass windows to fall on Hierarch Severius. The hierarch stood before a throne built to his specifications, a duplicate of the one in Imer. The Covenant of Menoth held a place of honor adjacent to this throne and elevated from the floor on a wide dais. Its chosen attendants stood unmoving but watchful, prepared to open the sacred relic's metal-inlaid cover if the hierarch needed to refer to its passages or to escort it should its presence be required elsewhere. The room was the largest hall of what had once been the Thunderhead Fortress, the old headquarters for the Order of the Golden Crucible. Efforts were underway to expand the temples of the city and build one at its heart more worthy of a hierarch. Even here the muffled sound of distant construction could be heard.

Vindictus offered his deepest bow to the hierarch, demonstrating the measure of his regard and respect. "Menoth watch over Your Holiness, and bless the Northern Crusade." This litany was immediately followed by the traditional refrain among those present and watching, "Mighty is the Creator, blessed his chosen priest!"

Severius spoke sharply to those around him. "Leave us." The others made a quick exodus, leaving only the Covenant's attendants and a pair each of Exemplar bastions and cinerators, who stood unmoving behind the hierarch's throne.

Both in their scrutator masks, the two great priests were in some regards similar, but any closer examination revealed many differences. The hierarch was attired in his more ornate vestments, with a weighted omophorion draped across his shoulders and the holy miter settled atop his head. His robes and armor were lined with gold that reflected the sun's light. Vindictus' armor had its own unique silhouette, with its solid mass around his chest and shoulders, and graceful pipes from his arcane turbine extended from his back. Near Severius was his Staff of Authority, standing perpendicular to the floor seemingly without support, as its base was set into a mount in the flooring designed for that purpose. The light shone upon this staff as well, and its Menofix gleamed as if lit by an inner fire.

"Vice Scrutator Vindictus, it would seem you have been busy." Hierarch Severius' strong voice betrayed no sign of his age. Since reading the Covenant aloud, the man was revitalized and more formidable than ever. "You recently returned from an excursion, one that brought surprising rewards. I find it puzzling you would not rush here to deliver this news personally."

"I did not wish to come to you with an incomplete account, Your Holiness. I would not distract you with trivialities."

"Come now! Capturing one of our great enemies is hardly trivial. There is no need for humility, Vindictus. Or to speak so formally when we are alone."

"You do me too much honor, Your Holiness." Vindictus showed no signs of lowering his guard. He had served Severius too long to trust that anything he said would not be used to gauge his commitment to the faith. In making the choices he had made, Vindictus had begun to cross a precarious bridge, and he must be very careful not to stumble. In the weeks and months ahead, Hierarch Severius would determine who he could trust to stand by him. Those he deemed a threat would be crushed.

"What I have heard of this account puzzles me." Severius added in a casual tone. "I am told Great Prince Vladimir Tzepesci sent a proposal to my attention, and yet I heard nothing of its contents. It would seem this messenger was intercepted . . . by your servants." Vindictus kept his head bowed but could still feel Severius' stare upon his brow, like a physical weight. This called to mind the circumstances two weeks earlier whereby he had embarked on this particular path.

A messenger rushed up to Vindictus, panting and wheezing. The vice scrutator had been occupied seeing to the refueling and repair of his warjacks, most particularly a Reckoner he had named "Refuter of Heresy" that had served him well in numerous hard-fought battles over the last two years. Vindictus took some pride in this machine, which had long been steeped in the cleansing prayers of the choir. He had augmented these sanctifications by ordering the words of the True Law inscribed in small but exacting print along its armored plates. Invariably the mechaniks failed to minister to the warjack with proper care, and he had taken it upon himself to supervise.

"Vice Scrutator!" While the youth's attire was unkempt, he wore a clean bronze shield embossed with a Menofix strapped to his upper left arm that marked him as a servant of the scrutators. This sigil gave him passage anywhere he was needed, a privilege that could be instantly revoked and the youth flogged to death if he abused it. "A Khadoran courier arrived at the front gate and insisted this message be brought to the hierarch. I convinced the guards to let me convey it."

Vindictus nodded as he took the sealed parchment. "You have done very well, my son. Menoth bless you. Now, go. Back to your post." He gestured to a nearby initiate who served as an aide and scribe. This man withdrew a slip of parchment from a pouch and pressed it into the youth's hand. It was a food voucher, which the boy gladly took before running off.

Vindictus opened the sealed papers while feel-

ing a sense of satisfaction that his precaution of putting people in place at all routes of ingress had proven worthwhile. Many outsiders, filled with an improper and exaggerated sense of their self-importance, sought to speak to the hierarch in person. Vindictus had taken it upon himself to serve as an intermediary and keep abreast of the goings-on in the city. This territory was freshly captured, its citizens only partially converted. The scrutators were in a state of heightened alert, as they knew conspiracies sprouted in every dark corner. The Llaelese were by tradition a treacherous and fickle people.

Even those "allies" who had helped them gain entrance to the city now resented their efforts to cleanse its streets and build proper temples. The Menites in this city were still a minority, and Vindictus often felt the stares of impudent citizens who watched, hidden, from upper windows. If he passed them on the streets they bowed and scraped and

tried to say the proper words of respect, but their voices betrayed insincerity and desperation. The city needed a good cleansing, but the hierarch insisted now was not the time. Not while industry could be coaxed from the grudging labors of these people.

Vindictus forced his mind from such thoughts to read the words on the parchment. It was plain to him that the hand of Menoth was behind this paper coming to him first. There in black ink at the bottom of the page was the signature of the Black Prince, ally of the Devourer, bane of the blessed, Vladimir Tzepesci!

The sigil was genuine, and Vindictus could discern that the words had been penned by the man's own hand. He had seen enough samples in manuscripts acquired at some difficulty to make that clear. The contents of the message were outrageous in their bald insincerity. The letter requested a clandestine meeting with the hierarch, allegedly to discuss a matter of "great importance, regarding a threat to those who are both faithful Menites as well as my rightful subjects." It was beyond belief. So incredible Vindictus almost laughed aloud.

His amazement turned to anger as he scrutinized several lines where Vladimir attempted to use their laws to safeguard his request. Clearly he had been studying Menite sacred texts, for he accurately described the old Law of Envoys and ended with assertions to his rightful claim as a sovereign of Umbrey. The letter generously allowed the hierarch to determine the time and location for their meeting.

Reading those lines again, Vindictus turned toward the nearest fire and almost threw the parchment on the flames, thinking it best destroyed. At the last moment he stopped. The wording of the message was cleverly done, quite proper in many respects. The proposal was likely an attempt to lure Hierarch Severius into an ambush, which obviously could not be allowed to occur. If Tzepesci actually expected that invoking the Law of Envoys would force the hierarch to attend this meeting, however, it presented an unusual opportunity.

Vindictus weighed the option of presenting the document to Severius, yet he hesitated. The hierarch was new to his position, not yet mindful of his singular importance to the faithful, as proven by his refusal to return to the safety of Imer. If shown this letter, Severius may well rise to the bait, just to see what Vladimir Tzepesci intended. That was an unacceptable risk.

The vice scrutator knew too well the insidious nature of the Tzepescis, who had sat on the Khadoran throne and nearly polluted all the north with their unholy practices. They had long ago turned away even from the Old Faith, that distant branch of Menites the Northern Crusade was eager to restore to the fold. Vindictus had captured and tortured members of the Tzepesci household before, and he had heard confessions of their heresies. They had made pacts with the Great Foe and traded their souls for power over the elements and over the blood-drenched soils of their lands. Vladimir walked and fought directly alongside the Devourer's prophet, the Crone of Crows, a creature as corrupt and twisted with unholy power as the Harbinger was exalted by Menoth's light.

No, he would not deliver this message, nor would he destroy it. Instead he would accept its terms. He would march forth to put his own hand in the lion's jaws. He knew precisely where to suggest they meet.

Vindictus realized he had hesitated too long to answer Severius' question. When the hierarch spoke again his tone showed the beginnings of anger. "You overstepped your station, Vindictus. It was not your decision to make. Or do you intend to usurp my authority by deciding when I should and should not be informed of certain matters?"

"No, Your Holiness!" Vindictus protested, his head still bowed low. "This was no act of disobedience."

"You have demonstrated loyalty in the past, but I have seen corruption take many forms and manifest in even the most devout. Did you allow your interest in the Tzepescis to color your decision?"

"I swear to you, I acted as I did only to protect you, Hierarch. The message was clearly an attempt to lure you into an ambush."

"Yet you did not think I would see it as such? I am fortunate to have someone of such *wisdom*." The sarcasm in his tone was biting.

Vindictus insisted, "I saw no need for you to be troubled by this when I could intervene in your stead. It is true, I have studied the Tzepescis extensively, and I have long been planning a means to bring that accursed family's heresies to an end. It seemed to me divine providence had granted me this opportunity."

There was another lengthy silence, as again Vindictus felt himself being judged. "A thin justification, Vindictus. We will put that aside, for now. I want to hear about the meeting you arranged."

Each side approached the rendezvous location with measured prudence. Immediately after Vindictus had sent his reply, he had ordered several groups of Daughters of the Flame ahead to the site. Then he had sent several phalanxes of Knights Errant to watch the perimeter. Their reports described the arrival of Khadorans entering the area on reconnaissance, including Widowmakers and more rustic trackers. Neither side could be assured they had spotted all their counterparts.

With these forces in place, Vindictus approached the location at the designated hour. He had brought elaborate banners and other regalia that would hopefully present the impression that the hierarch might be among them. Refuter of Heresy walked just ahead of Vindictus, while a Devout flanked him on the left and a Vigilant on the right. This escort would make it difficult for anyone observing their advance to see him clearly enough to identify him from a distance, even with the use of a spyglass. Among his soldiers walked two Castigators. Exemplar errants formed the largest human component of his retinue, led by Exemplar Errant Seneschal Bolias Nestore, while a smaller immediate bodyguard of Exemplar cinerators and bastions marched behind. The intent was to make his escort seem substantial enough to accompany someone as important as the hierarch without being so strong it would spook the Khadorans.

Vindictus had chosen the meeting location for its obscure history. It was a site he had gambled might appeal to Vladimir Tzepesci, as the Dark Prince considered himself a scholar as well as a warrior. It was an unremarkable-looking site amid the hills to the south of the Llaelese mountains, only a few hours from the mining town of Rynyr. There was little sign of past habitation aside from a few shattered pillars and the crumbling remains of several walls. Just below the soil rested more extensive ruins of an Umbrean city that had thrived before the Orgoth invasion. After its population had been enslaved and hauled away, it had been forgotten and eventually become buried, one of many places erased by the Orgoth. Vindictus had been intending to search the location for lost Menite relics and had studied the ground well.

Vindictus signaled to Seneschal Nestore. "Take your men to the position and await my signal. Do not get drawn into the fight, no matter what transpires."

The seneschal gestured across the far valley toward one of the tree-covered hills. "We watch that largest oak, Your Excellency?" At Vindictus' nod, the man turned and split away from the rest of the column, alongside several other Exemplar errants. They took a circuitous course, appearing to backtrack as they rushed to arrive at the designated location by a route unseen.

Soon they spotted the Khadorans waiting for them, just at the far side where a wide road had once passed between these hills and into the now-buried city. The Khadorans looked formidable, but the size of their force was similar to that of Vindictus' escort, if he included the errants already in place. As his column approached, Vindictus believed he saw the distinct silhouette of Drago, the ancient Berserker of the Tzepescis, among several other Khadoran warjacks. An honor guard of soldiers stood at attention, and at the center of them there was no mistaking Great Prince Tzepesci in his armor, ancient plate forged anew by his own hand.

"Halt, soldiers of the Protectorate!" Vladimir stepped forward, his blade still on his back. Most of his escort were heavily armored Iron Fangs, but several squads of Winter Guard with rifles were also present, their weapons slung. Both sides were tense. Vindictus had no doubt snipers watched them, even as his own errants had taken up positions with crossbows ready to fire on their counterparts.

The Devout and Vigilant each stepped aside just enough to reveal the vice scrutator. He enjoyed the look of surprise and then anger on the Khadoran warcaster's face. "Vindictus! What is the meaning of this? Where is Hierarch Severius?" He looked past the vice scrutator to the Cinerators behind, hoping to see the man he had anticipated meeting here. His men shifted uneasily but did not yet draw their weapons.

The Menite warcaster offered a slight bow. "Great Prince Tzepesci, I invite you to accompany us to Leryn. I am empowered to escort you there, where Hierarch Severius waits. You may bring up to six officers and servants to see to your needs. The rest of your retinue must remain behind."

Vladimir scowled at him and scoffed, "I gave my terms in my message. I will only meet with the hierarch here, on neutral ground. I have important and urgent information for your master. There is no time to waste."

"Then I suggest we hasten to Leryn immediately," Vindictus countered. "If the matter is of such importance, surely you can discuss it in a location where the hierarch's safety can be assured."

Vladimir hesitated as if weighing the option. Vindictus wondered if there was any chance the man might actually agree to such unfavorable terms. After a shared look with one of his nearest officers, Vladimir shook his head sharply. "You have made a mistake, Vindictus, and the lives my warning might have saved will be on your head." He turned to go.

Vindictus' voice was cold. "Wait a moment, Prince Tzepesci. I have not given you leave to depart. I need you to return with me to Leryn. My preference would be for you to do so of your own accord, but I do not intend to return without you."

The prince turned back sharply as angry muttering began among the nearest men. "What did you say? I am not certain I understood." His eyes had narrowed. "You would attack an envoy?"

Vindictus offered a shrug and said, "Your men are not covered by the protocols of envoy. If we fight, many will die. You can spare your people by accompanying me peacefully. It will be easier that way."

"Were it Hierarch Severius standing here making the same offer, I might accede. You, I do not trust." He drew the large sword from his back in a smooth movement, which was immediately mirrored in the soldiers behind him readying their weapons. "I suggest you withdraw. If you stay, we are quite willing to see this through to the bloody end."

"If that is how it must be, very well." Vindictus offered an even smaller bow than before and stepped backward. His warjacks moved into place to shield him from the Khadorans.

Chaos erupted. From one of the nearby hills there was a shout and the sound of several rifles firing. Vindictus'

Devout intercepted a shot meant for the warcaster, raising its shield to deflect, but altogether there was less incoming Widowmaker fire than anticipated. Vladimir and his officers were shouting queries but soon realized their vulnerability and sought cover as Exemplar Errant crossbow bolts began raining down into the clearing. Vindictus felt satisfaction knowing they and the Daughters of the Flame had clearly gotten the better of the Khadorans sent to cover the meeting from the higher vantage. There was no doubting Widowmaker capability, but in this case numerical superiority prevailed.

The Menite warcaster sent his will into the cortex of Refuter of Heresy and urged it to fire its massive cannon directly at Vladimir Tzepesci. The Reckoner responded quickly and eagerly, and it swung its cannon toward the enemy almost before the warcaster finished his thought. There was the boom of the Reckoner cannon and a great billow of smoke. Vladimir Tzepesci barely evaded the blazing projectile. Vindictus sensed the 'jack's enthusiasm to press forward and follow the blast with blows from its massive Consecrator, but he held it in check at his side.

> **DRAGO LOPED FORWARD LIKE A LIVING BEAST, CLEARLY WANTING TO RAGE HEADLONG INTO THE ENEMY.**

Vindictus knew this moment was crucial, as he had far fewer men in the immediate vicinity than Vladimir, having sent them to deal with the threats along the perimeter. Also, he was not yet where he needed to be. At a curt chop of his hand, his men began to back away, still facing the enemy. The Winter Guard fired their rifles, but their bullets could not penetrate the massive armor of the Exemplar cinerators who had formed a line before the warcaster and his 'jacks. The Guard were soon too preoccupied by crossbow bolts raining down upon them from the surrounding hills to do more than seek cover.

Vladimir's Destroyer fired in booming counterpoint to the Reckoner, its whistling shell seeking the vice scrutator. Protective runes of gold appeared around Vindictus as he drew on his holy power to shield himself. The shell missed him and exploded close by, while the nearby Vigilant moved between and used its shield-covered arms to absorb the impact of the blast. Air from the explosion washed around Vindictus and stirred up a whirlwind of dirt as his force continued to pull back. His attention was fully focused on the warjacks of his retinue, moving them like pieces on a chessboard. Urged on by their master, the Castigators ran

with alacrity despite their bulk to the extremes of either flank, taking positions behind pillars along this main row. They stood ready, holding their flame-covered fists like pugilists as they awaited the Khadoran heavies.

His men fanned out as they withdrew into a "V" shape, with the warcaster and his light warjack escort at the center in the back. The lane they backed into had been very deliberately chosen, and Vindictus felt a keen anticipation as he watched the enemy come forward like insects into a web. Vladimir displayed his arrogance as he advanced at the fore of his Iron Fangs while the power he drew flickered as an unholy aura around his person. He showed no fear or hesitation. The last time they had battled one another, other obligations had forced Vindictus to retreat. Now Tzepesci clearly expected cowardice from his enemy, and Vindictus was happy to exploit that prediction.

Drago loped forward like a living beast, clearly wanting to rage headlong into the enemy. Vladimir was likely holding it in check by force of will. The Destroyer and a Juggernaut also advanced in front of the prince. The Destroyer fired again, but its shell was intercepted by the Devout and caused only superficial damage. The Iron Fangs approached and overtook the 'jacks in an ordered line, disciplined as ever with their shields tightly set against those adjacent to them. They closed on the Exemplar cinerators, who stood stoically to receive them, flaming blades ready. The bastions just behind the cinerators were prepared to strike between their Exemplar brothers to cut down any foe that closed.

While Refuter kept to the side and continued to fire on the advancing Khadorans, the vice scrutator and his light 'jacks backed into a narrower area demarked by crumbled stone columns, between which several thick trees had sprouted in the centuries since any human had lived there. The Iron Fangs gave their battle yell and charged the awaiting Cinerators, Vladimir Tzepesci alongside them with his greatsword in hand. A darkness that warped the air like a mirage on desert sands lined his body as he entered battle, and glowing runes erupted as he invoked his sorcery. Drago and Vladimir fighting side-by-side carved easily through the Cinerator line and deftly blocked the blows of the Bastions behind them.

As a hole in the line was forced open, the Juggernaut pushed through, shouldering armored men aside like toys. Its eyes burned red with malevolence and the edge of its axe shimmered with cold. It charged straight toward the light warjacks escorting Vindictus as the Destroyer fired again, arcing another explosive shell toward the vice scrutator. The Devout once more intercepted the shell, but this time it staggered as the explosion tore a large gap through its shield and shattered part of its arm. Meanwhile the Vigilant moved protectively into the path of the charging Juggernaut, which towered over it as it drew back its freezing axe. The light warjack crouched and raised its shield-arms above it like a man might hold up his arms in a futile attempt to protect himself.

Vindictus stepped back calmly and mentally directed the Castigators, which he had sent back behind the trees and columns so their position would not be seen from Vladimir's perspective. He spoke another prayer as he urged them forward and sent holy sigils across all his people in the vicinity, lending strength to their legs and surety to their movements. The nearest Castigator barreled into the Juggernaut, and the entire earth shook with the weight of them smashing into the soil with the grinding sound of tearing metal. The rumbling did not stop there, and Vindictus smiled behind his mask to see the ground sagging and cracks opening in the earth beneath the 'jacks. With a great roar of collapsing dirt and stone, the ground opened and swallowed them. The crevice ended inches before the feet of the braced Vigilant, which now stood alone.

Simultaneously, his second Castigator came from the other direction, directly toward the Destroyer that had been firing with focused intensity at Vindictus. The Khadoran 'jack saw the Castigator a moment too late to evade its impact. The Castigator barreled its shoulder straight into the heavier machine and sent it flying into Vladimir Tzepesci. Both 'jack and warcaster toppled heavily on the ground, which also began to give way.

Vindictus stepped out from behind the protection of his escorting 'jacks to point at his enemy, calling forth the sonorous tones of Menite prayer. A ring of golden light shaped into runic text circled his outstretched hand and was mirrored on the ground where the toppled 'jacks and the warcaster had fallen. Vindictus clenched his fist to unleash a surge of power and the sagging ground tore itself apart with a massive explosion. The Castigator took advantage of the chaos to ignite a ring of fire around it, setting several of the nearest Iron Fangs on fire.

As the earth opened under their feet and rent a ragged gap in the entire lane between the two sides, Vladimir and the Khadoran warjacks disappeared, tumbling down into an ancient stone channel. The long passageway, smooth on the sides, had once carried massive quantities of clean water through this region from a collecting reservoir and aqueduct on the hill to the northeast. As the vice scrutator had predicted, the ground above the largely intact water channels could not sustain the weight of heavy warjacks in battle. Vindictus drew his sword Lawgiver and his flail Solace and walked closer to the precarious edge of the channel to gain a better vantage on his enemy below. He could only make out the Castigator that had fallen with them now engaged in a desperate clash with the Juggernaut.

There was a sudden noise like a growling beast, and Vindictus looked up to see to his startled dismay that Drago had not fallen with its master. The warjack had been near Tzepesci on the collapsing precipice but had apparently managed to scramble up from the edge in time. On spotting Vindictus, Drago let forth a triumphant howl of steam and was now racing forward along the solid ground along the edge of the chasm to close with the Menite warcaster.

Vindictus impelled his second Castigator, the one that had toppled the Destroyer into Vladimir, to intercept the maddened machine. Iron Fangs had managed to hem in the Castigator and circled it expertly, stabbing with their explosive-tipped lances. The warjack leaned forward and barreled through the nearest soldiers, smashing them underfoot or battering them out of the way as it moved to block the tenacious Berserker.

Drago raised its axes and leapt forward to attack with such fervor and intensity that Vindictus knew immediately Vladimir must still be conscious and controlling the machine. It whirled its axes with blinding speed to catch the Castigator high on the right shoulder and sever the pistons as if they were mere bones rather than steel. Smoke poured from its stacks as it hacked with its axes again and again into the enemy warjack, which fell back and collapsed as its engine was torn apart. It gave one last burst of fire as its inner reservoir of Menoth's Fury ruptured and collapsed. The glow of its eyes faded. Drago's own single eye looked demonic as the warjack raised its head and saw Vindictus. With a shriek of venting steam it ran forward again, nimbly vaulting over the nearest section of the chasm toward the Menite warcaster. Vindictus desperately sent both his Vigilant and Devout into its path.

The Berserker smashed the Vigilant aside into a nearby column and ignored the hasty swipe of the Devout's halberd as it passed. Vindictus ducked beneath its first axe, feeling his power field surge and respond to the proximity. His earlier blessings made the Khadoran warjack's movements seem almost slow and faltering, and yet there was a tremendous killing weight behind them. The eye contained a savagery that could not be born of steel. The ground bowed beneath Drago's feet, and Vindictus felt it giving way under himself as well.

This nearly distracted him as he tumbled to the side, swinging his flail into Drago's left leg. This dented the steel but unfortunately did not cause any real damage. He suddenly noticed Refuter of Heresy was moving up from where it had been standing on more solid ground. Its bond with Vindictus had impelled it to try to save its master and engage the frenzied enemy. Ordinarily these impulses were praiseworthy, but now Vindictus felt a moment of panic. The Reckoner was nearly as heavy as a Khadoran 'jack, and he had chosen its course into this region carefully. At the very moment he impelled it to step back, the ground beneath them cracked, moaned, and then fell away, tumbling all of them into the same stone channel where Vladimir and the other 'jacks had been dropped. Only the relatively agile Devout managed to evade the widening chasm.

Vindictus gained his feet quickly and took stock of the situation by seeing through the eyes of his 'jacks. Both his Castigators were destroyed, as the one fallen here in the channel had succumbed to the Juggernaut, which was damaged but still a threat. Vladimir was coming toward him now from further up the incline of the stone channel. His Destroyer lay on its side, struggling to right itself on crippled legs.

The vice scrutator urged Refuter of Heresy to its feet just in time for it to clash with Drago. It was all Vindictus could do to stumble out of the way; the channel was narrow for such a battle. Vladimir and the Juggernaut were approaching, and he had only the rattled Vigilant remaining to protect him. The Dark Prince was limping and blood was running down his left cheek from a gash on his temple, but his eyes were murderous as he closed with the vice scrutator and gripped his sword Dominion tight with both hands.

The cornered warcaster sent the Vigilant against the battered Juggernaut, not expecting the light 'jack to last long. He peered up out of the channel and found the hill and the tree he had mentioned earlier to his Exemplar errant seneschal. He took a precious moment to focus his holy energy and pointed at the tree. With a surge of power flames erupted along its dried branches, sending black smoke up into the sky. That was all he could manage before Vladimir was upon him. Their duel was an inverted parallel of the battle waged between Drago and Refuter of Heresy.

Vindictus barely evaded Dominion's edge, then he swept his flail Solace in an arc that Vladimir easily evaded before counterattacking with lightning swiftness. Vindictus interposed the edge of Lawgiver in time to deflect the heavier weapon. Despite Dominion's size and weight, Vladimir whirled it like a duelist's blade, and his bloodshot eyes and gritted teeth demonstrated he was in the battle frenzy for which his bloodline was feared. The Khadoran was clearly the superior swordsman, and it was all Vindictus could do to avoid the cutting edge of his weapon. Slipping on stone made slick from the thin rivulet of water running along the center groove of the channel, he nearly lost his footing evading Vladimir's next blow. His ankle twisted painfully, and he felt the bite of Dominion in his side as the blade pierced through both his power field and his protective prayers.

That was when he heard an echoing roar from up the channel. Vindictus kicked out desperately, knocking Vladimir's armored leg askew just enough to throw the man off his stride while mentally summoning his Devout. A swipe with Lawgiver forced Vladimir to parry lest the blade caress his

neck, and then the 'jack was scrambling along the chasm perimeter, trying to find an angle that would allow it to help.

At the vice scrutator's command, it lowered its halberd toward him, but the gap was too far to reach. Thinking quickly, Vindictus swung his flail instead, letting its chained heads whip around the halberd and clench tight. The Devout began to lift just as a great wall of water came rushing down the sluiceway. His hands nearly lost their grip as he was pulled up and out of the channel, the current pulling his torso and legs until he was free. The torrent was brief, a single massive surge let loose from the ancient reservoir whose crude controls Vindictus had earlier sent his seneschal to claim until his signal.

There was a debris grate just south of where they had been battling, and he could see the 'jacks and Vladimir washed up against it. The Khadoran warcaster was either dead or unconscious. Given the man's bloodline, Vindictus felt confident he was still alive. Thankfully, the engine fires of the warjacks had been extinguished. As Vindictus got to his feet he saw his Knights Errant making their way back to him, having finished cleaning up the remaining Khadorans. He caught the eye of his seneschal and nodded to the man, both a summons and a small gesture of approval.

When the knight approached, Vindictus told him, "Send the signal to the men and wagons. We'll need to extract Refuter, Tzepesci, and his fiendish Berserker from that." He waved toward the drain grate and the pile of machinery. "The rest we can leave behind. Make sure our 'guest' is comfortable for his return trip." He could not keep a note of satisfaction from his voice, even as he winced against the pain of his bleeding side.

In the audience hall of Hierarch Severius, the vice scrutator offered a more succinct version of the battle. Vindictus felt the hierarch's eyes upon him and gave the details as factually as possible, knowing the risk of being caught at embellishment. "It was an opportunity too great to let pass, Your Holiness. I apologize that I did not consult with you before launching the expedition. I offer as my feeble excuse that you trained us to seize the initiative when defending the faith or waging war on heretics."

Hierarch Severius was quiet for what seemed a long time. At last the older scrutator spoke. "A great victory, to be sure. I commend you." He paused briefly, then continued more severely, "Yet what of the Law of Envoy? From ancient times we have respected the sovereignty of entreating kings. Even in war, this law is sacrosanct."

Vindictus nodded heavily. "I realize my methods were unorthodox. I came to the decision at the outset that this man was not eligible as an envoy. I considered this carefully, Your Holiness. I am convinced he was abusing that station and intended to do harm to your person. He did not speak for Khador's empress, and his claims to his own sovereignty are dubious at best. The only power he serves is Zevanna Agha, that accursed crone. *She* most assuredly does not heed the True Law."

"Perhaps, perhaps . . ." Severius did not seem to find this explanation entirely to his liking. "I presume you have been questioning him. Have you discovered what excuse he was using as a pretext to meet with me? I would like to know the particulars of the bargain he intended to offer."

"He has not been forthcoming on that matter, I am afraid." In this Vindictus deceived by omission, as he had not questioned Vladimir closely on that topic, but it was a very mild distortion of the truth. "I am certain the entire arrangement was a farce. I wonder if his aim was to present himself to you and in that moment invoke unholy sorceries to summon the Crone of Crows. It is the only purpose I can imagine. I felt it imperative to determine the nature of their scheme before imperiling you, which is why I had not yet brought news. If you will allow me to return to him, I will continue to apply my arts to discern his true intent."

The hierarch replied sharply, "It seems your arts may be inadequate to this task. I think I may need to personally—"

They were interrupted when a pale, older priest rushed into the chamber. He offered profuse apologies and bowed repeatedly as he approached. Severius said in exasperation, "You have already intruded where you were not wanted, Sovereign Kovian. Speak quickly."

"Your Holiness, the prisoner . . . Vladimir Tzepesci . . ." He looked nervously to Vice Scrutator Vindictus before speaking again to Severius in a thin voice. "He has escaped. Many guards are dead, and we do not know where he is. The hunt for him has begun. I do not think he will get far."

Vindictus clenched his mailed fists against his desire to march from the chamber and flay the surviving guards to discover what had happened. "Your Holiness, if you will allow me, I will see to this. I will personally find and recapture Tzepesci."

Severius' voice was surprisingly mild. "It is likely too late for that." He glanced to the other priest. "Continue the search, and spare no manpower." The sovereign bowed again and hastened to exit. Severius watched him go and then turned his attention back to Vindictus. His voice took on an almost apologetic tone. "We will not catch him again, I predict. This means all your efforts have come to naught, Vice Scrutator Vindictus. There is a lesson in this, one we will take time and effort to elucidate between the two of us."

These simple words sounded to Vindictus' trained ear as chilling as a death sentence, for they contained the threat of a personal interrogation by the hierarch. If Vindictus were to come under such an application of their scrutator discipline, his position was forfeit, whatever the end results. Keeping his voice smooth, he said, "Your Holiness, while I did not discover Vladimir's purported reasons for seeking audience with you, I assure you that my efforts interrogating him were not wasted. I knew a man like Vladimir would not break under torture. It was not answers I sought, but an understanding of a different kind."

"Pray tell." The hierarch's bearing had not changed, but he allowed Vindictus to continue.

"I was studying the nature of the bond between Tzepesci and his ancient Berserker, Drago. As I suspected, this was fertile territory. The ancient cortexes such as those utilized by early Berserkers are not shielded the way modern cortexes are. By employing several of our most skilled and knowledgeable vassals, we were able to scrutinize that cortex closely, under unique stresses. We discovered that the arcane military locks protecting the cortex from outside interference would slip at times when Drago's master was suffering great pain. By careful examination, we further discovered a possible way to unlock the cortex protections remotely—for a short time. We would need to develop and engineer certain specialized pieces of machinery to accomplish this, but I am confident it is possible." He saw the hierarch's posture change as he said these things, subtly reassuring him that his words were being received with interest.

"That is remarkable. But ultimately, how useful? If we do anything to exploit such knowledge, they will simply change their cortex locks. It would not aid us beyond a single battle."

"That is true, Your Holiness. However, it will cost them precious time and resources to reconfigure all their cortex locks. Such measures are integral and must be modified individually. If we choose our timing carefully, I believe the gains will be great. Imagine what we could do in a battle where every enemy warjack was vulnerable to our commands."

He knew he had the hierarch. Severius crossed his arms behind his back in a manner that suggested he was begrudgingly pleased. "Very well. We will postpone our deeper dissection of your transgressions. Get to work on this cortex project immediately, but take precautions. I want no hint of this spoken outside our circle. Leave me now."

Vindictus bowed. "Yes, Your Holiness." He felt the hierarch's gaze upon his back as he left the chamber, and only when the doors sealed behind him did he allow himself to register the weight of having narrowly escaped something he feared more than death itself.

MISSION OF MERCY
KHADORAN-OCCUPIED LLAEL

It was a vision from the abyss of nightmare. The undead poured from their underground tunnels in the deep night and marched across empty fields. Alongside them were many dark constructs, machines created for no purpose except slaughter, the sound of their steam engines lost amid the wind of the rainstorm. The towns they approached were quiet and dark, unsuspecting, the citizens tucked inside their homes. The line of the thrall army spread far and wide.

The vision focused on a single town to the east, far from the occupying Khadoran garrisons. Windows were shuttered to keep out the chill rain and wind as the people within slept huddled beneath layers of blankets. In most of the houses the Menofix was placed prominently in the main family hall. Often it would be awash in the soft light of candles left to burn through the night within the darkened home. Now, though, cracks in the walls and seams in the shutters had let in enough wind to gutter the candles and extinguish them.

Mechanithralls and banes flooded into the town, and what ensued was a massacre. Some citizens awakened in time to defend themselves, but this availed them little. Even their deaths did not end the horror; the mangled bodies were collected by necrosurgeons and piled neatly onto wagons or dissected on the spot so that useful bits could be carved free and sorted. Houses were similarly disassembled, with metal and pieces of machinery pulled aside to be collected.

> **MECHANITHRALLS AND BANES FLOODED INTO THE TOWN, AND WHAT ENSUED WAS A MASSACRE.**

The vision pulled back and sped west, where other towns were attacked despite the protection of small Khadoran garrison forces. Even with the heroic efforts of the soldiers and militia who fought to stop the onslaught, the end result was the same each time. Further back amid the Cryxian throng were dark lords and masters, including a towering shape with tattered wings and a long bone-bladed sword. It seemed as though dark smoke-like tendrils extended from him, representing the spread of his dominion and influence and reaching toward various subordinates and minions that acted as he willed. This was a lich lord of Cryx, along with other, subordinate powers of similar malice but unique potential. Among these, directing the forces closer to the Black River, a trio of young witches invoked power drawn from a malevolent black sphere that floated upon the effluvium of darkness it oozed like blood.

The Harbinger, weeping silent tears, returned to her own mind.

She went immediately to Hierarch Severius to tell him of what she had seen, her cheeks still flushed with emotion from her vision. He asked her, "When will this take place? How much time do we have?"

The Harbinger shook her head, stirring the veils that covered her eyes. "You misunderstand, Hierarch. What I saw is not the future. It has already transpired. Cryx extends its claw and flows into the lands of Llael like a plague. There can be no mistaking their path. They have chosen to move against outlying communities, those poorly protected by Khadoran garrisons. Many towns and villages have been left vulnerable. The ones I witnessed were populated by Menites of the Old Faith. Many of those families moved here recently from Khador. These were such people as I was sent here to reach, strangled instead by Cryxians!" Her voice had lost its objectivity and filled with emotion.

"Why give us this vision so late?" Hierarch Severius spoke more to himself than to her.

She understood. He was jealous of her connection to the divine, as many priests were. It was natural. Divine power flowed through priests, like water through a tributary, but they did not have the privilege of true communion.

She explained, "The future is always shifting. It is not fixed. I sense this horror as I saw it was not certain until now. We lacked the insight to prevent this, and now the innocent pay the price."

The hierarch mused, "These villages, were they on Umbrean soil?"

"There were Umbreans among those I saw slaughtered."

"This must be why Tzepesci sought to speak with me. Somehow he knew of this. Damn Vindictus and his scheming!" the hierarch swore. "We could have used those people, true faithful, rather than the half-hearted converts and secret vipers in this city."

"There is no time for second guessing or regretting past decisions. What happened yesterday is done." She stopped speaking for a moment to bring her feelings under control. "I must go now; there is a very large Menite town still in the path of destruction. I have seen that among these faithful are several who have the warcaster potential. They will become weapons in Menoth's hand. I must protect them."

"I will come with you." Severius stood from his throne.

"It is your decision to make, Your Holiness, and I would appreciate your presence, but I believe you should remain here. Your strength will be needed in battle soon enough. This task is something I must do. I will take only a select group; the rest of our forces must remain to hold this city. We cannot risk them against this tide, not yet. Let me go to save those Menites not yet overcome. Word of our intervention will spread."

Severius nodded, acknowledging the prudence of her decision. "Very well; take whatever men you require. Go with my blessing, child of the Creator."

The Harbinger marched from Leryn at once, before dawn, bringing two strong interdictions. It was a sizable force but represented only a small sliver of the full crusade. She hoped it would be sufficient. Such details were not part of her divine visions. Only faith and instinct guided her, but she was certain she could not risk more than this.

The Testament joined her unasked, and in this she could not turn him away. He had his own dictates from the Creator. She had refused Grand Exemplar Kreoss' offer of assistance, although for a moment she thought he would insist on coming regardless. He had sent High Exemplar Gravus in his stead, along with the favored knights who comprised the First Exemplar Interdiction, men who had fought alongside him in Sul.

She had also selected High Executioner Reznik, whose more diverse forces provided much-needed flexibility to the Exemplar interdiction. This was the sort of task where his skills could be most useful.

They had never spoken, but she knew his mettle. A dark aura suffused his presence to her all-encompassing and eyeless vision, a lingering afterimage of all those he had executed in Menoth's name. Reznik was a killer, but his resolute certainty in battle would serve her.

Conspicuously absent was High Paladin Dartan Vilmon, and she missed his presence. He had not yet joined the Northern Crusade and remained in Sul, holding vigil as a self-imposed penance for his defiance of the hierarch in the final conflict in Caspia. She had personally forgiven him

this perceived sin, but his sense of honor required him to come to terms with it in his own way.

Dozens of warjacks came with them, both heavies and lights. As they marched from Leryn, the Avatar came forth unbidden to join them. She was not surprised to see it arrive and advance alongside the chosen acolytes who held the sacred chains connecting her to the earth and helping speed her own movement toward the west. The storm clouds still darkened the skies, but no rain fell on the Harbinger or the Avatar.

They crashed into a forward tendril of the Cryxian advance like the unforgiving fist of Menoth. The Avatar gleamed in the radiance of the sun breaking through the black clouds as it buried its blazing sword into the wreckage of a Reaper, cleaving through the enemy machine's torso and annihilating its engine. Holy fire consumed the helljack and it exploded to light afire several nearby mechanithralls seeking to swarm the sacred machine. The Harbinger's blessings added swiftness to the forward ranks of Temple Flameguard and Exemplars who charged into the Cryxian horde and set to work with spear and blade.

A swarm of helljacks and bonejacks received the crushing might of High Executioner Reznik's Crusaders, Vanquishers, and Dervishes. Surrounded by a ring of golden runes and then filled with Reznik's power, one of his Crusaders battered through a dense knot of bane thralls, carving a great swath of destruction through their ranks. Deliverer fire rained down around them, blowing the unholy creatures into scattered scraps of ancient rusted armor. Zealots inspired by their warpriests rushed to join the fray on that far right flank, hurling incendiary bombs into another group of advancing mechanithralls. The Testament fought in that quarter, and by his hand the dead became ash and the souls of the faithful were delivered to Urcaen.

They reached the largest Menite town just ahead of the larger Cryxian horde. The faithful poured from their homes weeping in praise and bowing down before the Harbinger, who looked beyond them to the enemy that approached. She could sense the unnatural presence of the undead along the horizon, could feel them mustering like a foul wind. She knew they would come soon, once their masters decided how to respond to the arrival of the Protectorate forces. They would not let this town go easily.

The Menite soldiers set to work with the locals establishing limited defenses. The townsfolk had received word of the horrors sweeping through Llael and had begun to do what they could. Their town had no proper walls, but a variety of barricades had been improvised. The Menites put their greatest effort into improving these in the time they had. Where walls could not be erected, the shields of the Flameguard and Exemplar Cinerators would serve instead.

Those citizens who could not bear arms against the enemy—the youngest and oldest, for the most part—were gathered in the stoutest building, a large and recently expanded Menite temple in the center of town. Its strong walls and castle-like battlements would serve as a last line of defense. The Harbinger had found among the town youths those with the prophesied warcaster potential, their souls shining like gemstones. It was rare for her to perceive them so clearly, yet here were no fewer than three she was certain would manifest the power, plus a dozen others the

hierophants said were possible candidates, good recruits for choir priests, at the very least.

Everyone else in the town had taken up what arms they could and joined the warpriests directing their efforts. The Testament walked among them, his silent and fearsome guise inspiring a fighting spirit equal to the awe they felt on seeing the Harbinger herself. She eventually took up a position just behind her soldiers outside the town, where her slender form collected the last rays of the day's light. The townspeople lit what fires they could and placed numerous torches along the outer battlements. Occasional fires from Flameguard testing their spears erupted across the lines, while the Menite warjacks stood rumbling and ready as the last glimmering of twilight faded from the sky and true darkness descended.

High Executioner Reznik was at the southernmost edge of their defending force with the greatest concentration of their warjacks, Exemplar bastions, and Exemplar cinerators. Fanning out to either side and taking what sheltered positions they could amid the somewhat flat and empty farmland outside the town were Knights Errant, who fired their bolts into the advancing Cryxian horde as the assault began. The first wave of mechanithralls rushed forward with typical reckless abandon. Mechanithralls existed for nothing else, mindless but too dangerous to ignore. Even one of those steam-powered fists could kill a man if it connected, and as a pair they could damage even hardened warjacks.

Redeemers fired into the closing swarm to explode dead flesh, steel, and ruptured piping. Behind the mechanithralls came bile thralls, disgusting undead horrors that could melt entire phalanxes of Flameguard or exemplars in a spray of caustic corruption. There seemed no end to them, and even the pyrotechnics of unrelenting Redeemer and Deliverer fire could not obliterate them all. Revengers standing with their polearms and shields at the farthest fringes of each warcaster's mental range channeled the fires of Menoth's wrath into the enemy through their arc nodes, as the warcasters set ablaze every enemy they could find.

Never had the Harbinger seen so many Cryxian thralls in one place, not even when she had ascended the Temple Garrodh to confront Asphyxious. While living bodies were little more than husks for the soul to be passed to Urcaen at death, many of these pitiful creatures had been deprived of even that final dignity; she sensed their souls had been torn free and imprisoned by necromancers. Their immortal essence would be wastefully burned as fuel to power more blasphemous death magic. Worse yet, the Harbinger knew the force she saw coming for this town was only a portion of a larger unholy army.

She looked past the advancing hordes even as she sent her will into her Redeemers to guide their rockets to the largest concentrations of the dead. She saw the Orgoth orb floating on its never-ending outpouring of liquid darkness, and alongside it the three women cursed to become soothsayers for the dragon king and Lich Lord Terminus. They were connected to the Orgoth artifact, the vile Egregore, and by the rites that bound them they possessed the ability to augur the future. They pushed the army forward and cloaked it in darkness, sending their power through the bonejacks racing alongside the mindless thralls.

The rising voices of the choir shielded the Protectorate warjacks from enemy magic even as the witch coven tested their defenses with unholy power. Flickering darkness shot forth from a Deathripper at the fore, falling upon a line of Exemplar cinerators that stood to intercept an incoming block of bane thralls. The knights turned to wraithlike darkness, allowing the bane thralls to pass through them as if they were nothing but shadows to tear into the Deliverers who had been safely shielded behind them. The Harbinger shouted out and let loose a great surge of spiritual power that rippled through the air as a golden ring. Where it passed, the foul sorceries of the enemy were dispersed and disintegrated. The cinerators regained their tangible forms and brought their blazing swords against the enemies, now ahead and behind. The battle quickly became chaotic.

The Harbinger joined her voice to the holy litany of the chanting choir priests. She sent her power to preserve those particularly devout souls who shone in her vision like lanterns of faith. She accepted their wounds into her flesh and suffered their pain even as those faithful again became whole. The rest who fell were left to the nearby reclaimers, who grasped the souls as bodies fell, passing residual spiritual energy to nearby warjacks. Adding his powerful voice to their harmony from next to her was her hierophant, a wizened older priest whose prayers mended the Harbinger's wounds almost as fast as they opened. She sent her power through her Revengers to instill the faithful with divine guidance, enabling even awkwardly thrust Flameguard spears find their mark against the nimble bonejacks that tried to evade them. Exemplar vengers swept around to run down the left flank, smashing through a line of bane knights.

The Testament was at her side, driving into the enemy and tearing a path through them with the weight of his smoldering weapon Requiem. The Avatar joined them from the other side, as did several Crusaders and Vanquishers, moving with almost eerie synchronicity as Reznik, too, joined their effort. A pair of skarlocks closed too near Reznik, their rune-covered corpse flesh gleaming with sickly light as they invoked their magic—until they were lit afire in retaliation for their temerity.

The Exemplar vengers charged ahead to shatter against swift-moving corpses shaped like mockeries of horses, Soulhunters, that had ran forward to harvest the souls of the Flameguard. The Harbinger pushed alongside the other warcasters as they parted the Cryxian tide, driving through Slayers, Harrowers, and Reapers. A cluster of mechanithralls spilled past the outer defenders, and the Harbinger unleashed a singular explosion of divine fury into their midst as they neared her floating form. A blaze of fire consumed them but left the faithful untouched.

She drove on toward the trio of witches she alone sensed within the darkness, scheming and coordinating this Cryxian assault. She could almost taste their confusion and fear as their very souls quailed within them. They did not yet have the armor of death to shield them from the awesome splendor of her divine manifestation. A sudden blaze of light consumed the entire area as the Harbinger fully unveiled her glory and consumed all the advancing abominations into roaring oblivion.

> **THE HARBINGER UNLEASHED A SINGULAR EXPLOSION OF DIVINE FURY INTO THEIR MIDST.**

Another Slayer leapt forward toward the Harbinger, empowered by the sorcery of the coven and seeking to block her advance. The Avatar intercepted and brought its sword down, ending the helljack's existence in two solid blows. A Stalker leapt for her but was smashed to pieces by the impact of the Testament's weapon. The Harbinger's acolytes rushed forward with her, driven by the holy inspiration of the woman connected to their hands by holy chains, and she saw before her one of the three witches. "Morgaen, I name you," she shouted. "Providence has come!" She plunged her sword into the body of the witch, feeling a keen sense of satisfaction. The woman screamed and her hands twisted into claws as she pushed at the blade, pulling herself off its length with a spurt of living blood.

Sudden absolute darkness enveloped the army, and for a moment even the Harbinger was bewildered by its intensity. It had poured forth from the Egregore, which extended a black tentacle of intangible force to seize the wounded Morgaen and pull her back toward it. Everything around the Menite army seemed enveloped in black as the darkness obliterated all light. The Harbinger had never before had her divine vision fail her; she could see only the Avatar, which had moved to stand close to her raising its shield protectively. Beyond the space of a dozen paces there was pitch blackness.

Suddenly the curtains of darkness fell away to reveal the normal night sky once more. The Harbinger saw no sign of the Egregore or its witches; without them, the Cryxian army had begun to falter and change its course. The mindless thralls still surged toward the town, where they were intercepted by the embattled defenders, but the machinery and more sentient of the dead were in retreat. The Harbinger had bloodied one of their masters and thus revealed their cowardice. They had no wish to taste the bite of her blade again.

"Fall back to the town. Ensure no horrors reach the temple," she called aloud. The soldiers around her gave a great shout as they realized the Cryxian attack was abating. Their blessed leader triumphed once more. The darkness had confused them for a time, but now they saw victory close at hand.

The Harbinger felt no disappointment at the Egregore's retreat, for the Cryxian horde she had seen was a humbling manifestation. Had the army driven with all its might at this town, she did not know if they would have prevailed. Lich Lord Terminus would not have retreated so soon. But now was not the time to reflect on dark thoughts; they had still to eliminate the last of the undead and secure their converts for the journey home. The fire of their faith was but a wavering light amid a greater darkness, and she must ensure it was not extinguished.

They exited the town in haste, knowing their position was far from secure. The citizens willingly packed up their belongings, assured that they would find a new home in the protected territory nearer to Leryn. All the same, the task of gathering and coordinating hundreds of civilians along with the massive army was not an easy one. As they marched from the town and began to move east, the Harbinger could sense Cryx following behind them. The undead had not yet sent forward any of their greater generals, but the outer remnants of the horde were like jackals, searching for any sign of weakness to exploit. The Menites sent the Exemplar vengers and a portion of the Temple Flameguard to the rear of the column to stand ready to intercept anything that ventured too close and to make certain the slowest of their stragglers were not left behind.

They had not traveled very far before they saw a disheveled line of refugees coming toward their column from the south, perhaps having heard of their triumph against the Cryxians. The downtrodden group of dirt and mud-covered citizens had clearly fled a destroyed town, bringing all that they could carry. Temple Flameguard halted them as they neared, but their spokesman pleaded with the officers long enough that eventually word reached the Harbinger.

High Exemplar Gravus rebuked the Flameguard captain who brought the news that the refugees sought an audience. "Do not trouble her with such as this. Tell them to stay back. We have barely enough supplies for our own people. Are they even Menites?"

"I do not think so, High Exemplar. The man who spoke to us wore Morrowan colors. A parish priest, perhaps?"

"A Morrowan priest?" Gravus was incredulous, and drew Reverence, his flail. "I'll deal with them."

"No, I will speak to this priest." The Harbinger's interruption prompted Gravus to pull his horse up short. His eyes were wide with surprise, but he simply bowed his head. He urged his horse to follow after her as she drifted serenely in the direction of the newcomers.

A Morrowan rector stood at the fore of the line, in similarly ragged robes as the rest of the refugees but carrying a heavily bound book. He bowed low as the Harbinger came forward to regard him. The line of refugees behind him stared up at her in wonder but also fear, whispering among themselves. Several made unfamiliar gestures. The fear coming from them in waves was jarring to her and quite different from the reverence she had received from the people of the town. She could immediately tell there was not a Menite among them. The priest implored, "Please, have mercy on us and take us into your protection, great lady." He attempted to speak with the same sonorous tone he likely used in congregation, but to her ear it sounded wavering and uncertain.

"I ask you, Rector Sirian," she began, prompting even more murmuring among those gathered as she gave his name unprompted. "Will you renounce your faith in Morrow and be cleansed in the glory of the True Faith? Will you bring your people back to the worship of the Creator, who set you forth in the dawn of mankind?"

His hands upon the book trembled. "What you ask . . . I am a priest of Morrow, my lady. We offer thanks to the Creator at the outset of every service! I will continue to do so. I will speak your praises, if only you will take us within your sheltering arms."

"I can unmake any vows you have made to lesser faiths, and you can begin your life anew in the service of the Creator. This is an opportunity for the salvation and redemption of those who follow you. Their lives rest in your hands, and your heart. Look upon me and put aside that blasphemous book. Cast aside your false symbols." Even as she spoke, the Harbinger felt a growing pressure inside her mind that she knew meant Cryx was gathering. She did not have long.

The priest trembled even more. As she hovered before him, the Avatar joined her, smoke plumes pouring from its stacks but looking like the walking embodiment of faith. Again the reaction of the refugees betrayed greater fear than wonder as they beheld the machine alongside the chosen prophet of the Lawgiver. The priest looked back to the people behind him and swallowed deeply. Finally he let the book in his hands fall to the ground. A gasp came from those nearest, but he shook his head and held up a hand to them. His shaking fingers pulled forth a silver chain bearing the sunburst symbol of Morrow from around his neck, and this too he dropped to the mud. He prostrated himself into the soil. "I will do as you ask. Save these people. Please."

The Harbinger's chest ached as she looked down from her high vantage. The man was possessed of a certain sort of courage and a proper regard for his followers. But his casting aside of his symbols was insincere. If anything, doing so had only reaffirmed his belief in Morrowan philosophies. His heart was closed to the Creator. He lied to her now, and he sought to lie to Menoth. Any vow he made would fail.

"I am sorry." Her voice was heavy with the sorrow she felt. "You are unwilling to embrace our salvation. I can see your heart, and it is false. You and your people will find no succor here." She could see High Exemplar Gravus moving his horse forward at these words, as his anger stirred. Once more she stopped him with a gesture. "Let them depart unharmed. They can reflect on their folly in the hours remaining to them. We must go." She addressed the refugees one last time, "I will see you again in Urcaen. Try to find the City of Man, and perhaps you will be given entrance if you demonstrate your regret and humility."

They screamed at her as she left, weeping and cursing her, and the entire clamor was like thorns on the heart of the Harbinger. She restrained her followers from retaliating, turning her back on the tumult to return to the vanguard of her soldiers. It was continually surprising how deeply Morrow's message had taken hold; even in the face of their destruction, such people could not set aside false teachings. Conversion without belief was empty and useless. Still, she would not entirely give up hope. She would continue to make these efforts, and some few would realize the rectitude of the True Law. The rest must suffer before they could understand, and she had to harden her heart to them. Mercy to those who needed to suffer would only cause them greater harm and delay their road to salvation. It was no mercy at all.

Leaving the Morrowan refugees to fend for themselves as the Cryxian horde followed after them, the Harbinger's interdictions and the rescued townspeople marched on toward Leryn.

No other nation in western Immoren has made such great advances from such humble beginnings as the Protectorate of Menoth. The Protectorate has risen from a defeated and oppressed Cygnaran minority to one of the great powers of the continent, stretching the reach of its military far beyond its original borders. While the Menite religion itself is rooted in antiquity, with ancient ceremonies and prayers taken from the earliest written words, this rise of the nation as a respected military power has occurred only within the last several decades. The Protectorate has been extremely successful in expanding and revolutionizing its military while staying true to its religious convictions. This transformation was made possible by the bold examples of several great leaders, some who have passed to the afterlife in Urcaen and others who yet walk among the faithful providing direct guidance.

Its successes are all the more remarkable given the Protectorate has the smallest population of all the Iron Kingdoms. Proof of the triumph of its efforts can be seen in accomplishments like the successful defense of Sul, the unprecedented invasion of Caspia, and the seizure of the Llaelese city of Leryn. By the strength of its army, the Protectorate of Menoth has taken control of its destiny, reshaped itself, and demonstrated its ability to fulfill its promise to strike down all who refuse to bow to the Creator of Man.

The nation has been preparing to unleash its crusades for decades, and the hour is at hand. Its military has been built into a tower of strength through the work of past hierarchs, and now at its pinnacle is a man who embodies the principles of the faith: Hierarch Severius. The first warcaster to rise initially to absolute control of the military and then to absolute authority over the entire nation, this leader has spent his entire lifetime working to see the Menite crusade realized. His people stand united behind him, willing to execute any order at his command and to strike down whatever enemy becomes the subject of his wrath.

The military continues to undergo radical reorganization and expansion. Already, the Protectorate armed forces show a blend of old and new ideas, pragmatic discipline mixed with religious ceremony. This is the nature of the Protectorate itself, which exists not for temporal power alone but also for the protection of the Creator's interests on Caen. The Protectorate is a theocracy on every level, with its priests assuming positions of rulership over daily governance as well as military doctrine. Although the majority of its standing army is made up of citizen soldiers compelled to serve, the Protectorate's elite forces draw from several ancient martial orders, each tightly integrated with the Temple of Menoth and its clergy.

Its diversity and the complexity of its ancient and modern influences make the Protectorate military difficult for its enemies to predict, a fact Protectorate leaders are adept at exploiting. While many of its military decisions prioritize mundane principles of logistics and long-term strategic interests, the Protectorate is just as likely to exert its strength for major religious goals. Some of these objectives are comprehensible only to prophets and others who can interpret divine portents. The faithful on Caen are part of the endless War of Souls the gods fight in Urcaen, even if they do not always understand their place or function. Via intermediaries such as the Harbinger of Menoth or members of the Reclaimant Order, Protectorate leaders have a unique perspective on divine will.

For this reason, soldiers in the Protectorate have learned to trust the priesthood implicitly. Those at the bottom of the chain of command are accustomed to fighting in ignorance of the ultimate purposes of their actions. Orders are not to be questioned but obeyed, accepted with the same faith

URCAEN AND THE WAR OF SOULS

As a deeply religious people, the citizens of the Protectorate of Menoth worry as much about the afterlife as they do their day-to-day lives. Menites believe reality is divided between Caen, the world of the living, and Urcaen, the world of the dead. While the Creator once walked Caen, he now exists solely in Urcaen, where he oversees a vast domain within which dwell the souls of every faithful Menite who has lived and died since mankind was created. This is the City of Man.

By its nature, Urcaen is imperfectly understood by the living; it is impossible for mortals to grasp its true scope and nature. Menites are taught that outside the great walls enclosing the City of Man lies an infinite hellish wilderness of untamed chaos, supernatural storms, and savage monstrous beasts. This is the domain of Menoth's ancient foe, the Devourer Wurm. Other lesser gods, such as Morrow and Thamar, have their own poorer domains in Urcaen, where their residents are envious of the shelter afforded to those who dwell in the City of Man.

War rages between the followers of these gods in Urcaen. This is the War of Souls, an epic and unending clash between the divine powers in the afterlife. Menites believe it is their destiny to live an eternity in service to Menoth in the City of Man after they die. Each of the faithful must play his part to preserve Menoth's realm from the depravities of the Devourer and the temptations set forth by the perfidious philosophies of Morrow and Thamar.

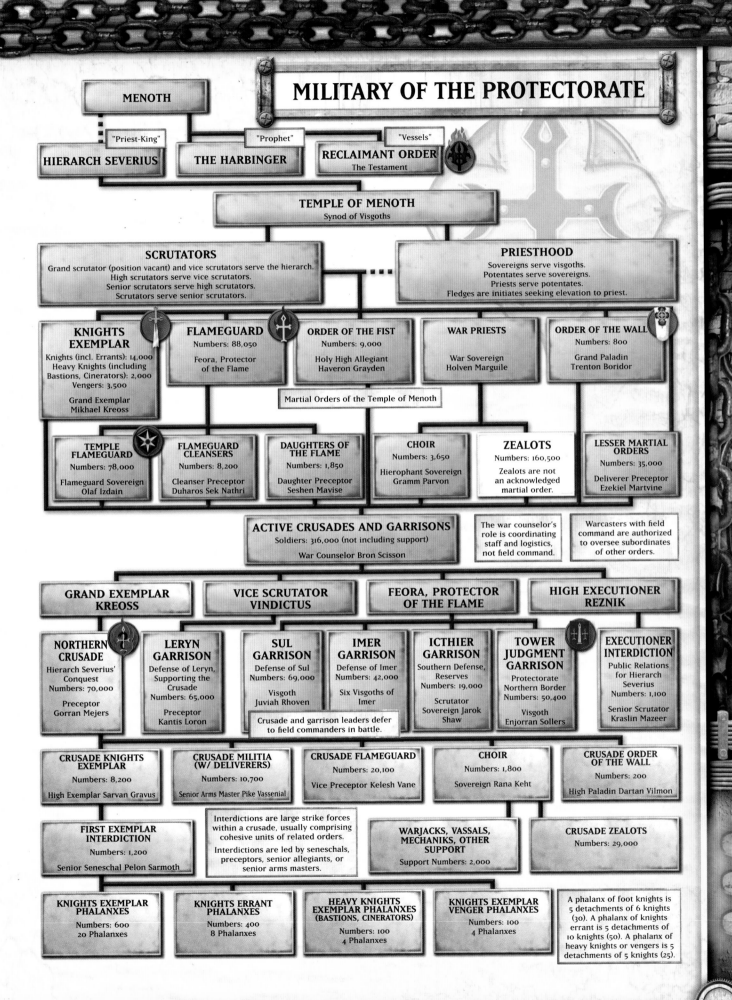

MILITARY OF THE PROTECTORATE

MENOTH

"Priest-King" — **HIERARCH SEVERIUS**

"Prophet" — **THE HARBINGER**

"Vessels" — **RECLAIMANT ORDER** / The Testament

TEMPLE OF MENOTH
Synod of Visgoths

SCRUTATORS
Grand scrutator (position vacant) and vice scrutators serve the hierarch.
High scrutators serve vice scrutators.
Senior scrutators serve high scrutators.
Scrutators serve senior scrutators.

PRIESTHOOD
Sovereigns serve visgoths.
Potentates serve sovereigns.
Priests serve potentates.
Fledges are initiates seeking elevation to priest.

KNIGHTS EXEMPLAR
Knights (incl. Errants): 14,000
Heavy Knights (including Bastions, Cinerators): 2,000
Vengers: 3,500
Grand Exemplar Mikhael Kreoss

FLAMEGUARD
Numbers: 88,050
Feora, Protector of the Flame

ORDER OF THE FIST
Numbers: 9,000
Holy High Allegiant Haveron Grayden

WAR PRIESTS
War Sovereign Holven Marguile

ORDER OF THE WALL
Numbers: 800
Grand Paladin Trenton Boridor

Martial Orders of the Temple of Menoth

TEMPLE FLAMEGUARD
Numbers: 78,000
Flameguard Sovereign Olaf Izdain

FLAMEGUARD CLEANSERS
Numbers: 8,200
Cleanser Preceptor Duharos Sek Nathri

DAUGHTERS OF THE FLAME
Numbers: 1,850
Daughter Preceptor Seshen Mavise

CHOIR
Numbers: 3,650
Hierophant Sovereign Gramm Parvon

ZEALOTS
Numbers: 160,500
Zealots are not an acknowledged martial order.

LESSER MARTIAL ORDERS
Numbers: 35,000
Deliverer Preceptor Ezekiel Martvine

ACTIVE CRUSADES AND GARRISONS
Soldiers: 316,000 (not including support)
War Counselor Bron Scisson

The war counselor's role is coordinating staff and logistics, not field command.

Warcasters with field command are authorized to oversee subordinates of other orders.

GRAND EXEMPLAR KREOSS

VICE SCRUTATOR VINDICTUS

FEORA, PROTECTOR OF THE FLAME

HIGH EXECUTIONER REZNIK

NORTHERN CRUSADE
Hierarch Severius' Conquest
Numbers: 70,000
Preceptor Gorran Mejers

LERYN GARRISON
Defense of Leryn, Supporting the Crusade
Numbers: 65,000
Preceptor Kantis Loron

SUL GARRISON
Defense of Sul
Numbers: 69,000
Visgoth Juviah Rhoven

IMER GARRISON
Defense of Imer
Numbers: 42,000
Six Visgoths of Imer

Crusade and garrison leaders defer to field commanders in battle.

ICTHIER GARRISON
Southern Defense, Reserves
Numbers: 19,000
Scrutator Sovereign Jarok Shaw

TOWER JUDGMENT GARRISON
Protectorate Northern Border
Numbers: 50,400
Visgoth Enjorran Sollers

EXECUTIONER INTERDICTION
Public Relations for Hierarch Severius
Numbers: 1,100
Senior Scrutator Kraslin Mazeer

CRUSADE KNIGHTS EXEMPLAR
Numbers: 8,200
High Exemplar Sarvan Gravus

CRUSADE MILITIA (W/ DELIVERERS)
Numbers: 10,700
Senior Arms Master Pike Vassenial

CRUSADE FLAMEGUARD
Numbers: 20,100
Vice Preceptor Kelesh Vane

CHOIR
Numbers: 1,800
Sovereign Rana Keht

CRUSADE ORDER OF THE WALL
Numbers: 200
High Paladin Dartan Vilmon

FIRST EXEMPLAR INTERDICTION
Numbers: 1,200
Senior Seneschal Pelon Sarmoth

Interdictions are large strike forces within a crusade, usually comprising cohesive units of related orders.
Interdictions are led by seneschals, preceptors, senior allegiants, or senior arms masters.

WARJACKS, VASSALS, MECHANIKS, OTHER SUPPORT
Support Numbers: 2,000

CRUSADE ZEALOTS
Numbers: 29,000

KNIGHTS EXEMPLAR PHALANXES
Numbers: 600
20 Phalanxes

KNIGHTS ERRANT PHALANXES
Numbers: 400
8 Phalanxes

HEAVY KNIGHTS EXEMPLAR PHALANXES (BASTIONS, CINERATORS)
Numbers: 100
4 Phalanxes

KNIGHTS EXEMPLAR VENGER PHALANXES
Numbers: 100
4 Phalanxes

A phalanx of foot knights is 5 detachments of 6 knights (30). A phalanx of knights errant is 5 detachments of 10 knights (50). A phalanx of heavy knights or vengers is 5 detachments of 5 knights (25).

MENITE PRIEST HIERARCHY

While the Protectorate of Menoth is a new nation, the ranks adopted by its priests are from ancient traditions and have been only slightly reinterpreted to suit the needs of the theocracy. The ranks used by Sul-Menite clergy are also shared by Menites elsewhere in the Iron Kingdoms, such as among the Old Faith in Khador. From lowest to highest, the priestly ranks are: fledge (also sometimes termed initiate), priest, potentate, sovereign, visgoth, and hierarch.

These ranks predate the Cygnaran Civil War, but historically very few hierarchs have existed outside the Protectorate of Menoth. This title has special religious significance and symbolism to the Menite faith, representing absolute theological authority. Traditionally the rank is bestowed only upon a priest who had the unanimous support of the visgoths, a conjunction that almost never happened. For example, the Old Faith in Khador has not titled anyone hierarch since before the invasion of the Orgoth, and for this reason its clergy are led by myriad visgoths.

The Protectorate was born from the civil war inspired by the first Sul-Menite to call himself hierarch in centuries, Hierarch Sulon. He united all the southern visgoths under his leadership and gathered the scattered faithful to Caspia. This set the precedent for those who would follow.

Visgoth Ozeall, who reluctantly assumed governance of the Protectorate after Sulon's death, set down the terms by which the nation would be run. By these laws, the leadership of the Protectorate rested in the hands of the Synod of Visgoths. Each visgoth had jurisdiction over a major aspect of the government. The laws stipulated that the Synod could choose to surrender its authority to a single senior priest who earned their unanimous support, who would thenceforth be called hierarch. Once approved, a hierarch would retain that title for life, and no mortal power could revoke his authority. In this regard, hierarch is not an inherited position, nor can it be passed to a chosen heir.

Severius is the sixth hierarch in the Protectorate's history and the first to transition seamlessly to the head of the Temple, an event

made possible by the guidance of the Harbinger of Menoth. In becoming hierarch Severius joined the esteemed company of his legendary predecessors: Hierarchs Garrick Voyle, Kilgor Ravonal, Caltor Turgis, Gevard Luctine, and Sulon.

In the Protectorate, an acknowledged hierarch becomes the ultimate voice of both secular and spiritual authority. Each hierarch relies upon the Synod of Visgoths to oversee the government bureaucracy, which is run on every level by subordinate priests. Visgoths maintain the peace, regulate theological doctrine, and ensure the smooth running of the Protectorate's industry, the health of its population, and adequate support for any garrisons or crusades. If required, visgoths join the crusades as military leaders, but more often they are occupied supervising the nation's infrastructure.

The number of active visgoths can change as required. The nine current visgoths are listed below.

- Juviah Rhoven, Visgoth and Overseer of Sul, Vice Scrutator
- Var Bodalin, First Visgoth of Imer, Vice Scrutator, Prime Curate over Scrutator Initiation
- Delcon Vesher, Second Visgoth of Imer, Vice Scrutator, Head of the Lyceum of the True Law
- Mishiva Nestore, Third Visgoth of Imer, Senior Scrutator, Overseer of the Vassals of Menoth
- Lars Elimon, Fourth Visgoth of Imer, Senior Scrutator, Overseer of Temple Defense and Armament
- Enjorran Sollers, Visgoth and Overseer of Tower Judgment, Senior Scrutator
- Ark Razek, Fifth Visgoth of Imer, Overseer of the Sul-Menite Artificers
- Morgimer Jasrun, Sixth Visgoth of Imer; Overseer of Mines, Quarries, and Menoth's Fury
- Brone Scarrel, Visgoth of the South, Overseer of Ancient Icthier

that assures each Menite of the place waiting for him in the afterlife.

Although not every Menite is equally pious, in the aggregate their beliefs bestow a degree of conviction, efficiency, and zealous fanaticism that strengthens them through the most difficult ordeals and setbacks. Enemies of the faith fear this zealotry, as other armies must rely on less certain traits like loyalty and duty—sometimes bought by coin. The Protectorate military has proven that faith has a tangible power. There is no army in western Immoren as singularly united.

THE MARTIAL ORDERS AND THE MILITIA

A staggeringly high percentage of the Protectorate's population serves at least part time in its military, considerably higher than is the case for any of its rivals. The Temple has been developing and stockpiling weapons since its foundation and is able to arm and equip a full third of the population. Training takes time, and the Sul-Menites have discovered that not every citizen is equally zealous, qualified, or capable of assisting the war effort. Leaders of the Temple are constantly evaluating the time required

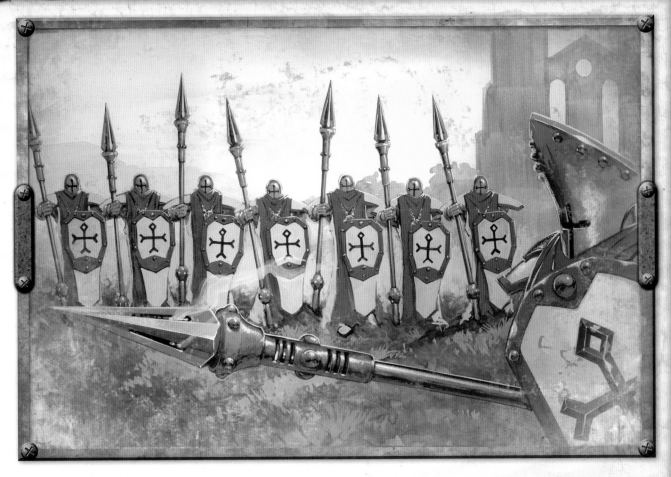

to train a professional soldier against the immediate need to field armed bodies. All the Protectorate's enemies have greater populations, resources, and manufacturing capacity—a fact of which the Synod is well aware.

Despite the large number of armed civilians bolstering the Protectorate's war efforts, at its core the military is most reliant on the strength of its smaller and highly trained martial orders. The backbone of the Protectorate military is the elite Knights Exemplar and, increasingly, the ranks of the Temple Flameguard. Members of these two orders are cognizant of the fact they exist solely to fight the battles of their faith. The leaders of the Exemplar order in particular have served as preeminent military leaders and advisors since the founding of the Protectorate.

The Temple Flameguard has assumed the role of the regular army of the Protectorate of Menoth. At one time charged with the defense of Menite temples and holy sites, the Flameguard has been newly expanded to execute the Protectorate's military ambitions.

The evolution of the Knights Exemplar has been more circuitous. These knights were predated by the Order of the Wall, an ancient order of independent Menite knights, but the paladins of the Order of the Wall refused to serve blindly and believed the dictates of faith must be adjudicated by one's conscience. Their beliefs regularly put them at odds with the priest caste. The Exemplar order was created with a code of absolute obedience to the clergy in reaction to this and eventually eclipsed the Order of the Wall, particularly in the Protectorate of Menoth. Scrutators came to rely on the Knights Exemplar to help them maintain doctrinal purity among the people and root out potential heretics and traitors. While the Order of the Wall still exists in small numbers, its impact on Protectorate politics and the military is negligible. It is preserved out of a sense of tradition and because these paladins are popular figures with the populace, but there is no question the Knights Exemplar have risen to become the preeminent warriors of the Temple.

While the Knights Exemplar still serve as the martial arm of the faith, over time it has become less occupied with keeping vigil on the faithful than with battling external enemies. The role of internal police force was shifted initially to the Temple Flameguard and later to the Order of the Fist. That order was created specifically for this task, its monks trained to blend into the civilian population and root out treachery from within. Working in tandem with the Order of the Fist, the Flameguard Cleansers and the Daughters of the Flame watch the citizenry and address both internal and external threats. The Knights Exemplar has evolved into a purely martial force regularly sent to do battle in foreign lands.

While the Exemplar knights are the Protectorate's preeminent fighting force, their code and training limits their numbers. Not every pious man or woman who would serve the Temple is suited to swearing the oath of the Exemplar. Similarly, the Temple Flameguard requires full-time dedication during at least the years of service for its professional soldiery. A large number of Protectorate citizens are allowed to aid the war effort without dedicating their lives to the task by joining its militia forces or volunteering when the battle priests sound the call to war. Caches of arms are maintained throughout the Protectorate to arm and equip these forces at a moment's notice.

While referred to as "voluntary," service in a time of crusade is compulsory, and the clergy are issued quotas for able-bodied men and women required to fill the ranks of the auxiliary fighting forces. The initiates of the Order of the Fist have proven adept at rounding up and enlisting those who have not demonstrated the devotion and piety expected of a citizen of the Protectorate. Nonetheless, the continual immersion of the populace in religious doctrine makes it relatively easy to gather large numbers of willing zealots and soldiers of all ages into service. These lay soldier forces make up the lesser military orders, such as the Deliverers.

There has been an ongoing struggle between respect for the traditions of each martial order and the establishment of a clear and centralized chain of command. Traditionally as long as the leaders of each order demonstrated their loyalty to the priest caste, and in particular to the Synod or hierarch, they were given complete autonomy over their organizations. Some of this remains, as each order can function as a self-contained organization. However, Hierarch Voyle realized the ability to conduct war on a larger scale would require the integration of the disparate elements of the Protectorate's fighting forces. It was with this task in mind that Severius was first promoted to grand scrutator and charged with the unification of the military orders.

Grand Scrutator Severius understood that reorganizing the Protectorate's military structure to support its crusades required careful attention to logistics and planning and created the office of war counselor. He appointed Bron Scisson to this post as the senior-most secular officer in the Protectorate military, not only to oversee the militias but also to work with the various martial orders to maintain the smooth running of the crusades. While War Counselor Scisson has no field authority, all elements of the Protectorate military are expected to cooperate with his staff in regards to supply, logistics, and personnel shifts. His office has none of the glory of those who march to battle, but without his efforts the Protectorate could not support its larger endeavors. The war counselor's staff has moved from Imer to Leryn to serve alongside Hierarch Severius, although couriers regularly convey coded messages back to the six visgoths of Imer to coordinate with the capital.

AN ARMY FORGED IN SECRET

Founded in the aftermath of civil conflict, the Protectorate of Menoth has always had a tumultuous relationship with Cygnar, the nation that forced its submission at its founding. By the terms agreed upon at the end of the Cygnaran Civil War in 484 AR, the Protectorate was forbidden to keep a standing army. These laws were never strictly enforced, but for decades the Protectorate seemed to accept them even while creating and expanding martial orders to protect the Temple and its adherents. The need for these groups was justified by ongoing fighting with tribal Idrians southeast of Cygnar, which continued even after the majority were pacified and converted to the worship of Menoth in 504 AR.

For many decades Cygnar seemed content with this arrangement, perhaps reassured that the Menites had inherited a resource-poor region and one inhabited by

CONTROL OF THE SEAS

The Protectorate of Menoth is not a naval power, although it does possess a small number of armed fighting vessels it employs to defend its docks in Sul and the coastline extending between Sul and Ancient Icthier. The majority of the Protectorate's ocean-faring vessels are working ships, including a fishing fleet based in Sul. Any of these ships could be rigged for battle if required, but the theocracy has largely surrendered control over the Gulf of Cygnar to the Cygnaran Navy. The visgoths are aware they would lose in any substantial engagement against Cygnar's formidable eastern fleet.

While this is seen as a weakness in the Protectorate's defenses, it has not proven to be important enough to address. Most of the military clashes between the Protectorate and its enemies take place on land, and there have been no substantial attempts by the Cygnaran Navy to strike at the smaller settlements dotting the Protectorate's coastline. Cryxian vessels occasionally make strikes against Protectorate shores, but these incidents are rare. It has proven to be more cost effective to allow Cygnar's navy to intercept Cryxian raiders rather than expending limited resources toward shipbuilding. Sul's docks are well defended and sheltered behind imposing walls, while the capital of Imer and its vital industry and mines are safely a hundred miles inland. The most vulnerable Protectorate target in this regard is the blessed city of Ancient Icthier, whose isolated location has thus far served to preserve it from attack.

Scrutators are an essential part of the Protectorate of Menoth's theocracy, forming the inner circle of the highest leadership among the priest caste. Their internal order is removed from the ordinary bureaucratic and liturgical concerns occupying the ordinary priesthood. While all priests are to be respected and obeyed by laymen, it is the scrutators who watch over the priests themselves. They are considered dark protectors of the faith, those who feel the difficult but vital calling to put all other considerations aside and focus on the preservation of the Temple by any means necessary. Being a scrutator is not a privilege but a responsibility—and one not bestowed lightly.

The scrutators consider their positions unenviable, as they cannot spend their time in the serene contemplation of the divine like ordinary priests. Instead, they must train to master the pragmatic arts of governance, torture, and interrogation; it is their purpose to test the faithful continually for any hints of treachery or heresy. Captured enemies must similarly be questioned for vital intelligence, punished for their transgressions, and executed. Scrutators believe that inflicting pain is the ultimate course to root out deception and discover truth.

This caste must abandon the indulgences of mercy and forgiveness, a fact symbolized by the masks they wear. These masks serve as a barrier between their human faces and the individuals they confront and interrogate. While all Menite priests wear ceremonial masks in honor of the one worn by Menoth, ordinary priests can remove them when speaking with friends or family. Scrutators are unmasked only when alone, as their station denies them the comforts of family or friendship. Among Menite citizens, a regular priest may be loved or adored as a teacher of Menoth's glory, but scrutators are universally feared.

The scrutators have achieved a prominence within Protectorate society that far exceeds their traditional status. Since ancient times it has been rare to see more than a single scrutator, who served by exacting judgment on captured criminals and heretics. They were executioners and torturers, and it was their task to root out those who had broken the law, whether temporal or divine. Shortly after the founding of the Protectorate of Menoth, the scrutator caste seized the reins of power. They became leading priests and the internal watchman of the clergy. It was natural that these formidable figures would rise to positions of authority. Every hierarch since the Protectorate's founding has served as a scrutator; the Synod believes only scrutators have the proper training and experience to make the difficult choices required to lead the nation and preserve the faith against the faithless.

numerous hostile tribesmen. Laws were enacted allowing the Protectorate to arm and train defenders of its temples and other holy places as well as to ensure the basic safety of its citizenry. The martial orders created under this pretext persist today, each of which remained tightly integrated to the Temple itself.

The adoption of laborjacks and eventually warjacks by the Protectorate happened early in the reign of Hierarch Gevard Luctine, but not without considerable dissention. Hard-line traditionalists insisted innovations like mechanika were anathema to Menoth according to the True Law, because of the arcane science required in their construction. Hierarch Luctine and his visgoths foresaw that such machines would be vital to the long-term prosperity and success of this new nation and argued it was their holy duty to find a way to purify their creation and use. These visionaries granted that mechanika and the arcane arts were unquestionably tainted but conjectured that they could be sanctified and blessed by the proper application of prayer, the engraving of holy scripture, and the constant ministrations of clergy tasked with cleansing them. By Menoth's grace would his people claim the might of these contrivances for him.

While laborjacks were incorporated into a number of industries to exploit the reliable strength and stamina of these machines, many more were outfitted with improvised weaponry to fight alongside the Protectorate's martial orders. Marching alongside these 'jacks were the first choirs, singing holy hymns to bless and sanctify the machines in battle.

It is doubtful Cygnar's governing authorities and spies were entirely fooled by pretenses that all the Protectorate 'jacks were committed to labor. However, they turned a blind eye to the mustering of temple soldiers and the arming of laborjacks so long as they were employed against savages dwelling on the fringes of the wastes. It is also likely these efforts obscured precisely how many 'jacks had been converted to battle readiness in addition to disguising the fact that the Menites were building new warjacks of their own design.

Aiding the clandestine efforts of the early Protectorate was Cygnar's almost exclusive focus on the great city of Sul, once eastern Caspia. The Protectorate lacked any meaningful secondary cities for many decades, so this was an understandable oversight. As a result, however, the Cygnaran crown was blinded to several significant developments many miles from the Black River. In 504 AR, a great earthquake struck the sands in the midst of a large battle between the Sul-Menites and a vast host of Idrian warriors. In the wake of this earthquake, which left the Menites standing but forced every Idrian to their knees, most of the Idrians present immediately converted to the worship of the Creator. This act of divine providence not only greatly increased and diversified the Protectorate's population but also brought the Idrian city of Imer and its surroundings into the theocracy.

Imer remained a primitive city for many decades, but several untapped mineral resources were discovered nearby shortly after the conversion of its populace. These included several rich veins of iron, copper, and tin in the foothills east and southeast of Imer. While it took many years to build the mines and other infrastructure to exploit these resources, they proved to be vital to the nascent Protectorate industry, particularly the eventual production of weapons and warjack components. Because most of the raw ore and other resources were initially processed in Sul, Cygnar never fully apprehended the extent of these mining operations and thus vastly underestimated the extent of the Protectorate's war industries until their fruits were revealed at the outset of the crusades.

More resources awaited discovery in the "barren" east, as discovered by Hierarch Caltor Turgis, who considerably broadened the Protectorate's borders during his reign from 535–549 AR. This period saw the construction of Tower Judgment on the northern border to stand as a looming bastion of the faith, the stronghold of the scrutators. In the south, Ancient Icthier was rediscovered and settled once again, bringing a wealth of forgotten sacred texts but also more tangible gains in precious stones. The diamonds and other gems gathered there helped open trade abroad by lining the pockets of Cygnaran inspectors and border guards.

As important as these findings were, it was the discovery and exploitation of Menoth's Fury, distilled from a less volatile oil bubbling up from the sands, that would rank among the greatest achievements of Hierarch Turgis' reign. With the proper distillation and refinery process, this oil became far more than a fuel for lanterns and cooking fires; it is a substance able to spark tremendous conflagrations. At its most refined, Menoth's Fury ignites immediately on exposure to air, adheres to surfaces with tenacity, and burns at an extremely high temperature that can melt steel. In time it became one of the signature weapons of the Protectorate, a substance synonymous with the wrath of the Lawgiver.

IGNITING THE GREAT CRUSADES

The Protectorate focused on expansion of its territories and the construction of infrastructure in the harsh south and east until the rise of Hierarch Kilgor Ravonal in 568 AR. Ravonal, the fourth Protectorate hierarch, was the first to preach the doctrine of true independence. Under his direction the clergy began to gather their nation's strength with the goal of restoring the word of Menoth to those kingdoms that had forsaken him. Ravonal preached it was not enough for the Protectorate to preserve the True Law; the heretics abroad must be cowed into submission just as the Idrians had been. He asserted that the Morrowan nations were cesspools of perfidy, lawlessness, and faithlessness and that their forcible conversion would be a mercy compared to the fate awaiting them in the afterlife.

Ravonal stockpiled resources and weapons purchased by the sale of diamonds abroad. He also ordered the expansion of the Knights Exemplar and the Temple Flameguard while ostensibly still heeding the treaties with Cygnar, as these groups were Temple protectors and therefore enabled the Protectorate to circumvent Cygnaran proscriptions against building a standing army. These two orders would become cornerstones of the Protectorate's new military. Ravonal also endorsed the creation of the Order of the Fist, an internal police force founded and led by the man who would succeed him, Garrick Voyle. The founding of the Order of the Fist freed the Knights Exemplar from their civil responsibilities, allowing them to focus solely on preparations for the imminent and necessary battles to come.

Following Ravonal's death, years of infighting among the Synod left the government ineffective until Hierarch Voyle's eventual rise to power in 588 AR. Voyle consolidated his power with the aid of his devoted monks, his scrutator allies, and his own formidable abilities. He was strongly influenced by his predecessor and continued the work Ravonal had begun.

Voyle's reign began immediately following the Scharde Invasions that had occupied Cygnar for four years. This war had tremendously taxed the Cygnaran Army and Navy and required them to spend time rebuilding and recruiting, distractions Voyle capitalized on as he began to expand the Protectorate's military strength substantially. He was later similarly able to exploit the era of Cygnaran confusion and unrest following Leto Raelthorne's coup.

As Ravonal had before him, Voyle understood that before the Protectorate could launch its crusades it must first lay a proper foundation for its armies. Key to this was his radical decision to move the capital of the Protectorate to Imer, which was entirely reconstructed under his direction

THE UMBER GUARD
FLAMEGUARD OF THE TENTH INTERDICTION

LEADERSHIP

- Preceptor Marvase Denjerin
- Temple Flameguard Senior Arms Masters Emanokar, Penthorne, and Malsythe
- Flameguard Cleanser Senior Arms Master Ard Corcoran
- Daughter of the Flame Senior Captain Laili Emonfoha

ASSETS

- 900 Temple Flameguard
- 200 Flameguard Cleansers
- 90 Daughters of the Flame
- 4 Heavy Warjacks, including 1 Guardian
- 6 Light Warjacks

Fiat Flamma "Let There Be Flame"

The Umber Guard earned its fame during the defense of Sul and the attack on Caspia, proving to be a resolute example the rest of the Flameguard could look to for inspiration. Feora has selected the Umber Guard to serve as the core of a dedicated interdiction under her personal supervision tasked to undermine Cygnaran defenses in the southern theater. Those who serve the Umber Guard do not know these actions have not been technically authorized by Hierarch Severius and are loyalty tests with Feora—nor would they care. They are hardened zealots who have been thoroughly integrated into the modern structure of the Flameguard. They understand the priests are the rulers of the theocracy, but they obey only their chain of command; by their training that command reaches no further than the Priestess and Protector of the Flame.

During the initial invasion of Sul by the Cygnarans, the Umber Guard both were among the most zealous defenders of the Great Temple of the Creator and protected Sulon's Remembrance, the tomb for that revered leader. This interdiction earned honor and prestige during these defensive battles and fought in the bloodiest and most protracted of the subsequent street-to-street battles. They learned very well the nature of the enemy and how best to thwart their advance through the city.

The interdiction is most famous, however, for its vital role in the subsequent counterattack on Caspia. The Umber Guard was at the forefront of the Menites chasing the Cygnarans out of Sul, and it was these soldiers who took the initiative to seize the Cygnaran gates before they could be closed. The subsequent invasion of Caspia would not have been possible without these heroic efforts, which earned those soldiers the personal commendations of both Feora and Grand Exemplar Kreoss.

The Umber Guard is now stationed in western Sul, posted to Sulon's Fortress. They helped protect this historical monument during its costly and delicate restoration from the lengthy defilement it endured when captured by Cygnarans and used as their field headquarters in the city. While some phalanxes of the interdiction are found at this site at all times, the majority are frequently sent on special missions, including into the outlying region north of Sul and sometimes clandestinely across the Black River and into enemy territory. They have been used to gauge the ongoing defensive situation with the Cygnarans as well as to intercept military supplies and conduct other harassment operations, such as burning crops and food warehouses. Their goal is to weaken the Cygnaran defenders at the Caspia garrison and Eastwall without provoking a substantial counterattack.

Many Flameguard phalanxes are made up of a single unit type, but the phalanxes of the Tenth Interdiction are mixed. This allows them to adapt to evolving needs better and to operate semi-autonomously. The bulk of the force remains Temple Flameguard, but it also includes a large attachment of Cleansers as well as a handpicked contingent of the most experienced Daughters of the Flame, who are most often chosen to conduct the most challenging espionage and sabotage missions.

into a modern city with full industrial capacity. This placed the central industries of the Protectorate farther from Cygnaran interference as well as closer to the vital mines in the eastern hills.

Work on the capital allowed Hierarch Voyle to implement several other reforms to strengthen the Protectorate military, including creating the House of Truth as the headquarters for the new Vassals of Menoth. This organization had its seeds in earlier efforts to capture foreign arcanists and force them to produce warjack cortexes for the Protectorate's armies. This practice had proven its worth, but Voyle greatly expanded its operations and included efforts to recruit and train both arcanists and mechaniks from among the Menite faithful. The captured wizards brought with them valuable lore and techniques from more mechanikally advanced nations, but the supply of these enslaved and reluctant workers was inadequate to the needs of the Protectorate's warjack industry. Even locally trained members of the Vassals were to be watched and scrutinized as closely as those captured abroad; working with arcane energies was still considered a corruptive influence requiring precautions. These measures reassured the more traditional and less pragmatic members of the clergy that such a compromise

would not violate the spirit of the True Law while providing substantial military gains.

Once the Protectorate war industry was proceeding apace, Hierarch Voyle began systematically to test King Leto's willingness to enforce the old treaties. He encouraged certain outlying Menite forces to conduct surgical strikes against Cygnaran targets, such as shipping along the Black River. These increasingly belligerent displays of the Protectorate's growing martial strength were carefully calculated to gauge the Cygnaran response. Simultaneously, Voyle sent ambassadors to Caspia to convey the impression that a peaceful resolution to these skirmishes would be considered. In all cases, the Cygnarans did not escalate the fighting but instead relied upon diplomatic methods to convey their displeasure. These interactions convinced Voyle the weak-willed Cygnaran king had a strong preference for peace at all costs and would never have the stomach for the casualties required to disarm the Protectorate by force. Accordingly, Voyle increased warjack production, weapons stockpiles, and the aggressive recruitment and training of battle-ready soldiers for the imminent crusade.

The perfect opportunity to unleash that crusade presented itself after Khador invaded Llael, forcing King Leto's army to dispatch a substantial fighting force north in defense of the beleaguered Cygnaran ally. Seizing the moment, Hierarch Voyle put aside all pretenses of obeying Cygnaran law to declare the independence of his nation, proclaiming that the Protectorate of Menoth would be beholden only to the True Law. The appearance of the Harbinger provided tangible proof Menoth approved of his plans. The Protectorate boldly struck at Cygnar while the older nation's military was strained by the war abroad. These initial attacks included the demolition of the Marchbridge to disrupt a vital rail line and assaulting Caspia's gates with the great siege engine Lawbringer.

LAUNCHING THE NORTHERN CRUSADE

In 606 AR, while much of the Protectorate's military might was occupied in clashes against Cygnar in the south, the Harbinger of Menoth informed Hierarch Voyle of a prophetic vision from Menoth regarding a danger in the north. She had received the divine mandate to confront a great darkness that threatened the realms of both the living and the afterlife, and she would therefore arm for war. The hierarch authorized the Northern Crusade and left it in the hands of Grand Scrutator Severius to ensure the Harbinger reached her destination. In addition, Severius was given several vital long-term objectives, including converting as many outsiders to the faith as possible, by any means necessary, and creating a permanent bastion for the faith in this region to be used for the ongoing conversion and arming of the faithful.

Among the Northern Crusade's greatest assets was the Harbinger's ability to sway the faithful regardless of their petty national allegiances. In the days leading up to the initiation of the Northern Crusade, the Harbinger called for Menites across western Immoren to make a pilgrimage to the Protectorate. The many thousands who answered her call greatly bolstered the population of the Menite nation and helped begin to bridge theological divisions between the Sul-Menites of the Protectorate and those who followed to the Menite True Faith of the north. It was hoped that wherever the Northern Crusade marched, the faithful would come to support the holy army. Because the crusade would be cut off from regular resupply, it was also imperative to establish a fortified stronghold in the north, one that would serve as a permanent conduit south for the influx of converted Menites from other nations.

The tremendous battle against dark forces the Harbinger had foreseen did in fact take place in the Thornwood Forest, at an ancient Orgoth temple called Garrodh. Here massive armies from several nations clashed, each with its own agenda and plans but all ultimately maneuvered there through the machinations of the Cryxian lich lord Asphyxious. This maddened undead lord sought to elevate himself to godhood by utilizing the temple's soul-capturing necrotech machinery to siphon all the souls from Menoth's realm in Urcaen to fuel his own power. Asphyxious intended to use the Harbinger as the gateway to those souls, drawing on her direct connection to Menoth.

Khadoran and Cygnaran forces were lured to this area to thwart the Cryxians but were largely unaware of the larger cosmological considerations. Because of this ignorance, their efforts only served to interfere with the sacred mission of the Menites. After an intense battle, the Harbinger was able to fulfill her purpose, although it cost her life. She sacrificed her own existence to end Asphyxious' ambition and in the process freed the souls of thousands of Menites imprisoned for centuries in the blasphemous Orgoth machinery.

This was a miraculous intervention, but the death of the Harbinger was a setback the Northern Crusade had not anticipated. Grief-stricken, the Testament and High Paladin Dartan Vilmon hastened to return the body of the Harbinger to Imer, where she was later resurrected by Menoth's will channeled through Hierarch Garrik Voyle. Meanwhile, Grand Scrutator Severius continued to lead the rest of the Northern Crusade and heroically battled to fulfill its secondary purposes even after being deprived of the Harbinger's blessed presence. The imperative for a stronghold in the north remained, and Severius would not turn aside from that objective. He proved the Protectorate's resolve to the Cygnarans when he annihilated the blasphemous city of Fisherbrook before marching farther north.

Fellig was the first city selected for conquest, but once again Khadoran and Cygnaran forces stood in the way of this holy cause, too locked in their centuries-long rivalry to recognize the divine purpose of Severius' followers. Although the Menites were unable to seize this city, they did succeed in destroying the monastery of Ascendant Angellia, a nearby site devoted to one of Morrow's minions. Having achieved this blow to undermine the faith of those who had forsaken their Creator, Grand Scrutator Severius led his battered and diminished force east in search of a more suitable site to establish a northern Protectorate stronghold.

His army made a long and harrowing trek to cross the Black River. There they met with reinforcements that had crossed the Bloodstone Marches to rendezvous with them. Given a fresh infusion of warjacks and a large column of Knights Exemplar and Temple Flameguard, the crusade marched north into Llael. After battling through tenacious Khadoran border defenders, they discovered fresh allies among the Llaelese Resistance who had taken refuge in the occupied nation's eastern countryside.

The Resistance was badly in need of aid and reinforcement to halt the advance of the Khadorans who had seized the rest of Llael. They had also become embittered toward Cygnar after watching those erstwhile allies retreat from the defense of Llael. Severius proved as able in diplomacy as upon the battlefield as he crafted agreements with these ragtag freedom fighters, giving him the stepping stone that would eventually provide the means to create his northern stronghold. He had already chosen the ideal location: the northwestern Llaelese city of Leryn.

Leryn had already served as a fulcrum for several notable events in the recent wars. Situated in the mountains, this extremely well fortified and isolated city had been a major element in the Khadoran planning for their invasion of the nation. The nearby town of Riversmet had been entirely annihilated solely to break the spirit of this city's defenders and provoke them to open their gates to the Khadorans. The impressive nature of its battlements and the difficulties involved in besieging it, combined with its self-sufficiency, made it ideal for the Northern Crusade's needs—if they could seize it.

Severius proved the strength of his own divine mandate in the days that followed. The Harbinger had prepared him for the difficulties that lay ahead by sending the Covenant of Menoth to him. This holy text was known to be capable of manifesting singular miracles and was part of long-held prophecies. Severius understood its purpose and set forth to unlock its final seals by marching to battle against the Khadorans standing between his army and Leryn. The bloodshed and strife of this conflict created the necessary conditions to unleash the book's power in its full glory, with Grand Scrutator Severius as its guiding hand. An imperishable rain of fire was unleashed to destroy the Khadoran army, but more importantly the invocation left a lingering holy aura on Severius. This heightened the warcaster's already formidable persuasive powers, as if his every spoken word was informed by the mandate of the Creator.

By the invocation of these miracles and with intelligence provided by the Resistance, Severius was able to seize Leryn without directly laying siege to its walls. He did so by confronting and converting two members of a ranking Greylord Ternion charged with governance of the city for the Khadoran military. Severius convinced them their only path to salvation required them to renounce their nation, rejoin the faith by putting aside their temporal allegiances, and open the gates to his army. After great trials and ordeals, the Northern Crusade had achieved its goal of finding a northern center of power, expanding the reach of the Protectorate into new lands far from its old borders.

RECLAIMING SUL AND THE INVASION OF CASPIA

As the Northern Crusade battled its way toward Llael, the majority of the Protectorate's military resources were tied up in southern conflicts. Tensions in the south reached a new peak on both Protectorate and Cygnaran soil in the wake of the Protectorate's declaration of independence. Cygnar took the unprecedented and extreme step of authorizing Lord Commander Coleman Stryker to round up and imprison its own Menite citizenry in a large area between Corvis and Caspia. These Menites were arrested on the grounds that they might be secretly collaborating with the Protectorate, regardless of whether there was any proof of collusion. The innocent Menites were put onto prison barges and shipped down the Black River toward their eventual relocation on Bloodshore Island, a prison previously reserved for Cygnar's most dangerous and hardened criminals.

The holy city of Sul became a vast staging ground for the largest Menite army assembled since the time of the priest-kings of old. Its ultimate goal was nothing less than the conquest of Caspia, Cygnar's imposing capital city, which sat across the river from Sul. With their greatest triumph at hand, however, the Menites' plans were thrown into chaos by a sudden Cygnaran attack that culminated in a full-scale invasion of Sul. For the first time in history, Sul's formidable walls were breached and fighting spilled into its sacred streets.

This event immediately prompted the establishment of two major crusades: the Reclamation of Sul Crusade and the Crusade in Defense of the Great Temple. Both these forces devoted to the protection and reclamation of the city were tested to their limits, yet in time their faith and devotion were rewarded. The Great Temple of the Creator and Sulon's Remembrance at the center of the city were kept safe from the interlopers and served to rally the city's defenders, who were eager to reclaim other sacred sites despoiled by the boots of unbelievers.

The Cygnarans lacked the resolve of the faithful, and when their leader Lord Stryker was injured in battle with Feora, Protector of the Flame, their will to fight crumbled. Swept up in holy fervor and encouraged by the examples of such great war leaders as Feora and Grand Exemplar Kreoss, the southern crusades drove the Cygnarans at last from the rubble-filled streets of Sul. So hasty was the retreat of the enemy and so closely did the Menites hound them at their heels that the Cygnarans could not seal the gates of Caspia in time. Menite forces overwhelmed the defenders at the bridge between Sul and Caspia and seized the battlements, enabling them to keep the bridge open. Menite soldiers stormed into the streets of Caspia for the first time since the Cygnaran Civil War.

FIRST EXEMPLAR INTERDICTION, LERYN
NORTHERN CRUSADE,
SERVING GRAND EXEMPLAR MIKAEL KREOSS

The promotion of Mikael Kreoss to grand exemplar brought new life and vigor to the Knights Exemplar brotherhood, and this is clearly demonstrated among the fighting men of the First Exemplar Interdiction. These soldiers would gladly lay down their lives for Kreoss, as he has fought and bled alongside them in countless battles. One common tale told among these knights is that the grand exemplar has not spent a single night in the Exemplar Fortress, their headquarters, since achieving his position: during the war he spent every day in battle alongside his brothers, and afterward he loaned his strength to the reconstruction of Sul, helping clear rubble and set stones with his own hands until he was called north. The fact that both the grand exemplar and the hierarch prefer to serve on the front lines rather than safely behind in the capital is a matter of pride to the First Exemplar Interdiction, and they gladly endured the long march to join their brothers in arms among the Northern Crusade.

The First Exemplar Interdiction is a large force of handpicked veteran knights. It includes a strong core of foot knights supported by Knights Errant alongside a small wing of Vengers cavalry and a smaller contingent of Bastions and Cinerators. Though composed solely of Exemplar knights, the First receives considerable support and fights alongside the other martial orders of the Northern Crusade. This force proved its mettle in the Caspia-Sul War when they fought directly alongside Grand Exemplar Mikael Kreoss for most of the major actions.

All who fought in the defense of Sul share a bond forged by the sight of their sacred city being brought to ruin and the miracle of its reclamation. Among the most famous of battles in which this force fought was the first defense of the Great Temple of the Creator in Sul shortly after the initial Cygnaran assault. Mustering a force of only a few hundred knights cut off from the rest of the city's brotherhood, Seneschal Pelon Sarmoth cut into the flank of Cygnaran attackers and battled through to rejoin the main defenders, including Kreoss, at the front of the Grand Temple. This was one of the hardest fought battles during the siege of Sul and represented a major turning point. These knights fought on despite being entirely surrounded by

Fidelitas et Ira
"Loyalty and Wrath"

Stormblades and other Cygnaran forces. They were able to hold long enough for Feora to arrive with a similarly ragtag assortment of Temple Flameguard. The Cygnarans routed and were forced to withdraw to the western city. Many believe that had this temple fallen, Sul would have followed.

The grand exemplar's duties leading the crusade often take him elsewhere, and in his absence the direct supervision and leadership of the First Interdiction fall upon Senior Seneschal Pelon Sarmoth, who reports to Kreoss directly. Sarmoth is greatly appreciated by the men as someone who has shown not only commitment to the cause but also fidelity to his subordinates. He has felt the death of every soldier under his command, and after battle he regularly stands vigil to recite the lengthy litany of the dead who have served under him. His memory for these names, a list now quite long, is seen as a sign that he takes no lives for granted even as he knows sacrifices are needed in war.

After the great casualties during the southern wars, the current members of the First Interdiction come from a wide variety of former interdictions and forces, each group the survivors of some greater calamity. This disparate set of backgrounds serves to bring them closer together and allows them justification to claim they represent the entirety of their order.

LEADERSHIP

- Grand Exemplar Kreoss, warcaster (not permanently attached)
- Senior Seneschal, Knight Exemplar Pelon Sarmoth
- Senior Seneschal, Knight Exemplar Venger Armides Marvant
- Senior Seneschal, Knight Exemplar Bastion Carvor Hazon

ASSETS

- 600 Knights Exemplar
- 400 Knights Exemplar Errants
- 100 Knights Exemplar Vengers
- 50 Knights Exemplar Bastions
- 50 Knights Exemplar Cinerators
- 8 Heavy Warjacks, 10 Light Warjacks

Caspia and Sul were once a single city, and it has long been the dream of many living on both sides of the river to reunite the City of Walls. Many Menite priests believe the entire city is a sacred relic of Priest-King Golivant. The chance to bring this fallen city once again under the dominion of the Temple of Menoth was a chance Hierarch Voyle could not let pass. He personally led Imer's vast garrisons from the capital to join the assault on Caspia. His arrival was fortuitous; despite his forces having claimed the outer gates, the City of Walls had proven to be extremely difficult to penetrate. The concentric defenses that had once thwarted even the Orgoth now stymied the invading Menites. Hierarch Voyle's arrival changed this as he shattered gateway after gateway by invoking the full potency and wrath of the Lawgiver.

In the end the capture of Caspia was not to be. Despite initial successes, the Harbinger had foreseen and attempted to counsel Hierarch Voyle that an unrelenting advance would divide the faithful and threaten the integrity of the Temple. Yet the hierarch was too blinded by the dream of uniting Caspia and capturing Castle Raelthorne to heed her warnings and pressed on.

This situation came to a head when Lord Commander Stryker stood in the way of the Menite advance and offered terms for a temporary truce. He showed his willingness to release thousands of the imprisoned Menites who had been captured under his orders. The Harbinger advised Hierarch Voyle that accepting these terms would work to the greater good of the Temple, bringing yet more converts and weakening the will of the Caspian defenders against the proof of Menoth's miraculous intervention. Once again Hierarch Voyle ignored her words, going so far as to order his followers to fire on the walls where the offered Menite prisoners had been positioned.

In silent disapproval, the Harbinger martyred her own flesh to provide succor to those injured, while High Paladin Dartan Vilmon of the Order of the Wall stepped forward to intervene for the helpless. The hierarch demonstrated both his hubris and how completely his fixation on conquest had overcome his rationality. He misunderstood Vilmon's stance as defiance and disobedience and struck at him with what should have been a fatal blow. This act was too much for the Harbinger to allow, as this paladin had spent his life in good works in the name of Menoth and had repeatedly endangered his own life to defend the god's chosen voice. In an act of miraculous intervention, the Harbinger took the paladin's injury upon herself and suffered what should have been a mortal wound.

Any hope that the shock of this might awaken Voyle to his ill-chosen path was quashed when the hierarch lashed out blindly against his Cygnaran enemy, holding Lord Stryker to blame for the Harbinger's fall. In the ensuing fight, the sheltering hand of Menoth was pulled aside and the previously invincible Hierarch Voyle fell at last to his adversary Lord Commander Stryker. The last moments of this battle are not well understood by the faithful, but some say it was the Harbinger's own infallible sword that ended Voyle's life. No one can answer the question of whether this means the Harbinger herself served as an instrument in the hierarch's fall. Most prefer to avoid confronting this difficult theological question and its ramifications.

Hierarch Voyle's body was returned to Sul and then to Imer, where he was buried with proper honor and dignity. Voyle will be remembered as a visionary who launched the great crusades and who strengthened the Protectorate of Menoth. Severius swore to continue his work and that of Hierarch Ravonal before him, and by the Harbinger's revelation he was chosen to be the next hierarch. It is left to Hierarch Severius to spread the Menite faith until all mankind has learned to recognize the Creator properly or is extinguished for their heresy.

As Sul was recovered and for the moment secure, the two southern crusades were ended, with the understanding these faithful could be called again at a moment's notice. While the southern territories consolidated their defensive garrisons, greater attention returned to the Northern Crusade, where Hierarch Severius remained.

ORGANIZATION OF GARRISONS AND CRUSADES

The Protectorate's active military forces are organized into garrisons and crusades. Garrisons include reinforcements for active forces and those reserved to defend Protectorate territories and resources. The largest garrisons are made up of large numbers of Temple Flameguard supported by smaller numbers of soldiers from the other orders. Although they can be allocated for offensive missions as needed, garrisons exist primarily to secure important cities or territories.

Crusades are large groups of mixed forces brought together for specific long-term objectives. Generally the most proactive of the Protectorate armies, crusades usually have a goal that requires the seizure of new territory or the destruction of a specific target. Crusades with defensive goals are unusual but not unprecedented, as demonstrated during the invasion of Sul by Cygnaran forces. The Crusade in Defense of the Great Temple was one such action, but even in that case the force conducted missions against the nearest Cygnaran elements to preempt a counterattack.

Crusades and garrisons are broken down into smaller functional groups called interdictions. These comprise smaller groups of forces called phalanxes, generally drawn from a single military order, but they can be mixed as needed to achieve objectives. The hierarch appoints crusade leaders, who in turn select interdiction leaders. By necessity crusades are trusted only to senior warcasters—those who have the ability to control warjacks as well as lead troops on the battlefield. All members of an interdiction are subordinate to its commander regardless of their martial orders.

At all levels of organization, priests in the Temple hierarchy act as officers within the Protectorate's armies. They command soldiers directly and organize logistics and supplies. Experienced lay soldiers can be promoted to positions of authority such as arms master or preceptor. Individuals at these ranks frequently lead individual phalanxes, but they must treat priests with respect regardless of their position. In any situation where the chain of command is uncertain, priests are obeyed before secular commanders.

A separate division of the priesthood leads the Protectorate's large zealot forces, which are considerably less organized and cohesive than the professional martial orders. These warpriests are the most numerous and least influential clergy and rarely have any larger responsibility beyond the rituals they conduct for the zealous local parishioners who have been gathered and armed for the war effort. The prayers of these warpriests help ensure success, and they offer last rites for the fallen. Above them are the priests ranked potentate or higher. Some warpriests are chosen to march in battle in choirs that empower sanctified warjacks with their holy prayers.

Even though higher-ranking priests are often occupied with matters of governance, it is not unheard of for them to enter battle alongside a threatened garrison or to be chosen to lend their power to an active crusade. These truly formidable and pious emissaries of Menoth often can wield singularly potent prayers, and their example inspires the soldiers to even greater heights of fervor and reinforces their strength and conviction on the battlefield.

Visgoth Juviah Rhoven of Sul, for example, was heavily involved in the battles between Caspia and Sul, applying his powers of prayer in both the southern crusades. Hierarch Voyle joined in the battle personally during the invasion of Caspia and is credited with crushing the bulk of Caspia's defenses almost single-handedly. While the fact that this action ended in his death underscores the risks, Rhoven's example stirred the Protectorate martial orders to its greatest united effort. Hierarch Severius has similarly shown no sign of leaving his active post with the Northern Crusade to return to the safety of Imer.

The Protectorate's military underwent significant organizational changes following the Caspia-Sul War. Hierarch Severius remained in Leryn to lead the Northern Crusade, so a large number of soldiers were sent to support his efforts. This is the only currently active crusade; those devoted to the reclamation of Sul have been officially disbanded and the bulk of their forces returned to the defense of the sacred city and of the Protectorate's border. Southern forces remain at their highest alert, ready to battle the enemy across the Black River, but the fighting in the south has calmed considerably and now occurs primarily in smaller engagements north of the walled cities. Operations in this quarter have taken on a more subversive and clandestine nature as each side seeks to undermine the other without provoking full retaliation. The uneasy truce between the two nations continues undefined, and Caspia and Sul remain officially at war.

Accordingly, a great number of the Protectorate's battle-ready warcasters have been reassigned to the Northern Crusade. These transfers include the Harbinger of Menoth, alongside the Testament, and Grand Exemplar Kreoss, who took with him a sizable contingent of handpicked Exemplar knights. The day-to-day oversight of the Northern Crusade has been left to the grand exemplar, who reports directly to Hierarch Severius on all matters. The massive garrison stationed at Leryn is commanded by Vice Scrutator Vindictus, who, like Severius, is blessed with the rare warcaster talent. This garrison supplies troops and material aid to the Northern Crusade throughout its ongoing battles.

High Executioner Reznik has been given command of an ancillary strike force and answers only to Severius. Some believe this arrangement reflects a rift between Severius and Grand Exemplar Kreoss, but others take it as a sign the hierarch wisely uses different tools for different ends. While no one can command the high executioner except the hierarch, Reznik has limited personal authority and commands only those men and women directly selected for his interdiction.

With so much of the Protectorate's military focused in the north, the absence of Feora, Protector of the Flame, is notable and has been widely interpreted among senior priests and martial officers as a sign of her disfavor with the hierarch. In fact, Feora's authority has become greater than ever before, as she has been left with the general oversight of all the southern garrisons. These include the garrisons at Sul, Imer, Icthier, and Tower Judgment. The top-level oversight of each of these regions is entrusted to visgoths and scrutators, but the garrisons' commanding officers are Feora's loyal subordinates. Feora has further established a protocol whereby members of the Flameguard's Incendium serve as intermediaries between top-ranking priests and

leading garrison officers. These measures were undertaken in the name of military efficiency and expediency but also allow Feora to control the flow of information and resource allocation to the bulk of the southern military.

These garrisons represent a sizable force that could be allocated to a new crusade should the need arise, but at the same time the Protectorate must defend its borders and cities. Certainly the protection of both Sul and Imer, in particular, is absolutely vital, especially with the home territory left potentially vulnerable after so many military assets were moved to the Northern Crusade. The visgoths in particular are uneasy with this arrangement and have counseled Severius to return south alongside some portion of his army to ensure the safety of the nation's interior. Thus far, the hierarch has ignored all such advice.

With the hierarch occupied by the Northern Crusade, Feora has taken to attending the Synod's meetings and now serves as Severius' unofficial proxy on military matters. This has given her a taste of the hierarch's responsibilities, which she has embraced enthusiastically. There is no question that Feora, Protector of the Flame, is presently the most influential and powerful military figure in the southern Protectorate. In many respects she is even held above the individual visgoths, several of whom periodically solicit her opinions.

The southern scrutators, including five of the nine visgoths, serve as Severius' eyes and ears in the south and watch Feora closely. As yet her actions seem to be in good faith, and she has not shown signs of ambitions beyond her station. Her influence over the remaining visgoths, however, is observed with growing concern.

PROTECTORATE OF MENOTH THEME FORCES

FEORA, PRIESTESS OF THE FLAME
NEW MODEL ARMY

WARJACKS
Protectorate non-character warjacks

UNITS
Choirs of Menoth, Flameguard units

SOLOS
Vassal Mechaniks, Flameguard solos

TIER 1

Requirements: The army can include only the models listed above.

Benefit: Flameguard units become FA U. Additionally, reduce the point cost of Guardian warjacks by 1.

TIER 2

Requirements: The army includes two or more Temple Flameguard units.

Benefit: Temple Flameguard units gain Advance Move. (Before the start of the game but after both players have deployed, a model with Advance Move can make a full advance.)

TIER 3

Requirements: The army includes two or more Daughters of the Flame units.

Benefit: You gain +1 on your starting roll for the game.

TIER 4

Requirements: Feora's battlegroup includes three or more warjacks with the Continuous Effect: Fire 🔥 weapon quality.

Benefit: For each warjack in Feora's battlegroup with the Continuous Effect: Fire 🔥 weapon quality, place one wall template anywhere completely within 20" of the back edge of Feora's deployment zone after terrain has been placed but before either player deploys his army. When a model enters or ends its activation in the wall area, it suffers an unboostable POW 12 fire damage roll 🔥 and the Fire continuous effect 🔥. Models within the wall template gain concealment. These wall templates leave play after the first round of the game.

FEORA, PROTECTOR OF THE FLAME
DEFENDERS OF THE TEMPLE

WARJACKS
Protectorate non-character warjacks

UNITS
Choirs of Menoth, Flameguard units, Visgoth Juviah Rhoven & Honor Guard

SOLOS
Vassal Mechaniks, Flameguard solos

TIER 1

Requirements: The army can include only the models listed above.

Benefit: Flameguard units become FA U.

TIER 2

Requirements: The army includes two or more Temple Flameguard units.

Benefit: Add a unit attachment to one Temple Flameguard unit free of cost. This unit attachment ignores FA restrictions.

TIER 3

Requirements: The army includes one or more Daughters of the Flame units and one or more Flameguard Cleanser units.

Benefit: Flameguard units gain +2 SPD during your first turn of the game.

TIER 4

Requirements: The army includes Visgoth Juviah Rhoven & Honor Guard.

Benefit: Your deployment zone is extended 2" forward.

THE HIGH RECLAIMER
THE FLAMES OF RECLAMATION

WARJACKS
Protectorate non-character warjacks, Avatar of Menoth

UNITS
Flameguard Cleansers, Holy Zealots, Deliverer units

SOLOS
Reclaimers, Vassal solos

TIER 1

Requirements: The army can include only the models listed above.

Benefit: The FA of Reclaimer solos increases by +1 for each unit included. Reduce the point cost of Castigator warjacks by 1.

TIER 2

Requirements: The army includes three or more Reclaimer solos.

Benefit: Reclaimer solos each begin with one soul token.

TIER 3

Requirements: The army includes two Flameguard Cleanser units.

Benefit: Flameguard Cleanser units gain Advance Move. (Before the start of the game but after both players have deployed, a model with Advance Move can make a full advance.)

TIER 4

Requirements: The High Reclaimer's battlegroup includes two or more heavy warjacks.

Benefit: For each heavy warjack, place one 3" AOE cloud effect anywhere completely within 20" of the back edge of High Reclaimer's deployment zone after both players have finished deploying their armies but before the first player takes his first turn. These cloud effects leave play after the first round of the game.

TESTAMENT OF MENOTH
SANDS OF FATE

WARJACKS
Protectorate non-character warjacks, Avatar of Menoth

UNITS
Exemplar Errants, Holy Zealots, Idrian Skirmishers

SOLOS
Exemplar Errant Seneschals, Reclaimers, Vassals of Menoth, Idrian solos

TIER 1

Requirements: The army can include only the models listed above.

Benefit: Holy Zealot units gain Advance Deployment ⊙.

TIER 2

Requirements: The army includes two or more Exemplar Errant units.

Benefit: You gain +1 on your starting roll for the game.

TIER 3

Requirements: The army includes two Idrian Skirmisher units.

Benefit: Reduce the point cost of Idrian Skirmisher units by 1.

TIER 4

Requirements: The army includes Avatar of Menoth.

Benefit: Models/units in the army gain Incorporeal ⊙ during your first turn of the game.

HIGH EXEMPLAR KREOSS
INTERDICTION STRIKE FORCE

WARJACKS
Protectorate non-character warjacks, Fire of Salvation

UNITS
Choirs of Menoth, Exemplar units

SOLOS
Vassal Mechaniks, Exemplar solos

TIER 1

Requirements: The army can include only the models listed above.

Benefit: Exemplar Venger units become FA 2. Additionally, reduce the point cost of each Exemplar Venger unit by 1.

TIER 2

Requirements: The army includes High Exemplar Gravus.

Benefit: Place High Exemplar Gravus and Exemplar Venger units after normal deployment. These models are placed at the same time as your models with Advance Deployment ⊙ (if any). These models must be placed within your normal deployment zone.

TIER 3

Requirements: The army includes two or more Exemplar Errant units.

Benefit: Models/units in the army gain Pathfinder ◐ during your first turn of the game.

TIER 4

Requirements: Kreoss' battlegroup includes two or more warjacks with Arc Node ⊛.

Benefit: Friendly models/units can begin the game affected by Kreoss' upkeep spells. These spells and their targets must be declared before either player sets up models. Kreoss does not pay focus to upkeep these spells during your first turn.

GRAND EXEMPLAR KREOSS
CRUSADERS OF SUL

WARJACKS
Protectorate non-character warjacks, Fire of Salvation

UNITS
Deliverer Sunburst Crews, Exemplar units, Flameguard units, Visgoth Juviah Rhoven & Honor Guard

SOLOS
Vassal Mechaniks, Exemplar solos

TIER 1

Requirements: The army can include only the models listed above.

Benefit: Knights Exemplar units become FA U.

TIER 2

Requirements: The army includes two or more Knights Exemplar units.

Benefit: Knights Exemplar units gain Advance Move. (Before the start of the game but after both players have deployed, a model with Advance Move can make a full advance.)

TIER 3

Requirements: The army includes four or more Exemplar units.

Benefit: Add one Knights Exemplar Seneschal or Knights Errant Seneschal solo to the army free of cost. This solo ignores FA restrictions.

TIER 4

Requirements: Kreoss' battlegroup includes Fire of Salvation.

Benefit: Your deployment zone is extended 2″ forward.

GRAND SCRUTATOR SEVERIUS
LEGIONS OF THE FAITH

WARJACKS
Protectorate non-character warjacks, Blessing of Vengeance

UNITS
Choirs of Menoth, Holy Zealots, Temple Flameguard, Deliverer units

SOLOS
Hierophant, Wracks, Exemplar solos, Vassal solos

TIER 1
Requirements: The army can include only the models listed above.

Benefit: Wracks in this army can be placed up to 20″ from the back edge of Severius' deployment zone.

TIER 2
Requirements: The army includes two or more Temple Flameguard units.

Benefit: Add a unit attachment to one Temple Flameguard unit free of cost. This unit attachment ignores FA restrictions.

TIER 3
Requirements: The army includes two or more Vassal Mechanik solos.

Benefit: Up to one heavy warjack gains Advance Move for each Vassal Mechanik solo in the army. (Before the start of the game but after both players have deployed, a model with Advance Move can make a full advance.)

TIER 4
Requirements: Severius' battlegroup includes Blessing of Vengeance.

Benefit: Friendly models/units can begin the game affected by Severius' upkeep spells. These spells and their targets must be declared before either player sets up models. Severius does not pay focus to upkeep these spells during your first turn.

HIERARCH SEVERIUS
THE NORTHERN CRUSADE

WARJACKS
Protectorate non-character warjacks, Avatar of Menoth, Blessing of Vengeance

UNITS
Choirs of Menoth, Temple Flameguard, Exemplar units

SOLOS
Hierophant, Wracks, Exemplar solos, Vassal solos, Covenant of Menoth

TIER 1
Requirements: The army can include only the models listed above.

Benefit: Reduce the point cost of Crusader and Templar warjacks by 1.

TIER 2
Requirements: This army includes the Covenant of Menoth.

Benefit: You gain +1 on your starting roll for the game.

TIER 3
Requirements: This army includes two or more medium-based Exemplar units.

Benefit: Medium-based Exemplar units gain Advance Move. (Before the start of the game but after both players have deployed, a model with Advance Move can make a full advance.)

TIER 4
Requirements: Severius' battlegroup includes three or more heavy warjacks.

Benefit: Warjacks gain +2 SPD during your first turn of the game.

HIGH ALLEGIANT AMON AD-RAZA
WANDERERS OF THE FAITH

WARJACKS
Protectorate non-character warjacks

UNITS
Holy Zealots, Idrian units

SOLOS
Allegiants of the Order of the Fist, Reclaimers, Idrian solos, Vassal solos

TIER 1

Requirements: The army can include only the models listed above.

Benefit: Idrian Skirmisher units become FA U. Additionally, the FA of Allegiant of the Order of the Fist solos increases by +1 for each unit included.

TIER 2

Requirements: The army includes two or more Idrian Skirmisher units.

Benefit: Add a unit attachment to one Idrian Skirmisher unit free of cost. This unit attachment ignores FA restrictions.

TIER 3

Requirements: The army includes three or more Allegiant of the Order of the Fist solos.

Benefit: Allegiant of the Order of the Fist solos gain Advance Deployment (►).

TIER 4

Requirements: The only warjacks in Amon's battlegroup are light warjacks.

Benefit: Each warjack in Amon's battlegroup is automatically allocated 1 focus point at the start of your first Control Phase. This focus is in addition to any points Amon allocates.

THE HARBINGER OF MENOTH
ARMY OF THE RIGHTEOUS

WARJACKS
Protectorate non-character warjacks, Avatar of Menoth

UNITS
Choirs of Menoth, Holy Zealots, Temple Flameguard

SOLOS
Hierophant, Paladin solos, Vassal Mechaniks

TIER 1

Requirements: The army can include only the models listed above.

Benefit: The FA of Paladin of the Order of the Wall solos increases by +1 for each unit included.

TIER 2

Requirements: The army includes Avatar of Menoth.

Benefit: You gain +1 on your starting roll for the game.

TIER 3

Requirements: The army includes High Paladin Dartan Vilmon.

Benefit: For each Paladin solo, place one wall template anywhere within 20" of the back edge of the Harbinger's deployment zone after terrain has been placed but before either player deploys his army. The walls are linear obstacles that grant cover.

TIER 4

Requirements: The Harbinger's battlegroup includes three or more heavy warjacks without ranged weapons.

Benefit: Reduce the point cost of heavy warjacks without ranged weapons by 1.

HIGH EXECUTIONER SERVATH REZNIK
JUDGMENT OF FIRE

WARJACKS
Protectorate non-character warjacks

UNITS
Choirs of Menoth, Exemplar Cinerators, Flameguard Cleansers

SOLOS
Hierophant, Reclaimers, Wracks, Vassal solos

TIER 1
Requirements: The army can include only the models listed above.

Benefit: Wracks can be placed up to 20″ from the back edge of Reznik's deployment zone. Additionally, reduce the point cost of Reckoner warjacks by 1.

TIER 2
Requirements: This army includes two or more Flameguard Cleanser units.

Benefit: Flameguard Cleanser units gain Advance Deployment ⬤.

TIER 3
Requirements: This army includes three or more units.

Benefit: Add three Wrack solos to the army free of cost. These solos ignore FA restrictions.

TIER 4
Requirements: Reznik's battlegroup includes two or more heavy warjacks.

Benefit: Warjacks in the army gain +2 SPD during your first turn of the game.

VICE SCRUTATOR VINDICTUS
MISSIONARIES OF WAR

WARJACKS
Protectorate non-character warjacks

UNITS
Choirs of Menoth, Exemplar Errants, Holy Zealots

SOLOS
Allegiants of the Order of the Fist, Exemplar Errant Seneschals, Hierophant, Reclaimers, Vassal Mechaniks

TIER 1
Requirements: The army can include only the models listed above.

Benefit: The models/units units in your army gain Pathfinder ⬤ during your first turn of the game.

TIER 2
Requirements: The army includes two or more Exemplar Errant units.

Benefit: Add a unit attachment to one Exemplar Errant unit free of cost. This unit attachment ignores FA restrictions.

TIER 3
Requirements: The only warjacks in the army have SPD 5 or greater.

Benefit: You gain +1 on your starting roll for the game.

TIER 4
Requirements: Vindictus' battlegroup includes three or more heavy warjacks.

Benefit: Heavy warjacks in Vindictus' battlegroup gain Advance Deployment ⬤.

The Protectorate military displays significant strength despite their relatively small numbers, due perhaps in large part to their remarkable success at recognizing and fostering warcaster talent. It is no small frustration to their enemies, particularly the Cygnarans, that this fanatical nation is able to maintain a strong and diverse retinue of powerful warcasters.

Many priests are content to credit this achievement as a sign of Menoth's favor, but it seems more likely that the focused meditations and training undertaken by Sul-Menite priests opens their minds to the possibility of contact with the cortex. The tremendous force of will required to channel their holy powers reinforces the potential. Many priests, even those who do not possess the warcaster talent, have proven adept at recognizing that power in others before it manifests. Senior warpriests who have accompanied warcasters in battle for many years often develop a particularly uncanny ability to sense latent potential.

An individual capable of warcasting is rare even among the clergy, but the Protectorate has managed to unearth such jewels from among its population and polish them to readiness. Had they been born in another kingdom, these individuals may never have recognized their true potential. It doubtless helps that Protectorate citizens are required to join the war effort if asked; nearly a third spend time assisting garrisons or crusades, which can bring them into close contact with both warjacks and those sensitive to the talent to control them.

The Protectorate's final advantage in the discovery of potential warcasters is derived from their unique culture. The priesthood keeps itself frighteningly well informed about the activities of the people. Indeed, no other nation of the Iron Kingdoms polices its citizenry as closely. With supernatural manifestations viewed as potential heresy, many parents willingly give up a child who demonstrates unexpected gifts. Most of these unfortunate nascent potentials are put to death, but those who harbor the talent for warcasting may be fortunate enough to find themselves placed under the tutelage of the masters of the Lyceum and use prayer to discipline their talents.

The development of a warcaster in the Protectorate is as much a matter of martial training as it is of theological indoctrination and purification. All warcasters are taught to channel the divine magic of the Creator, but each possesses a unique set of abilities and affinities. Some theologians hypothesize that each warcaster represents a specific passage or interpretation of the Canon of the True Law.

Warcasters who manifest their ability later in life, typically while training with one of the Protectorate's martial orders, usually remain with their order. Instructors specializing in tutoring warcasters are summoned from Imer or Sul to oversee the training if necessary, but most major monasteries and temples have senior warpriests capable of helping a new warcaster master his art and integrate it into their regular fighting discipline.

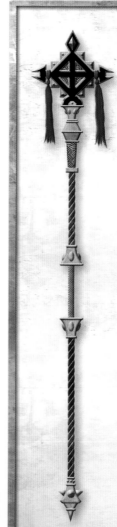

SACRED WEAPONRY

Given the standing and importance of warcasters and ruling priests in the Protectorate's military, it is no wonder the weapons they carry are singularly potent tools of war. Each of these priceless relics is more than a tool designed to kill; it is also a work of art and a symbol of station. These arms inspire the faithful even as they strike fear in the hearts of the enemy.

Crafting a weapon perfectly suited to the individual fighting style, station, and needs of each warcaster is the responsibility of Visgoth Ark Razek, the overseer of the Sul-Menite Artificers. Each weapon is as unique as the warcaster wielding it, including examples such as the chained Oblivion wielded by Amon Ad-Raza, the spear Justifier wielded by Grand Exemplar Kreoss, and Feora's fire-spewing halberd, Apocalypse.

Sacred symbolism illuminates these weapons and is particularly dense and elaborate on the great staves wielded by the highest priests. Every ruling priest has in his possession such a staff, which embodies his authority. The Menofix—the symbol of Man, Menoth's greatest creation—is prominently displayed on these staves and other great weapons as a reminder of the god's purpose, scrutiny, and wrath.

TESTAMENT OF MENOTH

Each martial and spiritual order within the Temple of Menoth's hierarchy has its own initiation and promotion ceremonies, and an individual warcaster must ascend through these ranks just as any other member must. Given their unique powers and responsibilities, it is natural for these warcasters to attain esteemed ranks quickly, so long as they remain true to their order's code and the True Law. Several orders are led by warcasters, who are in turn subordinate only to the Synod and the hierarch. Indeed, for the first time in the Protectorate's history, the ruling hierarch is himself a warcaster. Some priests have interpreted the rise of Hierarch Severius to this position of authority as proof that the final crusades of their faith are now upon them.

HIGH ALLEGIANT AMON AD-RAZA
PROTECTORATE WARCASTER

Let our faith be our armor, our fist be our sword.

—*Prayer of the Order of the Fist*

AMON

SPD	STR	MAT	RAT	DEF	ARM	CMD
6	8	7	4	16	14	8

 OBLIVION

	POW	P+S
	6	14

FOCUS	6
DAMAGE	17
FIELD ALLOWANCE	C
WARJACK POINTS	+6
SMALL BASE	

FEAT: UNION

His spirit always centered even in the heat of battle, High Allegiant Amon Ad-Raza is able to open his mind utterly to the warjacks of his battlegroup. When the time comes, his calm erupts into a terrible storm that washes away all who would stand against him.

While in Amon's control area, warjacks in Amon's battlegroup gain Perfect Balance. For each focus point Amon spends during his activation, allocate 1 focus point to a warjack in his battlegroup that was in his control area when he spent the focus. Union lasts for one round.

AMON

 Pathfinder

Groundwork – While knocked down, this model is not automatically hit by melee attacks and its DEF is not reduced.

Perfect Balance – This model cannot be targeted by combined melee attacks, combined ranged attacks, or free strikes. Models do not gain back strike bonuses against this model. When knocked down, this model can stand up during its activation without forfeiting its movement or action if it is able to forfeit its movement or action to stand up.

OBLIVION

⊘ Magical Weapon

⊙ Reach

Chain Weapon – This attack ignores the Buckler and Shield weapon qualities and Shield Wall.

Smite (★Attack) – Instead of making a normal damage roll, the model hit is slammed d6″ directly away from this model and suffers a damage roll with POW equal to this model's current STR plus the POW of this weapon. The POW of collateral damage from this slam is equal to this model's STR.

Thresher (★Attack) – This model makes one melee attack with this weapon against each model in its LOS and this weapon's melee range.

SPELLS	COST	RNG	AOE	POW	UP	OFF
CONVECTION	2	10	–	12	NO	YES

When Convection destroys a living enemy model, allocate 1 focus point to a warjack in this model's battlegroup that is in its control area.

FLAGELLATION	2	SELF	–	–	YES	NO

When making melee attacks, this model ignores both focus points overboosting the target's Power Field and spell effects that add to its DEF or ARM. Models damaged by this model lose Tough and cannot be healed for one round.

MOBILITY	2	SELF	CTRL	–	NO	NO

Models in this model's battlegroup currently in its control area gain +2 SPD and Pathfinder ⬤ for one turn.

SYNERGY	2	SELF	CTRL	–	YES	NO

While in its control area, models in this model's battlegroup gain a +1 cumulative bonus on melee attack and melee damage rolls for each other model in the battlegroup that hit an enemy model with a melee attack this turn while in this model's control area.

TACTICAL TIPS

UNION – A warjack cannot exceed normal focus allocation limits as a result of Union.

PERFECT BALANCE – If the model forfeits both its movement and action for other effects, either voluntarily or as required, it cannot use Perfect Balance to stand up for free.

SMITE – The slammed model is moved only half the distance rolled if its base is larger than the slamming model's.

THRESHER – The melee attacks are all simultaneous.

CONVECTION – A warjack cannot exceed normal focus allocation limits as a result of Convection.

Amon Ad-Raza learned to survive on the fringes of Protectorate society, his nomadic Idrian family constantly on the move in a futile attempt to escape Menite rule. If not for the hardships he endured early in life, it is possible the young man would never have found the strength to walk his true path as a servant of the Lawgiver. He first discovered the Word of the True Law while infiltrating a Protectorate settlement in search of food, where he overheard the sermons of Menite monks. Moved by the power of their words and heeding the acclamation in his

soul, Amon entrusted his destiny to the will of Menoth from that fateful day forward. He soon found his true calling in the teachings and philosophy of the Order of the Fist.

Amon's combination of unshakable faith and unparalleled determination made him a prodigy among the order. He honed his body to achieve feats beyond the reach of most of his brothers: his flesh shattered blades as if he were made of stone; his graceful movements flowed like currents in the sea; and his strength focused the unrelenting might of the crashing tides. Amon's ascension to the rank of high allegiant resonated with the will of a divinely guided hand, for in mere years he began counseling students beside the very same masters who had instructed him.

It was none other than Hierarch Garrick Voyle who took note of the young allegiant. Seeing the potential within Amon, Voyle pushed the monk to his limits to test every talent, ability, and aspect of the young man's spirit. Surpassing the hierarch's expectations, Amon triumphed over each trial, including conquering the cortex of a warjack with his mind. Using every ounce of his superior mental discipline and control, Amon projected his will into the mind of the machine, confirming the hierarch's suspicions: Amon was a born warcaster.

Voyle declared, "One who controls the titans of war should be an instrument of Menoth's will, not cloistered in a temple tutoring monks and breaking stones!" Soon Amon was displaying his skills on the field, leading his battlegroup to war. As his legend grew among the Idrian tribes, more of his people began to convert, and in time Amon earned the esteemed rank of high allegiant.

Amon wears little armor in battle, instead relying on his monastic conditioning to shrug off blows that would fell a lesser man while maintaining a calm that eludes description. Focusing the holy clarity of his training, Amon's unstoppable attacks are charged with the very fury of his faith.

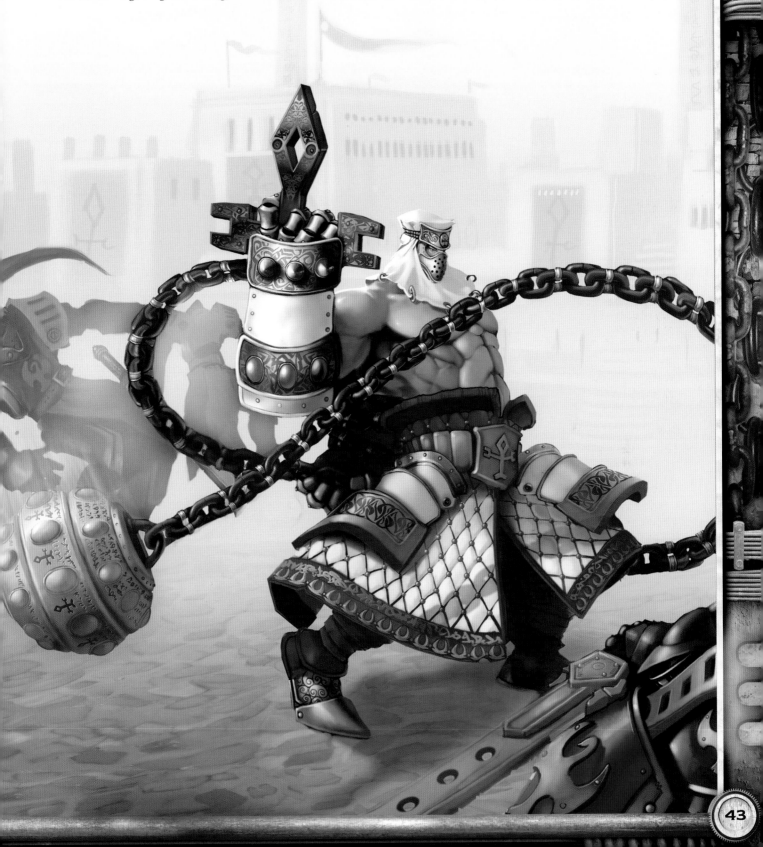

FEORA, PRIESTESS OF THE FLAME
PROTECTORATE WARCASTER

Menoth's glory is unto a flame in the hearts of the faithful. Some are guided to greatness by his light, while others are utterly consumed by the spiritual conflagration.

—Feora, Priestess of the Flame

FEORA						
SPD	STR	MAT	RAT	DEF	ARM	CMD
6	7	6	5	15	17	9

FLAMETHROWER			
RNG	ROF	AOE	POW
SP 8	1	—	12

×2

TRUTH	
POW	P+S
6	13

CONSEQUENCE	
POW	P+S
6	13

FOCUS	6
DAMAGE	16
FIELD ALLOWANCE	C
WARJACK POINTS	+6
SMALL BASE	

FLAMETHROWER
🔥 **Continuous Effect: Fire**

🔥 **Damage Type: Fire**

TRUTH
🔥 **Critical Fire**

⚔ **Magical Weapon**

CONSEQUENCE
🔥 **Critical Fire**

⚔ **Magical Weapon**

FEAT: SCORCHED EARTH

Using her talent for controlling flame, Feora has learned how to focus her holy fury into a singular burst of fiery wrath. The resulting conflagration, guided by her will, engulfs any enemy unfortunate enough to be close by, forcing them to feel the smoldering hatred of her prayers.

Enemy models currently in Feora's control area suffer the Fire continuous effect 🔥.

FEORA
🔥 **Immunity: Fire**

Inspiration [Flameguard] – Friendly Flameguard models/units in this model's command range never flee and immediately rally.

SPELLS	COST	RNG	AOE	POW	UP	OFF
BLAZING EFFIGY	4	8	*	14	NO	NO

Enemy models within 2″ of target friendly Faction warjack suffer a POW 14 fire damage roll 🔥.

ENGINE OF DESTRUCTION	2	SELF	–	–	NO	NO

This model gains +2 SPD, +4 STR, and +4 MAT for one round.

HEX HAMMER	3	SELF	CTRL	–	YES	NO

When an enemy model casts a spell or uses an animus while in this model's control area, after the spell or animus has been cast or used the enemy model suffers d3 damage points.

IGNITE	2	6	–	–	YES	NO

Target friendly model/unit gains +2 to melee attack damage rolls. Affected models gain Critical Fire 🔥 on their normal melee attacks.

IMMOLATION	2	8	–	12	NO	YES

Immolation causes fire damage 🔥. On a critical hit, the model hit suffers the Fire continuous effect 🔥.

WALL OF FIRE	2	CTRL	WALL	–	YES	NO

Place the wall template anywhere completely in this model's control area where it does not touch a model's base, an obstruction, or an obstacle. When a model enters or ends its activation in the wall area, it suffers an unboostable POW 12 fire damage roll 🔥 and the Fire continuous effect 🔥. Models within the wall template gain concealment.

TACTICAL TIPS

IGNITE – When this spell is cast on cavalry models, it affects mount attacks.

WALL OF FIRE – The wall is not an obstacle.

Forged in the blessed fires of faith, Feora is known for her iron will and blazing temper. An unfathomable vessel of divine power, she demonstrates a ferocity in battle that is without compare. She is a living example to the Temple Flameguard, who attend her with absolute devotion.

Feora was a child when she first manifested her affinity for and control over flame. Recognizing her ability as a gift directed by the hand of the Creator, her prominent family quickly stifled any disparaging rumors that her powers might be sorcerous in nature and therefore impure. They had long been associated with the Temple Flameguard and arranged for their young daughter to be tutored by the order's most influential and powerful clergy.

Ultimately, Feora entered the ranks of the most promising individuals within the Flameguard—the Incendium. This body of elite soldiers is hand-chosen to receive both spiritual training and martial instruction. As Feora's talents

as a warcaster developed, several scrutators took particular interest in the powerful young woman, who in time became a preeminent leader within the Temple. When the standing Priest of the Flame passed on to his reward in Urcaen, Feora was chosen to lead the Flameguard.

She has been preparing her temple for war since the day of her appointment to this post and has been instrumental in reshaping the order into a true fighting force. She considers the nation of Cygnar to be both inherently flawed and a bastion of heretical Morrowan teachings; that such a government claims authority over the Protectorate galls her. Feora holds her people to the high standard of discipline she herself exemplifies and is a captious commander, but because her actions mirror her words, she has the respect of her troops.

As one might expect from such a driven and intense individual, Feora prefers to lead from the front, entering the fray with a zealot's righteous fanaticism and laying purifying flame upon the wicked with fists fueled by her warcaster armor.

Powerful though she is, Feora has one significant fault: her ambition and intolerance of disobedience has made her so possessive of power that she trusts no one else and has long resented those of higher station. Her promotion through the Flameguard ranks has seen her become increasingly distant as she cements her hold on the order. In truth, the Temple Flameguard answer to her alone, and it may be only a matter of time before Feora begins to believe herself the Protectorate's true leader.

FEORA, PROTECTOR OF THE FLAME
PROTECTORATE EPIC WARCASTER

Sul stands. The flame of the Temple goes unquenched.

—Feora to Hierarch Voyle

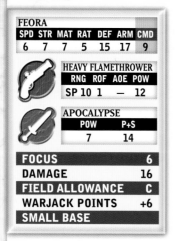

FEORA						
SPD	STR	MAT	RAT	DEF	ARM	CMD
6	7	7	5	15	17	9

HEAVY FLAMETHROWER			
RNG	ROF	AOE	POW
SP 10	1	—	12

APOCALYPSE	
POW	P+S
7	14

FOCUS	6
DAMAGE	16
FIELD ALLOWANCE	C
WARJACK POINTS	+6
SMALL BASE	

FEAT: WILD FIRE

The ultimate master of fire's all-consuming power, Feora can transmute flame into raw energy to strengthen her warjacks. She delivers her allies from the blazes around her by siphoning the flames and sending them leaping across the battlefield to her enemies.

Feora gains 1 focus point for each enemy model currently in her control area suffering the Fire continuous effect 🔥 and can immediately allocate that focus to warjacks in her battlegroup in her control area. Feora can then remove the Fire continuous effects from any number of models in her control area. For each Fire continuous effect Feora removes, choose one model in her control area to suffer the Fire continuous effect 🔥.

FEORA

🔥 **Immunity: Fire**

Caustic Presence [Fire] – Fire continuous effects 🔥 that affect enemy models in this model's control area cannot expire.

Inspiration [Flameguard] – Friendly Flameguard models/units in this model's command range never flee and immediately rally.

Righteous Flames – An enemy model that ends its activation within 2" of this model suffers the Fire continuous effect 🔥.

Warjack Bond – One non-character warjack in Feora's battlegroup begins the game bonded to her. When a model is hit by a ranged or melee attack made by the warjack while the warjack is in her control area, the model hit suffers the Fire continuous effect 🔥.

HEAVY FLAMETHROWER

🔥 **Continuous Effect: Fire**

🔥 **Damage Type: Fire**

APOCALYPSE

🔥 **Critical Fire**

🔥 **Magical Weapon**

🔥 **Reach**

SPELLS	COST	RNG	AOE	POW	UP	OFF
CLEANSING FIRE	3	8	3	14	NO	YES
Cleansing Fire causes fire damage 🔥. On a critical hit, models hit suffer the Fire continuous effect 🔥.						
CONVECTION	2	10	–	12	NO	YES
When Convection destroys a living enemy model, allocate 1 focus point to a warjack in this model's battlegroup that is in its control area.						
ESCORT	2	SELF	CTRL	–	YES	NO
Warjacks in this model's battlegroup beginning their activations in its control area gain +2" movement. This model gains +2 ARM while one or more warjacks in its battlegroup are within 3" of it.						
FIRE STEP	2	SELF	*	13	NO	NO
Enemy models within 2" of this model suffer a POW 13 fire damage roll 🔥. After the damage is resolved, place this model completely within 3" of its current location. Fire Step can be cast only once per activation.						
IGNITE	2	6	–	–	YES	NO
Target friendly model/unit gains +2 to melee attack damage rolls. Affected models gain Critical Fire 🔥 on their normal melee attacks.						

TACTICAL TIPS

WILD FIRE – A warjack cannot exceed normal focus allocation limits as a result of Wild Fire.

CONVECTION – A warjack cannot exceed normal focus allocation limits as a result of Convection.

IGNITE – When this spell is cast on cavalry models, it affects mount attacks.

Feora was both humbled and exalted by her travails in the besieged city of Sul. She rallied her followers to defend sacred sites and led them to feats of bravery and sacrifice.

In the final days of the siege, there was a moment in which Feora faced certain death. A confrontation with the Cygnaran warcaster Allister Caine left her buried beneath the wreckage of her Devout. Trapped, helpless, and surrounded by enemies, she experienced full self-awareness—and did not like everything she saw. She realized her drive and ambition, though necessary to transform an unready populace into a true army in the name of Menoth, had distracted her from her true path: forging the Flameguard into the greatest fighting force in the Protectorate and rising on their efforts to a position where she could lead the theocracy. She was also reminded that the original purpose of her order was the protection of the great holy places of Menoth, now threatened by the invading Cygnaran army.

With this clarity of purpose burning anew in her heart, Feora managed to find the strength to escape the warjack's impossible bulk even as the Daughters of the Flame who had witnessed her fall rushed to her side. She insisted they take her to one of the beleaguered outer garrisons and gather the surviving Flameguard. At the head of this ragged force Feora marched to the courtyard of the Great Temple of the Creator where the Cygnarans pressed forward in a seemingly unstoppable advance. As she led her warriors into the Cygnaran flank, Feora unleashed the full power of flame backed by renewed faith and pain, filling her warjacks with power and annihilating whole ranked masses of the enemy. The Cygnarans balked and routed, and the temple was preserved.

Only months later, Feora marched alongside Hierarch Voyle into the heart of Caspia itself. The armies of the Lawgiver seemed unconquerable as they laid waste to their enemies in Cygnar's capital. In their moment of triumph Feora saw Lord Commander Stryker strike down Voyle—and their seemingly assured victory. Grand Exemplar Kreoss withdrew the army in response, and Feora reluctantly joined the retreat to Sul.

Feora was shocked by Voyle's death, as he had been instrumental in her rise to power. That such a powerful man could be killed in the moment of his triumph was deeply troubling. Still worse, Feora's ambition to take the hierarch's place was dashed when Severius, a man with little patience for disrespect and whom she had personally insulted, ascended to supremacy. Nevertheless, Feora's ambition remains undimmed, and she knows there may be political opportunities for her in overseeing the southern garrisons while the hierarch focuses on extending his crusade north. This may be her best chance to advance her agenda and establish a solid foundation for her future rule.

THE HARBINGER OF MENOTH
PROTECTORATE WARCASTER

I am the Harbinger of Menoth, his vessel on Caen. Through me the Creator speaks, and he has much to say.

—The Harbinger of Menoth to the Synod, 603 AR

HARBINGER						
SPD	STR	MAT	RAT	DEF	ARM	CMD
6	4	3	1	14	14	10

PROVIDENCE		
	POW	P+S
	8	12

FOCUS	10
DAMAGE	17
FIELD ALLOWANCE	C
WARJACK POINTS	+5
LARGE BASE	

FEAT: GODHEAD

Calling upon Menoth's blazing glory, the Harbinger becomes a radiant beacon on the battlefield that burns away the impurities of any heretic who dares to approach her sacrosanct form.

For one round, advancing enemy models that end their movement in the Harbinger's control area closer to her than they began suffer an unboostable POW 14 fire damage roll 🔥.

HARBINGER

Awe – While in this model's command range, living enemy models suffer –2 to attack rolls.

Divinity – This model cannot be knocked down and never suffers Blind. Its front arc extends to 360°.

Martyrdom – When a friendly Faction non-warcaster warrior model in this model's command range is disabled, this model can suffer d3 damage points to cause the disabled model to heal 1 damage point.

PROVIDENCE

🌀 **Magical Weapon**

Guided – Attacks made with this weapon automatically hit.

SPELLS	COST	RNG	AOE	POW	UP	OFF
CATACLYSM	4	8	5	20	NO	YES

Target enemy model is automatically hit. Reduce the base POW of Cataclysm by 1 for each full inch between the target and this model. Blast damage affects only enemy models. Cataclysm has no effect if the target model is out of range.

CRUSADER'S CALL	3	SELF	CTRL	–	NO	NO

Friendly faction models beginning a charge while in this model's control area this turn gain +2″ movement.

FEAR OF GOD	2	10	–	–	YES	YES

Target enemy model/unit cannot give orders, receive orders, or make special attacks.

GUIDED HAND	2	6	–	–	NO	NO

Target friendly model/unit gains an additional die on each model's first melee attack roll this turn.

PURIFICATION	3	SELF	CTRL	–	NO	NO

Continuous effects, animi, and upkeep spells in this model's control area immediately expire.

TACTICAL TIPS

MARTYRDOM – A disabled model that heals damage is no longer disabled.

CATACLYSM – Modify the POW before calculating blast damage. Even if this spell is channeled, its damage is still based on the range of the target from the Harbinger.

CRUSADER'S CALL – Apply movement bonuses only during a model's activation.

In late 603 AR, three scrutators and a score of Knights Exemplar arrived in a small village just north of Ancient Icthier to escort a teenaged girl to Imer. Calling herself the Harbinger of Menoth, she said the Creator had come to her in a vision and declared her too holy to touch the earth, and she had floated above it ever since. As the Harbinger travelled to Imer, word spread and whole communities emptied as the faithful followed her.

At sunset the visgoths assembled in the Sovereign Temple of the One True Faith and faced the young woman floating in the blood-red sunlight. Without leave she described her visions and the voice that filled her. She claimed to wear a blindfold because to see the world through Menoth's eyes was overwhelming. She singled out individual visgoths by name, speaking of things they hid even from each other. Finally she turned to Hierarch Garrick Voyle and smiled just as the great sand clocks struck the tenth hour of her trials. The hierarch pointed to the floor where her shadow stood, unchanged after all that time. Voyle stepped down and bent his knee to ask if she would serve as his personal spiritual advisor.

The years that followed reinforced the fact that the Harbinger is a direct conduit of the god, as countless miracles have transpired in her presence. Though unburdened with worldly trifles, she unreservedly endorsed Hierarch Voyle when he called for a pilgrimage to witness her divinity—an event meant to heal the rift between the Protectorate and those of the Old Faith. The appearance of the Harbinger of Menoth is heralded as the single greatest religious event in western Immoren since the discovery of the Canon of the True Law.

The Harbinger proved her commitment to the faithful when she went forth to confront a darkness in the Thornwood prophesied to threaten all Menites, both living and dead. There she released the souls of thousands of Menites captured and enslaved by the Orgoth and gave her life to save them before they could be used as fuel for an even greater evil instigated by the lich lords of Cryx. All of the Protectorate mourned when her body was returned to Imer, and hundreds of thousands witnessed the miracle of her resurrection by Menoth's will. The god's message was clear: the Harbinger had not yet fulfilled her divine destiny on Caen.

When Voyle prepared to lead a crusade into Caspia itself, the Harbinger reminded him of Sulon's final prophecy: doom would befall any hierarch who entered Caspia before the divided city was made whole. Voyle ignored her warning, and she silently accompanied him in what he believed to be his moment of triumph. Hours later Voyle stood on the edge of total victory in Caspia when hubris overwhelmed his devotion to the Lawgiver, leading to his death. Recovering from her own wounds received in the conflict, the Harbinger saw Hierarch Voyle buried with full state honors and decreed Severius his replacement, ensuring a smooth transition.

She has journeyed north to join the new hierarch and renew their efforts to reach the faithful in enemy lands. She has proven her willingness to wade personally into battle, where she is immeasurably powerful and possesses the ability not only to command warjacks but also to decimate whole companies of men with divine magic and her unerring sword, Providence.

Completely infused with the glory of Menoth, she is a beacon to the devoted that has reinvigorated all Menites who have beheld her with their own eyes. With the Harbinger leading the way, the crusade continues to storm across western Immoren uniting the faithful while releasing the wrath of the Lawgiver on those who defy Menoth.

THE HIGH RECLAIMER
PROTECTORATE WARCASTER

He is nameless and without identity or mercy. He is the High Reclaimer. Heretics flee his approach in terror, but no soul can escape his grasp.

—*High Exemplar Mikael Kreoss*

HIGH RECLAIMER						
SPD	STR	MAT	RAT	DEF	ARM	CMD
5	7	6	4	14	15	8

CREMATOR	
POW	P+S
7	14

FOCUS	5
DAMAGE	18
FIELD ALLOWANCE	C
WARJACK POINTS	+6
SMALL BASE	

FEAT: RESURRECTION

Though the High Reclaimer's primary purpose is to usher souls into the next existence, he has been given the authority to return them from death in order to carry out Menoth's will. This is among the greatest of miracles granted by the Creator of Man, only bestowed on those who will fight to preserve the faith.

Return d3 + 3 friendly destroyed Faction troopers to play. Place those models in formation in their original units completely in the High Reclaimer's control area.

HIGH RECLAIMER

Terror

Oath of Silence – This model does not have the Commander advantage.

Reclaim – This model gains one soul token for each friendly living Faction warrior model destroyed by a continuous effect, an enemy attack, or collateral damage from an enemy attack in its control area. During your Control Phase, after this model replenishes its focus but before it allocates focus, replace each soul token with 1 focus point.

Soulstorm – While this model has one or more soul tokens, enemy models entering or ending their activations within 2″ of it immediately suffer 1 damage point.

CREMATOR

Continuous Effect: Fire

Magical Weapon

Reach

SPELLS	COST	RNG	AOE	POW	UP	OFF
ASHES TO ASHES	4	8	*	10	NO	YES

If target model is hit, it and the d6 nearest enemy models within 5″ of it suffer a POW 10 fire damage roll.

BURNING ASH	1	CTRL	3	–	NO	NO

Place a 3″ cloud effect anywhere completely within this model's control area. While in the AOE, living enemy models suffer –2 to attack rolls. The AOE remains in play for one round.

IMMOLATION	2	8	–	12	NO	YES

Immolation causes fire damage. On a critical hit, the model hit suffers the Fire continuous effect.

SACRIFICIAL LAMB	1	CTRL	–	–	NO	NO

Remove one friendly living Faction model in this model's control area from play to allocate 1 focus point to each warjack in this model's battlegroup that is currently in its control area. Sacrificial Lamb can be cast only once per turn.

TACTICAL TIPS

RESURRECTION – You cannot return models to a unit that has been completely destroyed. Remove all damage from returned models. They can activate normally this activation.

SACRIFICIAL LAMB – A warjack cannot exceed normal focus allocation limits as a result of Sacrificial Lamb.

Menoth creates, and he destroys. It is the job of the Reclaimant Order to assist in the latter. They are an extension of Menoth's will, and they return souls to the Shaper of Man to add strength to his wars in Urcaen.

Even other religious orders of the Protectorate balk at the unbending standards and principles to which reclaimers adhere. Their severe masks of iron are bolted shut anytime their wearers walk from the unadorned cells in which they live and eat in solitude. Their last spoken words are their oath to the order before their masks are sealed, and forever after no words escape their lips. Even their prayers are silent.

One man who took the Oath of the Reclaimer's Last Breath has risen above his peers. Through this man the divine power of Menoth flows without effort as he sends forth clouds of burning ash and causes the unworthy to burst into flame, consumed with brutal agony before their lives are snuffed out and their souls sent to Urcaen. Hierarch

Voyle publicly recognized him as the High Reclaimer, a title denoting absolute unity with the will of the Lawgiver. Never before had a man of this order demonstrated the warcaster talent, and it was immediately obvious that he would bring tremendous strength to the upcoming crusades.

The High Reclaimer's sole weapon is a ceremonial torch called Cremator. It is kept aflame by a continuous supply of concentrated Menoth's Fury. One crushing blow from the High Reclaimer's great weapon smashes limbs and collapses torsos, rends warjack armor like mortified flesh, and ignites anything it does not immediately demolish.

Those soldiers who have marched at his side in battle attest that they know his will without being told. To prepare for each upcoming conflict, the High Reclaimer spends countless hours in meditation and tests his limits with a rigorous regimen of exercises and fasting that tempers his body into corded muscle and sinew akin to iron.

No one is safe from reclamation. It is said Menoth whispers to the High Reclaimer during his prayers, naming those who are to be returned to him. Enemies, allies, even so-called innocent bystanders are oft reclaimed with no more foreknowledge than the sudden pressure of a crusader's grip or Cremator's hiss as it delivers a killing blow. Even lesser reclaimers know they must not be deficient in their duties, for failure means their own reclamation, perhaps by the High Reclaimer himself.

TESTAMENT OF MENOTH
PROTECTORATE EPIC HIGH RECLAIMER WARCASTER

The language of Urcaen is unknown to all men but one, for he has seen the face of the Creator and lived. How can any hope to stand against him?

—Grand Exemplar Mikael Kreoss

TESTAMENT						
SPD	STR	MAT	RAT	DEF	ARM	CMD
5	7	6	4	14	16	8

REQUIEM		
	POW	P+S
	7	14

FOCUS	5
DAMAGE	18
FIELD ALLOWANCE	C
WARJACK POINTS	+6
SMALL BASE	

FEAT: ESSENCE OF DUST

The Testament of Menoth opens the intangible gates between Caen and Urcaen as easily as drawing back a curtain. Using these supernal portals, he moves his army between worlds by rendering the living no more substantial than dust in a guided wind.

Friendly Faction models currently in the Testament's control area gain Incorporeal (⊕). When declaring charges and slam power attacks, an affected model can ignore other models when determining LOS. Essence of Dust lasts for one turn.

TESTAMENT

⊙ Terror

Oath of Silence – This model does not have the Commander advantage.

The Omegus – Enemy models cannot gain soul tokens from models destroyed in this model's control area.

Reclaim – This model gains one soul token for each friendly living Faction warrior model destroyed by a continuous effect, an enemy attack, or collateral damage from an enemy attack in its control area. During your Control Phase, after this model replenishes its focus but before it allocates focus, replace each soul token with 1 focus point.

Urcaen's Gate – Once per turn during your Control Phase, after replenishing focus but before focus allocation, this model can spend one soul token to be placed anywhere completely within 3˝ of its current location.

REQUIEM

⊙ Continuous Effect: Fire

⊙ Magical Weapon

⊙ Reach

SPELLS	COST	RNG	AOE	POW	UP	OFF
ASHEN VEIL	2	6	–	–	YES	NO

Target friendly model/unit gains concealment. Living enemy models suffer −2 to attack rolls while within 2˝ of an affected model.

DUST TO DUST	3	10	–	13	NO	YES

When a warrior model is boxed by Dust to Dust, center a 3˝ AOE cloud effect on it, then remove the model from play. The AOE remains in play for one round.

HALLOWED AVENGER	2	6	–	–	YES	NO

When an enemy attack destroys or removes from play one or more friendly Faction models within 5˝ of target warjack in this model's battlegroup, after the attack is resolved the affected warjack can charge an enemy model, then Hallowed Avenger expires.

REVIVE	3	CTRL	–	–	NO	NO

Return one destroyed friendly Faction Grunt to play with one unmarked damage box. It must be placed in this model's control area in formation and within 3˝ of another model in its unit.

TACTICAL TIPS

ESSENCE OF DUST – Remember, models lose Incorporeal when they make melee or ranged attacks.

DUST TO DUST – The boxed model does not provide a soul or corpse token.

REVIVE – Remember, the Grunt can activate normally with its unit this turn. If all models in the Grunt's unit have been destroyed, it cannot be placed within 3˝ of a model in its unit and therefore cannot return to play.

He fought back their press with his weapon Cremator, baptizing it in the ephemeral ichor of ghosts and fallen souls and transforming the metal with every strike. Finally the dead thinned to reveal an ancient tomb-like city, a shadow of Icthier, inscribed with Menite scripture never before seen by mortal eyes. The throng of ancient faithless were thwarted by the perimeter of the hallowed grounds, allowing the High Reclaimer respite to discover a temple dedicated to the Creator.

At his arrival, the heavy doors to the vast shrine opened, revealing a lone tablet atop an ancient altar: the Omegus. Lifting the ancient tablet from its resting place of eons, the High Reclaimer began to read the text inscribed there in a tongue unknown to men. His mind reeled as it filled with the Creator's laws of the dead. Saturated with energy as old as life itself and imbued with the knowledge to wield it, the High Reclaimer set out to pass through Urcaen's gates back into the world of the living.

He was prepared for an arduous return through the masses, but when the High Reclaimer exited the temple he found an army of Menite souls holding back the restless tides—fallen soldiers of the faith had cleared a path for him. As he walked, they moved with him as a barrier against the

When the High Reclaimer pushed open the gates of Imer and disappeared into the blasted wastes of the Stormlands, most believed he had gone to his death. Many feared he had chosen to reclaim himself in this time of great need. They were not wholly mistaken.

Battling the whipping winds and flesh-scouring sands of the marches, the High Reclaimer pushed himself to the limits of life to open the forgotten and unseen Gates of Urcaen through which he would be reborn. Stepping into the dominion of the dead beyond the walled City of Man where the faithful are protected in death, he waded through relentless hordes of unclaimed, suffering terrible wounds as they clawed at him for the warmth of his living body.

raging unfaithful. As one fell, two more replaced him, until the High Reclaimer again reached the gates between worlds.

Once again among the living, the High Reclaimer had become something else—a testament of Menoth's will. He was bestowed this title by the Harbinger and his given name buried so that he exists only as an embodiment of the True Law.

Clad in new vestments and wielding his otherworldly weapon, the Testament of Menoth is a champion of faith unlike any other. Having accomplished the impossible—crossing the gates between life and death—he is able to step between those worlds for a short time without paying heed to either as long as a soul lights his way.

The Testament's divine power was forged in the fire of sacred oaths and tempered by the ancient words writ on the Omegus. With a mere gesture he can draw back the curtain between worlds to return fallen Menites to life and banish infidel souls to the hellish wastelands of Urcaen, far from the reach of their lesser gods. The living fear him, the dead remember him, and Menoth's will guides him. The Testament has come to bring a new word to the realm of man.

HIGH EXEMPLAR KREOSS
PROTECTORATE WARCASTER

If you didn't believe in the Creator before, you will today.

—Long Gunner Sergeant Terschel Bannock to a fresh recruit sent into battle against the Knights Exemplar

KREOSS						
SPD	STR	MAT	RAT	DEF	ARM	CMD
5	6	7	4	14	15	8

SPELLBREAKER	
POW	P+S
8	14

FOCUS	7
DAMAGE	18
FIELD ALLOWANCE	C
WARJACK POINTS	+5
SMALL BASE	

SPELLBREAKER

⊘ **Magical Weapon**

⟳ **Reach**

Chain Weapon – This attack ignores the Buckler and Shield weapon qualities and Shield Wall.

Dispel – When this weapon hits a model/unit, upkeep spells on the model/unit hit immediately expire.

FEAT: MENOTH'S WRATH

High Exemplar Kreoss stands in perfect harmony with the Old God. With but a few chanted words from an ancient litany, Kreoss unleashes the anger of man's creator to smite all who oppose him to their knees.

Enemy models currently in Kreoss' control area are knocked down.

SPELLS	COST	RNG	AOE	POW	UP	OFF
CLEANSING FIRE	3	8	3	14	NO	YES
Cleansing Fire causes fire damage 🔥. On a critical hit, models hit suffer the Fire continuous effect 🔥.						
DEFENDER'S WARD	2	6	–	–	YES	NO
Target friendly Faction model/unit gains +2 DEF and ARM.						
IMMOLATION	2	8	–	12	NO	YES
Immolation causes fire damage 🔥. On a critical hit, the model hit suffers the Fire continuous effect 🔥.						
LAMENTATION	3	SELF	CTRL	–	YES	NO
Enemy models pay double the focus or fury point cost to cast or upkeep spells while in this model's control area.						
PURIFICATION	3	SELF	CTRL	–	NO	NO
Continuous effects, animi, and upkeep spells in this model's control area immediately expire.						

TACTICAL TIPS

DISPEL – Because they expire immediately, upkeep spells that had an effect when the model was hit or damaged will have no effect.

Though few are blessed enough to know Menoth's will directly, the god's mandates are set in stone and passed from one generation to the next by orders devoted to divine service. These have perfected the means to prepare the Lawgiver's chosen followers for the wars of Caen. Mikael Kreoss, a high exemplar of the Knights Exemplar, is a prime example of Menoth's worldly influence embodied by mortal man.

Kreoss was born into a community of the Old Faith in the rugged north of Khador. Bereft of his mother from birth, the young Mikael aspired to become a paladin of the Order of the Wall to serve as a guardian of the people after debtors conscripted his father into forced labor. The elder Kreoss was overwhelmed with the unrelenting work to reduce his debt while trying to raise his son alone. At last, in hopes of giving his child a better life, he entrusted Mikael to the care of a group of visiting Protectorate pilgrims who took him south to the Protectorate to provide him a proper upbringing surrounded by the faithful.

Mikael channeled the pain of separation from his family into a quest for perfection. So strong was his conviction that he sought to enter the priesthood. As an acolyte, he encountered a band of heathens robbing a sacred crypt. Enraged, Mikael assailed them with no more than his fists and his faith, cracking bones with his bare hands. Towering over his quaking foes, the Khadoran-born Menite seemed a wrathful, unstoppable giant. After crushing these desecrators, he prayed to Menoth for direction at the adjoining temple. While in vigil, Mikael Kreoss realized his destiny rested with neither the clergy nor the paladins he had admired as a youth. A visiting member of the Knights Exemplar overheard the acolyte at prayer and was impressed enough to invite Kreoss to join their brotherhood. Exemplars say their initiation is their true birth, when old lives and family are put aside. Kreoss left his past behind to pursue his true calling.

Mikael Kreoss quickly rose in Menoth's grace and in the opinion of the ruling visgoths. His efforts were effective in stamping out heretics and blasphemers wherever they were rooted. Even before the Protectorate initiated its larger crusades, Kreoss dedicated himself to going where "the wayward masses spurned Menoth's laws." Kreoss believes every man and woman lives as a gift of the Creator, and those who take Menoth for granted are unworthy of their flesh. He has sent many a dissenting soul to Urcaen for judgment.

High Exemplar Kreoss' concentration is unmatched as he directs interdictions of thousands of zealous soldiers and warjacks to key points in a battle. So strong is his faith that a mere touch from his blessed weapon can revoke the unwholesome sorcery granted by lesser gods to their wayward followers.

Among the people of the Protectorate, Kreoss has become a living legend. When the decision was made to renew war with the Cygnarans, thousands gathered to listen to him stir the faithful in preparation for battle. His flowing robes and thick rune-inlaid armor enhance his impressive physique, while his unwavering faith makes him a leader upon whom the scrutators can rely with absolute confidence.

GRAND EXEMPLAR KREOSS
PROTECTORATE EPIC WARCASTER

My sword, my suffering, and my soul all belong to the Creator. Claim them he may; they will ever serve him.

—*Grand Exemplar Mikael Kreoss*

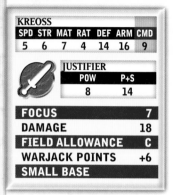

KREOSS						
SPD	STR	MAT	RAT	DEF	ARM	CMD
5	6	7	4	14	16	9

JUSTIFIER	
POW	P+S
8	14

FOCUS	7
DAMAGE	18
FIELD ALLOWANCE	C
WARJACK POINTS	+6
SMALL BASE	

FEAT: STRENGTH OF ARMS

In battle Grand Exemplar Kreoss issues commands underscored by a righteousness impossible to ignore. Following his divine example, Kreoss' forces push themselves beyond mortal limitations.

When a friendly Faction model makes a melee attack against an enemy model while the enemy model is in Kreoss' control area, the attack automatically hits. While in Kreoss' control area, friendly Faction models can make one additional melee attack during their combat actions. Strength of Arms lasts for one turn.

KREOSS

Aegis – This model is immune to continuous effects.

Elite Cadre [Exemplar] – Friendly Exemplar models gain Aegis.

Imperishable Conviction – When a friendly Faction model in its control area is destroyed by an enemy attack, this model heals 1 damage point.

JUSTIFIER

 Magical Weapon

Reach

Armor Piercing (★Attack) – When calculating damage from this attack, halve the base ARM stats of models hit that have medium or larger bases. This attack gains +2 to damage rolls against models with small bases.

Smite (★Attack) – Instead of making a normal damage roll, the model hit is slammed d6″ directly away from this model and suffers a damage roll with POW equal to this model's current STR plus the POW of this weapon. The POW of collateral damage from this slam is equal to this model's STR.

SPELLS	COST	RNG	AOE	POW	UP	OFF
CASTIGATE	2	SELF	CTRL	–	NO	NO

For one round, enemy models lose the Arc Node advantage while in this model's control area.

CHASTEN	2	8	–	12	NO	YES

Enemy upkeep spells and animi on target model/unit damaged by Chasten expire.

CLEANSING FIRE	3	8	3	14	NO	YES

Cleansing Fire causes fire damage. On a critical hit, models hit suffer the Fire continuous effect.

INVIOLABLE RESOLVE	2	6	–	–	YES	NO

Target friendly Faction model/unit gains +2 ARM and Fearless.

SACROSANCT	2	6	–	–	YES	NO

Target a friendly Faction model/unit. When an enemy non-warcaster, non-warlock warrior model destroys one or more affected models with an attack, immediately after the attack is resolved the attacking model is knocked down

TACTICAL TIPS

SMITE – The slammed model is moved only half the distance rolled if its base is larger than the slamming model's.

CASTIGATE – This does not effect models that can channel spells that do not have Arc Node.

INVIOLABLE RESOLVE – Fleeing models that gain Fearless immediately rally.

Mikael Kreoss is a man of faith and few words who lives his life according to a strict code, the oath of the Knights Exemplar. Duty to the Creator and fealty to his priests on Caen has consumed him and burned away whatever imperfections once corrupted his mortal soul. No other man alive so perfectly exemplifies what it means to be a warrior serving in Menoth's name.

When Grand Exemplar Bane Hurst gave his life to protect the Harbinger of Menoth against Cryxian despoilers, Hierarch Garrick Voyle did not hesitate to appoint Kreoss as the new leader of the Knights Exemplar. For ten days and ten nights, Kreoss remained in isolation at the Sovereign Temple of the One Faith, praying and purifying himself. Priests attended him, and he was set to trials that pushed his spirit and tugged at the very fabric of his soul. Scrutators watched him, measured his actions, and weighed his prayers. Finally satisfied in his absolute commitment to his faith, the scrutators released him to take his new vows. Kreoss emerged from the Temple wearing a brilliant armor of gold and steel and holding aloft the shining spear Justifier.

Since that day, Kreoss has led the exemplars at the fore of the great crusade. He thrusts his legions through Cygnar's defenses like Justifier's piercing blade, leaving a swath of ash and cinders where infidel encampments once stood. The Protectorate's forces look to him as a guiding light of righteousness, and the scribes of the True Faith record each of his valorous deeds, keeping a careful tally of the dead he sends to Urcaen.

This grand exemplar is an enigma to other leaders of the Protectorate. While he does his duty without hesitation, he is not above questioning the actions of the church. Kreoss is a courageous and fearsome warrior but does not possess the ruthlessness common to the Menite hierarchy. This may, in fact, be one of his greatest strengths, and it has already made him a hero to the common people of the Protectorate. Kreoss joined others in mourning the loss of a great leader when Hierarch Voyle was killed, but he had little sympathy for the hubris and callous disregard displayed by the late hierarch toward those who shared his faith.

Menites are often the instrument of their own contrition, and Grand Exemplar Kreoss is no exception. He takes the weight of the crusade on his own shoulders, continually pushing himself to assure its success, even at the cost of countless sleepless nights of prayer and contemplative vigil. Over the years, many friends have bled out their last under his command, and he has always been grateful of their sacrifices. All Menites are his brothers in battle, and he is determined to avenge the fallen and the lost. With every death stoking the warrior's furnace within him, his rage and fury have become the spear and shield of Menoth's vengeance.

HIGH EXECUTIONER SERVATH REZNIK
PROTECTORATE WARCASTER

He is nothing but a blunt instrument of the hierarch released to obliterate any who offend. Pray your name never earns a place on his writs.

—Grand Exemplar Mikael Kreoss

REZNIK						
SPD	STR	MAT	RAT	DEF	ARM	CMD
5	7	7	4	14	17	7

CONFESSOR		
	POW	P+S
	7	14

FOCUS	6
DAMAGE	17
FIELD ALLOWANCE	C
WARJACK POINTS	+6
MEDIUM BASE	

FEAT: JUDGMENT DAY

Heresy and blasphemy provoke the righteous wrath of High Executioner Servath Reznik, who delivers Menoth's final fire of judgment to those who would draw upon sorcerous power in defiance of the Lawgiver. Reznik strips away the arcane strength of his enemies and leaves them quaking and frail, awaiting the sentence of death.

Enemy models currently in Reznik's control area lose all focus and fury points. While in Reznik's control area, enemy models cannot upkeep spells or be allocated focus and those casting spells suffer the Fire continuous effect 🔥. Judgment Day lasts for one round.

REZNIK

☠ Terror

Excruciator – Once per turn during this model's activation, when it boxes a living enemy warrior model with a melee attack you can place a Wrack into play within 3" of this model. If you do, remove the boxed model from play.

Witch Hound – If a model in this model's battlegroup in its control area is hit by an enemy magic attack, immediately after the attack is resolved one model in this model's battlegroup in its control area can make a full advance and make one normal attack.

CONFESSOR

⚔ Magical Weapon

➤ Reach

Purgation – Gain an additional die on attack and damage rolls with this weapon against models with an enemy upkeep spell on them.

SPELLS	COST	RNG	AOE	POW	UP	OFF
ENGINE OF DESTRUCTION	2	SELF	–	–	NO	NO

This model gains +2 SPD, +4 STR, and +4 MAT for one round.

HEX BLAST	3	10	3	13	NO	YES

Enemy upkeep spells and animi on the model/unit directly hit by Hex Blast immediately expire.

IGNITE	2	6	–	–	YES	NO

Target friendly model/unit gains +2 to melee attack damage rolls. Affected models gain Critical Fire 🔥 on their normal melee attacks.

IRON AGGRESSION	3	6	–	–	YES	NO

Target friendly warjack can run, charge, or make slam or trample power attacks without spending focus and gains boosted melee attack rolls.

PERDITION	2	6	–	10	NO	YES

When an enemy model is damaged by Perdition, immediately after the attack is resolved one warjack in this model's battlegroup that is currently in this model's control area can make a full advance toward the nearest enemy model. A model can advance as a result of Perdition only once per turn.

TACTICAL TIPS

Excruciator – This Wrack does not begin with a focus point on it. Because the boxed model is removed from play before being destroyed, it does not generate a soul or corpse token.

Hex Blast – Because they expire immediately, upkeep spells and animi that had an effect when the model/unit was hit or damaged will have no effect.

Ignite – When this spell is cast on cavalry models, it affects mount attacks.

Those who have spurned the Lawgiver often enjoy a false sense of security outside the Protectorate of Menoth, thinking themselves safe from the scrutators. These faithless learn their mistake at the edge of the high executioner's sword. Servath Reznik readily imposes his will on foreign soil. He brings sworn writs demanding the execution of those guilty of sacrilege, sorcery, or religious treason, both inside and outside the Protectorate's borders.

The high executioner embodies ancient ways of the faith, and his masked visage recalls the time before the rise of the Twins, when priest-kings reigned and citizens understood that impiety would be met with suffering and death. He was raised in Khador's northern mountains among the strictest sects of the Old Faith, who saw the local scrutator as judge and jury.

There he learned that the ministrations of wrack or execution invoked with the proper prayers might divest a soul of sin as it fled to Urcaen and gain redemption in the City of Man despite mortal failings. The way of the priest did not suit Reznik, however, and he soon abandoned the north. He sojourned south, where he had heard that those of purer faith had carved a nation amid sun-blasted sands.

At that time not yet hierarch, the monk and scrutator Garrick Voyle saw Reznik's true soul in his eyes: here walked an instrument of faith who could kill eagerly and without mercy. In that hour Servath Reznik become high executioner, and in the early days of Voyle's hierarchy Reznik proved by numerous example the hierarch would brook no insubordination or lack of resolve. To this day stories still circulate of Menite villages burned to the last man, woman, and child at Reznik's hands, with none left to describe the reasons for such punishment.

The Protectorate's leaders have little love for Reznik. Only Hierarch Severius tolerates his presence, understanding what sort of weapon his predecessor wrought in him. Reznik's single-mindedness and almost inhuman appetite to punish the faithless has earned the enmity of Grand Exemplar

Kreoss. Word of his purpose has spread to every Menite community across western Immoren. He has earned a kind of fearful adoration from those who relish divine retribution, and they bring him the names of suspected heretics.

Severius' great work in Llael has prompted Reznik to swear anew his vows of service. He has joined his strength to the Northern Crusade to carve a stronghold from this stubborn soil. The days ahead will provide ample opportunities to exercise his function and spread the fire of the Lawgiver across the darkened lands.

GRAND SCRUTATOR SEVERIUS
PROTECTORATE WARCASTER

This man embodies my voice on the battlefield. None shall question his authority, lest they incur my wrath.

—Hierarch Garrick Voyle to the assembled Synod of the Nine Visgoths

SEVERIUS						
SPD	STR	MAT	RAT	DEF	ARM	CMD
5	5	4	5	14	14	9

STAFF OF JUDGMENT		
	POW	P+S
	8	13

FOCUS	8
DAMAGE	16
FIELD ALLOWANCE	C
WARJACK POINTS	+6
SMALL BASE	

FEAT: DIVINE MIGHT

Endowed with the authority to pass judgment on his fellow man, Grand Scrutator Severius may invoke the prohibitions of Menoth to deny the use of profane magics in his presence.

For one round, enemy models cannot cast spells and lose the Arc Node advantage while in Severius' control area. While in Severius' control area, enemy models with the Focus Manipulation ability do not replenish focus points during their controller's next turn.

SEVERIUS

Convert (★Action) – RNG CMD. Target living enemy non-character trooper model. If the model is in range, it must pass a command check or it becomes a friendly Faction solo under your control for the rest of the game. The converted model cannot activate this turn.

Sacred Ward – This model cannot be targeted by enemy spells.

STAFF OF JUDGMENT

⬡ Magical Weapon

⬡ Reach

SPELLS	COST	RNG	AOE	POW	UP	OFF
ASHES TO ASHES	4	8	*	10	NO	YES

If target model is hit, it and the d6 nearest enemy models within 5" of it suffer a POW 10 fire damage roll 🔥.

DEATH SENTENCE	2	8	–	–	YES	YES

When a friendly Faction model misses target enemy model/unit with an attack, it can reroll the attack roll. Each attack roll can be rerolled only once as a result of Death Sentence.

DEFENDER'S WARD	2	6	–	–	YES	NO

Target friendly Faction model/unit gains +2 DEF and ARM.

EYE OF MENOTH	3	SELF	CTRL	–	YES	NO

While in this model's control area, friendly Faction models gain +1 to attack and damage rolls.

IMMOLATION	2	8	–	12	NO	YES

Immolation causes fire damage 🔥. On a critical hit, the model hit suffers the Fire continuous effect 🔥.

VISION	2	6	–	–	YES	NO

The next time target friendly Faction model is directly hit by an attack, it suffers no damage roll from the attack, then Vision expires.

Scrutators require a singular strength of presence; they belong to the inner circle of priests responsible for policing the clergy itself, who in turn control the entire Protectorate of Menoth. They must be able to snap the minds of the faithless and overwhelm them with feelings of piety, servitude, and fear of a divine reckoning. Scrutators cannot show the slightest weakness or doubt. Grand Scrutator Severius is the stoutest pillar holding up the grand Temple of Menoth. Severius answered only to the hierarch and was given command over the entirety of the Protectorate's military.

Severius has single-handedly converted thousands of heathens and infidels to the True Law. In past decades he marched far afield into other nations as an unofficial ambassador of the faith—one too powerful to ignore and too dangerous to confront. After a particularly fruitful trip to Khador in the 570s, he was banned from that nation for the thousands who abandoned the Motherland and answered his call to join the Protectorate. Since the Protectorate has mounted increasingly militant and aggressive crusades, Severius has ceased these missions to focus on leading Menite forces in battle. Conversion remains a priority, but he conducts it now on subjugated villages and towns whose defenders have been slaughtered or driven away.

In a parallel to Menoth's ancient war with the Devourer, Severius lives to battle the enemies of his faith. He has a powerful thirst for the blood of blasphemers and brings a commanding presence and undeniable genius to the battlefield. His warjacks come alive with the same fervor as his converts. His plans are laid well in advance, for he has a brilliant grasp of both strategy and tactics. Indeed, Severius has a plan in motion that will not come to fruition until far past his lifetime. While he is a visionary, he is also deeply traditional and strives to return the world to a state ordained by Menoth at the dawn of civilization.

Age may have withered the warcaster and stolen his former strength, but what he lacks in bodily prowess he makes up for with divine power. As the blaze of Menoth's wrath, he is able to breach the minds of non-believers with a single word. So potent is his righteousness, he wades through otherwise deadly arcane attacks as if they were no more than illusion. Severius is the eye of the hurricane and a center of focused spiritual control willing to annihilate anything around him that threatens his faith.

Severius' divine nature is so strong that if he so chooses, he can thunder the Litany of Menoth declaring the Creator's glory. With a great boom, this divine rite reverberates to all enemy warcasters within earshot, rending their blasphemous connection to their impure mechanika. The litany proves that all things are Menoth's and neither pagan sorcery nor heathen witchcraft can stand against him. Through Grand Scrutator Severius, Menoth's glory is unmistakable, and his voice shall be heard.

HIERARCH SEVERIUS
PROTECTORATE EPIC WARCASTER

Death and destruction are not our purpose. We require only submission to the Creator. However, those who refuse to bow will burn.

—Hierarch Severius

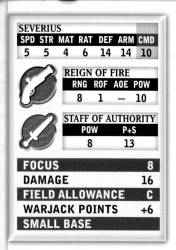

SEVERIUS						
SPD	STR	MAT	RAT	DEF	ARM	CMD
5	5	4	6	14	14	10

REIGN OF FIRE			
RNG	ROF	AOE	POW
8	1	—	10

STAFF OF AUTHORITY	
POW	P+S
8	13

FOCUS	8
DAMAGE	16
FIELD ALLOWANCE	C
WARJACK POINTS	+6
SMALL BASE	

FEAT: FIRES OF COMMUNION

With his divinely appointed authority, Hierarch Severius can invoke the most sacred rites of his faith to call down curtains of holy fire from on high. Unholy blasphemies are transfigured to ash. The living who have followed false gods feel overwhelmed by shame and are compelled to prostrate themselves before the hierarch and obey his commands.

Either you take control of d3 + 3 living enemy Grunts currently in Severius' control area, or d3 + 3 undead models currently in Severius' control area suffer a POW 12 fire damage roll 🔥. Decide before rolling. You choose the models affected. Controlled models become friendly solos for one turn.

SEVERIUS

Admonisher – When this model directly hits an enemy model with a melee or ranged attack, the d3 nearest enemy models within 5" of the model hit suffer a POW 10 magical damage roll.

Warjack Bond – One non-character warjack in Severius' battlegroup can begin the game bonded to him. Once per turn, when the warjack is directly hit by an attack it can immediately spend 1 focus point not to suffer a damage roll from the attack.

REIGN OF FIRE

🔥 **Damage Type: Fire**

🌀 **Magical Weapon**

Spiritual Channeling – This attack can be channeled through an arc node. If a model cannot channel spells, it also cannot channel attacks as a result of Spiritual Channeling.

STAFF OF AUTHORITY

🌀 **Magical Weapon**

🎯 **Reach**

SPELLS	COST	RNG	AOE	POW	UP	OFF
AWARENESS	3	SELF	CTRL	–	NO	NO

While in this model's control area, the front arcs of models in its battlegroup are extended to 360° and when determining LOS those models ignore cloud effects, forests, and intervening models. Awareness lasts for one round.

CREATOR'S WRATH	2	SELF	–	–	YES	NO

This model gains an additional die on melee attack and melee damage rolls. When making a melee attack, it ignores spell effects that add to the target's DEF or ARM.

FEAR OF GOD	2	10	–	–	YES	YES

Target enemy model/unit cannot give orders, receive orders, or make special attacks.

HEX BLAST	3	10	3	13	NO	YES

Enemy upkeep spells and animi on the model/unit directly hit by Hex Blast immediately expire.

HOLY WARD	2	6	–	–	YES	NO

Target friendly Faction model/unit gains +2 DEF and cannot be targeted by enemy spells or animi.

INFLUENCE	1	10	–	–	NO	YES

Take control of target enemy non-warcaster, non-warlock warrior model. The model immediately makes one normal melee attack, then Influence expires.

TACTICAL TIPS

FIRES OF COMMUNION – The enemy models you take control of activate normally this turn. If a unit commander is affected by this feat, its controller chooses another model in that unit to become the unit commander. The model chosen remains the unit commander even after Fires of Communion expires and control of the affected models returns to your opponent.

SPIRITUAL CHANNELING – The attack does not become a spell or magic attack in any way as a result of this ability.

HEX BLAST – Because they expire immediately, upkeep spells and animi that had an effect when the model/unit was hit or damaged will have no effect.

Demonstrating steadiness and surety that belie his age, Severius inspires his followers to transcend their humanity and become an extension of the Creator's will. Those who attend him can feel the power of unchecked divinity in his words and deeds. When he raises his staff against his enemies, righteous fire blazes forth to grant them a final lesson in pain and humility. While believers look on his robed form with an awe and adoration that gives rise to tears, others see him as an incarnation of pure terror and a reminder that the Shaper of Man can just as easily reduce his creation to ash if it displeases.

The death of Hierarch Voyle could have been a cataclysmic blow to the Protectorate. To see the most potent Menite since the days of the priest-kings struck down by a heathen the very moment victory over their oppressors seemed assured was staggering. The priesthood froze in despairing disbelief in those first terrible hours. The visgoths and senior priests remembered too well the years of chaos and uncertainty in the wake of Hierarch Ravonal's passing and the bloody struggle that had followed as Voyle seized the reins of power. The presence of the Harbinger of Menoth, however, reassured the priests in Sul and Imer and reminded them they did not lack for guidance. To them she said, "The next hierarch walks among you, carving a new domain in the north, uniting the faithful." The rise of Severius marks the first time a hierarch gained power so quickly and with such irrefutable approval from the Creator.

Severius no longer refuses authority as he had as grand scrutator, when he had removed himself from the political arena to demonstrate his determination to fight on the battlefield. He takes the burdens of leadership in stride, knowing the Protectorate must heed a single voice in this time of war. Likewise, Severius knows his place remains at the fore of his crusade. He will never step from the field of battle and his role as the anointed priest-general.

This hierarchy shall differ dramatically from Ravonal's and Voyle's. Theirs was a time of preparation, of building the machinery of war, readying the martial orders, and constructing factories and mines to support the coming crusades. Hierarch Severius will take up the weapons his predecessors forged and leave the trivial matters of the Temple bureaucracy to the Synod.

Before his elevation to hierarch, Severius spoke the words inscribed in script of blazing fire within the Covenant of Menoth outside Leryn, invoking its terrible power as foretold by prophecy and confirmed by the visions of the Harbinger. This unleashed power awaits his command to turn any enemies of the faithful to ash, while imbuing his voice with the authority of his god. He can

pierce the hearts of those who have faltered in their faith, restoring them to Menoth. He has witnessed the return of the Testament from Urcaen and has vowed to employ the Harbinger to swell the ranks of the faithful. The path of the future lies open and clear to him.

The hierarch has taken it as his life's work to unite the Menites of western Immoren and spread the True Faith to all humanity. Those answering his call will usher in a new age by hammering the cathedrals of Morrow to rubble and erecting new temples to the Lawgiver. The younger, wayward faith will bow to Menoth or perish utterly.

VICE SCRUTATOR VINDICTUS
PROTECTORATE WARCASTER

The forgiveness of Menoth is the greatest gift that can be bestowed upon the impious, for his Law holds dominion over this world and the next. That they do not wish that forgiveness is of no consequence.

—*Vice Scrutator Vindictus*

VINDICTUS						
SPD	STR	MAT	RAT	DEF	ARM	CMD
6	6	7	4	15	16	9

LAWGIVER		
	POW	P+S
	6	12

SOLACE		
	POW	P+S
	6	12

FOCUS	6
DAMAGE	16
FIELD ALLOWANCE	C
WARJACK POINTS	+6
SMALL BASE	

FEAT: PENITENCE

When Vice Scrutator Vindictus marches to war his prayers ensure those who harm the faithful will suffer for their impious temerity. When he voices passages of the True Law, his followers become the vessels for his righteous wrath and deliver holy retribution to any who strike them.

When one or more friendly Faction models are damaged by an enemy attack while in Vindictus' control area, immediately after the attack is resolved the attacker suffers 1 damage point. Penitence lasts for one round.

VINDICTUS

🌙 Pathfinder

Death Toll [Holy Zealot] – When this model destroys a living enemy model with a melee attack, after the attack is resolved you can add one Grunt to a friendly Holy Zealot unit in this model's command range. The Grunt must be placed in formation and within 3″ of this model. The destroyed model is removed from play but does not provide a soul or corpse token.

Sacrificial Pawn [Holy Zealot] – When this model is directly hit by an enemy ranged attack, you can choose to have one friendly, non-incorporeal Holy Zealot model within 3″ of this model directly hit instead. That model is automatically hit and suffers all damage and effects.

LAWGIVER

⚙ Magical Weapon

Blessed – When making an attack with this weapon, ignore spell effects that add to a model's ARM or DEF.

SOLACE

⚙ Magical Weapon

Chain Weapon – This attack ignores the Buckler and Shield weapon qualities and Shield Wall.

No Menite alive is so occupied with the fate of the souls of heathens as Vice Scrutator Vindictus. When others among the Protectorate leadership look out upon a sea of faceless heretics, the vice scrutator sees potential devotees ready to swell the ranks of the faithful. Vindictus preaches with word and deed together; when an unbeliever cannot hear the truth of Menoth's words, he is well prepared to communicate in the language of agony.

The vice scrutator feels compelled to turn the wicked to the path of the True Faith wherever they may be found. He sees

SPELLS	COST	RNG	AOE	POW	UP	OFF
DEFENDER'S WARD	2	6	–	–	YES	NO
Target friendly Faction model/unit gains +2 DEF and ARM.						
IMMOLATION	2	8	–	12	NO	YES
Immolation causes fire damage 🔥. On a critical hit, the model hit suffers the Fire continuous effect 🔥.						
RIFT	3	8	4	13	NO	YES
The AOE is rough terrain and remains in play for one round.						
SACRIFICIAL LAMB	1	CTRL	–	–	NO	NO
Remove one friendly living Faction model in this model's control area from play to allocate 1 focus point to each warjack in this model's battlegroup that is currently in its control area. Sacrificial Lamb can be cast only once per turn.						
TRUE PATH	3	SELF	CTRL	–	NO	NO
Friendly Faction warrior models/units beginning their activations in this model's control area gain +2″ movement and Pathfinder 🌙 during their activations. True Path lasts for one turn.						

TACTICAL TIPS

DEATH TOLL – The added Grunt can activate normally this turn.

SACRIFICIAL LAMB – A warjack cannot exceed normal focus allocation limits as a result of Sacrificial Lamb.

it as his holy duty to tend to the flocks of mankind born without a chance to witness the glories of Menoth's nation on Caen. Thousands of priests tend to the Protectorate's flocks, but few make it their life's mission to spread the Creator's word across the face of Caen. To this end, Vindictus periodically travels far from the borders of his homeland, bringing armies loyal to the Lawgiver against the unbelievers and capturing those he believes he can convert by the ministrations of pain.

Vindictus has traveled deep into the heartlands of the enemy to preach and has delivered many zealots to the True Faith since the beginning of the great crusade. His sermons are filled with the language of penitence to best evoke the wrath of Menoth toward those who spurn their creator. More than one Cygnaran farm town or Khadoran mining village has been torn apart by those newly converted who are desperate to prove their devotion with the blood of their unrepentant neighbors. The holy zealots who follow Vindictus fight with the strength of fanatics and martyrs, eager to emulate the man who delivered them to the True Faith. The vice scrutator himself can be more forgiving. Even in the chaos of battle he will stay his hand, sparing those who fall before him should they accept the Creator as their rightful master.

A powerful warcaster, Vindictus possesses divine powers is the clarity of his vision and the scope of his lore. He has studied the darkness that is the enemy and understands their heresies and occult rituals. He has taken on the burden of understanding the tainted agreements and pacts made by those who have turned from Menoth and sought easier and more corrupt paths to power. These are dangerous studies, but Vindictus has proven he has the strength of will and conviction to confront them and to use this lore to root out and punish the blasphemous. He is a master at finding the weakness in the hearts of his enemies and using their faltering convictions to destroy them. Vindictus intends to show all people of Caen the Creator's glory—or personally send their souls to the afterlife.

WARJACKS OF THE PROTECTORATE

The Protectorate of Menoth has always had a unique and contentious relationship with mechanika and warjack development. A strict interpretation of the faith's doctrine indicates *all* arcane works are heretical. After the rise of the warjack in Cygnar and Khador, however, Protectorate visgoths and hierarchs determined that military dominance is impossible without mechanikal superiority. As Menoth intended his people to be victorious, it was his will that a way be found to sanctify these machines of war.

The Protectorate's earliest application of mechanika was with peacetime laborjacks. Under tremendous agricultural and industrial burdens, Menites resigned themselves to this vital assistance. The clergy sought to reconcile their beliefs with the necessities of life, and some began to inscribe prayers of atonement and penance into the hulls of the steamjacks. Any zealots who continued to decry the mechanika were silenced by direct order of Hierarch Luctine early in his reign, conclusively ending the theological debate.

In the early decades the Protectorate's leadership were concerned with maintaining the appearance of accord with the treaties they had signed with Cygnar. Prohibited from possessing dedicated weapons of war, the fledgling martial orders soon began arming laborjacks for battle and defense, smuggling warjack-grade cortexes and other refined machinery from Khador and other nations. The Protectorate quickly had a handful of functional warjacks composed of black-market parts and a few simpler components manufactured in secret.

In time the Menites became bolder and expended less effort on disguising their activities. Within a few decades they were producing a small number of their own warjacks, the cortexes created by kidnapped foreign experts. These enslaved arcanists, eventually organized as the Vassals of Menoth, would in time become critical to the Protectorate's war efforts. While this organization still relies on such captives, it also includes a number of Protectorate citizens born with arcane abilities, individuals who at one time might have been put to death in childhood. A strong stigma associated with crafting arcane machinery remains within the culture even today, and many who join the ranks of the Vassals do so to avoid reclamation.

Despite the formidable number of warjacks the Protectorate constructs in its dedicated factoriums, its production capabilities lag behind those of its enemies. Many in the Protectorate think of its warjacks as precious weapons blessed by Menoth. The sight of an ornately decorated warjack trailing plumes of smoke, inscribed with the words of the Creator and accompanied by choirs chanting holy prayers, inspires awe in faithful and heretic alike.

VIGILANT CONCEPTUAL DESIGNS

PROTECTORATE WARJACK ADORNMENT

PRAYER SIGILS

Many warjacks that have survived multiple engagements are decorated with intricately ornamented blessed sigils to which lengths of prayer cloth are attached. The cloth is covered with script containing passages from the True Law. These blessings are believed to call Menoth's regard upon those fighting in the vicinity, and they ensure that his wrath falls on their enemies.

ORNAMENTED MENOFIX

Intricate Menofixes are other common blessed adornments utilized by soldiers in the field to recognize warjacks that endure and perform particularly well in battle. Sometimes they are set with large gemstones or glass beads that refract sunlight to represent the sacred flame of the Creator.

DERVISH
PROTECTORATE LIGHT WARJACK

Its blades are an effortless extension of my will; its movements are my movements. In its simple mind I find a brother in battle.

—High Allegiant Amon Ad-Raza

DERVISH						
SPD	STR	MAT	RAT	DEF	ARM	CMD
5	9	6	4	13	16	—

SWORD (L)
	POW	P+S
	4	13

SWORD (R)
	POW	P+S
	4	13

DAMAGE

1	2	3	4	5	6
	L			R	
L	L	M	C	R	R
	M	M	C	C	

FIELD ALLOWANCE	U
POINT COST	4
MEDIUM BASE	

DERVISH

Side Step – When this model hits with an initial attack or a special attack, it can advance 2" after the attack is resolved. This model cannot be targeted by free strikes during this movement.

SWORD

Combo Strike (★Attack) – Make a melee attack. Instead of making a normal damage roll, the POW of the damage roll is equal to this model's STR plus twice the POW of this weapon.

HEIGHT/WEIGHT: 8′7″ / 3.5 TONS
ARMAMENT: SWORDS (RIGHT AND LEFT ARMS)
FUEL LOAD/BURN USAGE: 365 LBS / 7 HRS GENERAL, 80 MINS COMBAT
INITIAL SERVICE DATE: 595 AR
CORTEX MANUFACTURER: VASSALS OF MENOTH
ORIG. CHASSIS DESIGN: SUL-MENITE ARTIFICERS

TACTICAL TIPS

COMBO STRIKE – This ability cannot be used while either of this model's arm systems is locked. A model with a crippled weapon system cannot use it to make chain attacks or special attacks, including power attacks.

A work of divine inspiration, the Dervish uses the unparalleled reflexes of its Devout chassis wholly for offense: instead of protecting, every motion of the warjack is meant to end life. The 'jack falls upon the enemies of the faithful like an iron-forged maelstrom of butchery, its twin blades working in tandem to sow death across the battlefield. The Dervish has marked its successes with a wake of shorn limbs and fallen soldiers since the day it emerged from the hidden foundries, becoming notorious for its death-dealing capabilities during the vicious fighting between Protectorate and Cygnaran forces in the streets of Sul.

The light and agile Dervish is the perfect addition to a crusading army on the move. It possesses greater reflexes than any other Protectorate warjack developed to date and is constructed to have supreme flexibility. Bringing its blades to bear at blinding speeds, the Dervish weaves through battle, sidestepping attacks in the same motion it uses to dispatch enemies in its path.

This killing machine of the first order was obviously designed solely for war. Unable to justify the existence of the machine as part of any Protectorate defensive force, the Synod decreed the Dervish would be constructed in secret and only in small numbers. Now in the days of the crusade, these warjacks have been called to the front lines to carve a bloody swath through the Protectorate's enemies.

DEVOUT
PROTECTORATE LIGHT WARJACK

It is not enough to thwart the attacks of the faithless; they must also be punished for their affront to the Creator. The Devout exemplifies this divine imperative.

—Visgoth Terren Eommes

HEIGHT/WEIGHT:	8'7" / 3.9 TONS
ARMAMENT:	POLE AXE (RIGHT ARM), GREAT SHIELD (LEFT ARM)
FUEL LOAD/BURN USAGE:	387 LBS / 7 HRS GENERAL, 75 MINS COMBAT
INITIAL SERVICE DATE:	579 AR
CORTEX MANUFACTURER:	VASSALS OF MENOTH
ORIG. CHASSIS DESIGN:	SUL-MENITE ARTIFICERS/CYGNARAN ARMORY

Faith alone is not always sufficient to shield the righteous from their enemies, and so the Devout was crafted to protect the Protectorate's leaders from heretics. Every component lends to the Devout's ability to protect its master: It is light enough to keep up with fleet-footed warcasters, and it uses its enhanced mechanikal reflexes to intercept attacks or bring weapons to bear against a foe drawing too close to its ward. Its massive shield is sanctified with holy inscriptions from the Canon of the True Law to protect its controller from the accursed magic of heathen sorcerers.

When the Vassals of Menoth were commanded by the Synod to produce a warjack capable of guarding a warcaster, they wasted no time in applying their considerable expertise to the task. After rejecting the workhorse Repenter chassis as too cumbersome, they chose instead to design the Devout from the ground up to ensure its suitability to its vital purpose. Though the Devout prototype still made extensive use of smuggled components, its cortex was developed entirely within the Protectorate.

The Devout's whip-like reflexes and heavy shield make it the perfect bodyguard: like a faithful hound, its every reaction is tuned to the flow of battle as it positions itself between the warcaster and those who would strike him.

DEVOUT

Defensive Strike – Once per turn, when an enemy model advances into and ends its movement in this model's melee range, this model can immediately make one normal melee attack against it.

Shield Guard – Once per round, when a friendly model is directly hit by a ranged attack during your opponent's turn while within 2" of this model, this model can become the target of the attack and be automatically hit instead. This model cannot use Shield Guard if it is incorporeal, knocked down, or stationary.

Spell Barrier – Anytime during its activation while B2B with its controlling warcaster, this model can spend 1 focus point to use Spell Barrier. If it does, the warcaster cannot be targeted by enemy spells for one round.

GREAT SHIELD
+2 Shield

POLE AXE
Reach

DEVOUT						
SPD	STR	MAT	RAT	DEF	ARM	CMD
5	9	6	4	13	16	—

GREAT SHIELD	
POW	P+S
1	10

POLE AXE	
POW	P+S
4	13

DAMAGE

1	2	3	4	5	6
		L		R	
L	L	M	C	R	R
	M	M	C	C	

FIELD ALLOWANCE	U
POINT COST	5
MEDIUM BASE	

TACTICAL TIPS

SHIELD GUARD – If this model cannot become the target of the attack for some reason, it cannot use this ability.

SPELL BARRIER – The warcaster and this model do not need to remain B2B.

REDEEMER
PROTECTORATE LIGHT WARJACK

Never again shall you fear being outnumbered by heretics. Under a hail of blessed fire their numbers will wither to nothing, scattered by Menoth's hand.

—Senior Scrutator Vorn

REDEEMER						
SPD	STR	MAT	RAT	DEF	ARM	CMD
5	9	6	5	12	17	—

SKYHAMMER			
RNG	ROF	AOE	POW
16	3	3	12

BATTLE MACE	
POW	P+S
4	13

DAMAGE

1	2	3	4	5	6
	L			R	
L	L	M	C	R	R
	M	M	C	C	

FIELD ALLOWANCE	U
POINT COST	6
MEDIUM BASE	

SKYHAMMER

Inaccurate – This model suffers –4 to attack rolls with this weapon.

HEIGHT/WEIGHT: 9′10″ / 4.85 TONS
ARMAMENT: SKYHAMMER ROCKET POD (LEFT ARM), BATTLE MACE (RIGHT ARM)
FUEL LOAD/BURN USAGE: 154 LBS / 5.5 HRS GENERAL, 1.2 HRS COMBAT
INITIAL SERVICE DATE: 545 AR
CORTEX MANUFACTURER: VASSALS OF MENOTH
ORIG. CHASSIS DESIGN: ENGINES EAST/KHADORAN MECHANIKS ASSEMBLY (MODIFIED BY THE SUL-MENITE ARTIFICERS)

Armed with numerous devastating long-range rockets, the Redeemer was designed to deliver judgment from afar. This warjack carries an ample supply of Menite-manufactured explosives and a mechanikal rig to launch them. Borrowing technology developed for the Repenter's ignition system, the Redeemer uses vented heartfire to light the propellants. The simple rockets are launched recklessly into enemy ranks to explode in a cascade of deadly debris that leaves enemy infantry with horrible lacerations and extensive burns that are notoriously difficult to heal. The Redeemer can deliver devastating salvos of rocket fire, though the inaccuracy of its weapon usually spreads the projectiles across a wide area, and it wields a brutal mace for close fighting.

In the earliest decades after its production, the Redeemer was instrumental in expanding the borders of the Protectorate to the east and south. It was often employed against rugged and determined bands of Idrian holdouts who refused to convert. Since that time the warjack has been more actively turned against Cygnar and other enemies of the Protectorate, deploying to support both border defenses and active assaults abroad. Many Cygnarans still wait hopefully for long-lost kin, not knowing their bodies lie unrecognizable in the battlefields, torn apart by Redeemer fire.

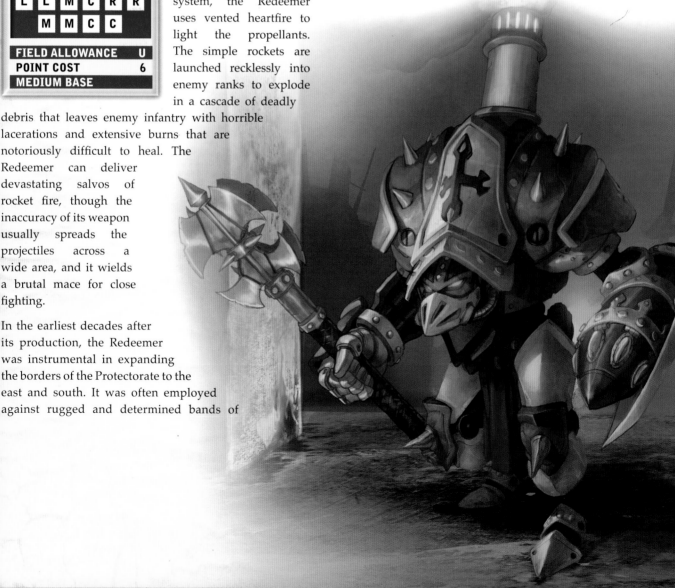

REPENTER
PROTECTORATE LIGHT WARJACK

Our enemies rightly fear its fire, as the cleansing flame inflicts unimaginable pain.
Such excruciation forces repentance before death claims them.
—Grand Scrutator Severius

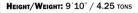

HEIGHT/WEIGHT:	9′10″ / 4.25 TONS
ARMAMENT:	FLAMETHROWER (LEFT ARM), WAR FLAIL (RIGHT ARM)
FUEL LOAD/BURN USAGE:	165 LBS / 6 HRS GENERAL, 1.5 HRS COMBAT
INITIAL SERVICE DATE:	533 AR
CORTEX MANUFACTURER:	VASSALS OF MENOTH
ORIG. CHASSIS DESIGN:	ENGINES EAST/KHADORAN MECHANIKS ASSEMBLY (MODIFIED BY THE SUL-MENITE ARTIFICERS)

The Protectorate of Menoth uses the volatile oil known as "Menoth's Fury" in great abundance, a fiery reminder of the faith's burning wrath. Older warjacks like the Repenter are outfitted with the crudest and least refined supply of Menoth's Fury, as it is readily available in quantity. The Repenter was first used to police the borders of the Protectorate, and it brought these scourging flames to bear against any who dared to trespass.

FLAMETHROWER

🔥 **Continuous Effect: Fire**

🔥 **Damage Type: Fire**

WAR FLAIL

Chain Weapon – This attack ignores the Buckler and Shield weapon qualities and Shield Wall.

REPENTER

SPD	STR	MAT	RAT	DEF	ARM	CMD
5	9	6	5	12	17	—

FLAMETHROWER

	RNG	ROF	AOE	POW
L	SP 8	1	—	12

WAR FLAIL

	POW	P+S
R	4	13

DAMAGE

1	2	3	4	5	6
		L		R	
L	L	M	C	R	R
	M	M	C	C	

FIELD ALLOWANCE	U
POINT COST	4
MEDIUM BASE	

When they designed the Repenter decades ago, the Sul-Menite artificers armed the light warjack with a great three-headed flail. Into its other arm they integrated a rudimentary flamethrower. That first model was little more than a pipe and an ignition system attached to a reservoir with a simple pump, but newer versions utilize fanning spray nozzles and refined mechanikal systems to propel the blazing fluid a considerable distance. The latest weapon foregoes an external igniter and instead vents superheated heartfire directly into the fuel.

Arguably as important as the damage wrought by this fire is the impact of a Repenter's blaze on enemy morale. Those of weak faith who face the Protectorate in battle have no fortitude for seeing their friends burned alive, screaming in terror while allies try desperately to extinguish the hungry flames. The Repenter is a favored vehicle for delivering Menoth's wrath to any enemies who defy his will.

REVENGER
PROTECTORATE LIGHT WARJACK

We carry the words of the Lawgiver to the living, enact his will on Caen, and strike with his fist.

—Hierarch Caltor Turgis to his scrutators

REVENGER						
SPD	STR	MAT	RAT	DEF	ARM	CMD
5	9	6	5	12	17	—

REPULSOR SHIELD		
L	POW	P+S
	1	10

HALBERD		
R	POW	P+S
	4	13

DAMAGE

1	2	3	4	5	6
	□	□			
	□	□	□		
□	□	□	□	□	
	L	A	A	R	
L	L	M	C	R	R
	M	M	C	C	

FIELD ALLOWANCE	U
POINT COST	6
MEDIUM BASE	

REVENGER
⬡ Arc Node

REPULSOR SHIELD
⊕2 Shield

Repel – When this model hits an enemy model with this weapon during its activation, the model hit is pushed 1″ directly away from this model. When this model is hit with a melee attack made by a model in its front arc, after the attack is resolved the attacking model is pushed 1″ directly away from this model. This model loses Repel while this weapon system is crippled or locked.

HALBERD
⊘ Reach

Powerful Charge – This model gains +2 to charge attack rolls with this weapon.

HEIGHT/WEIGHT:	9′8″ / 4.45 TONS
ARMAMENT:	REPULSOR SHIELD (LEFT ARM), HALBERD (RIGHT ARM), ARC NODE
FUEL LOAD/BURN USAGE:	165 LBS / 5.5 HRS GENERAL, 1.2 HRS COMBAT
INITIAL SERVICE DATE:	546 AR
CORTEX MANUFACTURER:	VASSALS OF MENOTH
ORIG. CHASSIS DESIGN:	ENGINES EAST/KHADORAN MECHANIKS ASSEMBLY (MODIFIED BY THE SUL-MENITE ARTIFICERS)

Menite artificers crafted the powerful repulsor shield to protect this vital weapon in battle. Aided by priests, the artificers inlaid runes of protection on the warjack's shield. If the powerful runes come into contact with an enemy, the foe is immediately rebuked and hurled away. This has given the Revenger the ability to distance itself from superior combatants like heavier 'jacks so that it may retaliate from a safe distance.

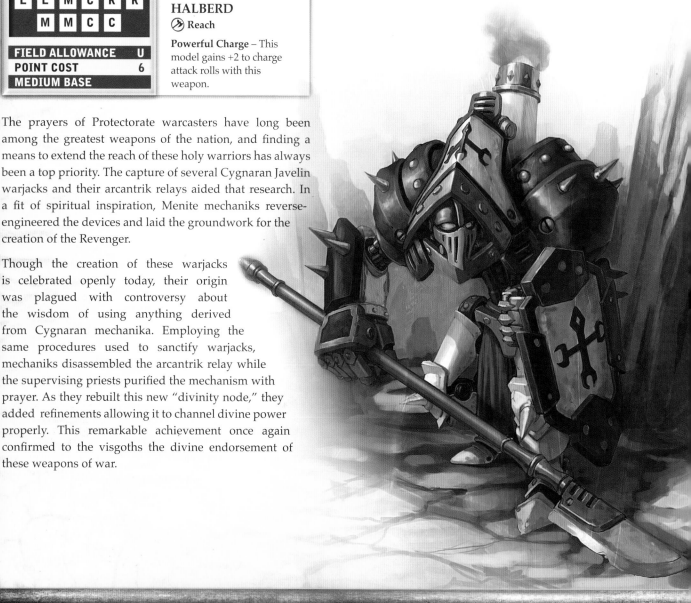

The prayers of Protectorate warcasters have long been among the greatest weapons of the nation, and finding a means to extend the reach of these holy warriors has always been a top priority. The capture of several Cygnaran Javelin warjacks and their arcantrik relays aided that research. In a fit of spiritual inspiration, Menite mechaniks reverse-engineered the devices and laid the groundwork for the creation of the Revenger.

Though the creation of these warjacks is celebrated openly today, their origin was plagued with controversy about the wisdom of using anything derived from Cygnaran mechanika. Employing the same procedures used to sanctify warjacks, mechaniks disassembled the arcantrik relay while the supervising priests purified the mechanism with prayer. As they rebuilt this new "divinity node," they added refinements allowing it to channel divine power properly. This remarkable achievement once again confirmed to the visgoths the divine endorsement of these weapons of war.

PROTECTORATE LIGHT WARJACK

The Vigilant shall shield our bodies as the Creator shields our hearts.
—Visgoth Ronev Gant

TACTICAL TIPS

While both its Shield Fists are functional, this model has a +4 ARM bonus from its shields.

HEIGHT/WEIGHT: 9'10" / 5.0 TONS

ARMAMENT: TWIN SHIELD FISTS

FUEL LOAD/BURN USAGE: 470 LBS / 5 HRS. GENERAL, 50 MINS COMBAT

INITIAL SERVICE DATE: 535 AR

CORTEX MANUFACTURER: VASSALS OF MENOTH (CURRENTLY)

ORIG. CHASSIS DESIGN: ENGINES EAST, KHADORAN MECHANIKS ASSEMBLY (MODIFIED BY THE SUL-MENITE ARTIFICERS)

Built on one of the oldest Menite warjack chassis designs still in service, the Vigilant was among the first warjacks to serve alongside the nascent Protectorate military. In those days the Protectorate still outwardly adhered to Cygnaran prohibitions against the creation of steamjacks dedicated to war. Armed defensively, the Vigilant obeyed those proscriptions nearly to the letter while providing Protectorate warcasters with a weapon of brutal simplicity.

VIGILANT

Girded – This model does not suffer blast damage. Friendly models B2B with it do not suffer blast damage.

SHIELD FIST

Open Fist

+2 Shield

VIGILANT						
SPD	STR	MAT	RAT	DEF	ARM	CMD
5	9	6	5	12	17	—

SHIELD FIST		
L	POW	P+S
	2	11

SHIELD FIST		
R	POW	P+S
	2	11

DAMAGE

1	2	3	4	5	6
		L		R	
L	L	M	C	R	R
	M	M	C	C	

FIELD ALLOWANCE	U
POINT COST	4
MEDIUM BASE	

Its twin fist-mounted shields make the Vigilant incredibly durable, able to withstand punishment that would cripple much heavier machines. The tremendous area covered by its towering shields provides nearly unassailable shelter from enemy artillery fire, making it a favorite among warcasters; indeed, more than one 'caster has been saved by a Vigilant's armored presence. Warcasters also appreciate the 'jack's low-maintenance operation and utility: a Vigilant is as adept at carrying loads in a supply train as it is at hurling enemy combatants about like rag dolls. The relatively small warjacks' ability to maneuver nimbly around barricades and weather tremendous fire in vicious street fights made it crucial to the Protectorate's defense during the siege of Sul.

After decades of service, the Vigilant is as dependable today as it was the day it first walked off the assembly line. Some Vigilants have been in continuous military service more than fifty years. The Vigilant's uncomplicated weaponry and cortex make it easy and inexpensive to manufacture, ensuring its place in the Menite military for years to come.

BLESSING OF VENGEANCE
PROTECTORATE CHARACTER LIGHT WARJACK

Reserve pity and mercy for forgivable mistakes. Those who violate the True Law earn only righteous vengeance.

—Grand Scrutator Severius

BLESSING OF VENGEANCE						
SPD	STR	MAT	RAT	DEF	ARM	CMD
5	9	7	5	12	17	—

REPULSOR SHIELD (L)

	POW	P+S
	1	10

HALBERD (R)

	POW	P+S
	4	13

DAMAGE

1	2	3	4	5	6
	L	A	A	R	
L	L	M	C	R	R
	M	M	C	C	

FIELD ALLOWANCE	C
POINT COST	7
MEDIUM BASE	

BLESSING OF VENGEANCE

Arc Node

Affinity [Severius] – Once per turn, when Severius channels a spell through this model, he gains +2 to that spell's damage rolls.

Defensive Strike – Once per turn, when an enemy model advances into and ends its movement in this model's melee range, this model can immediately make one normal melee attack against it.

Imprint: Bushwhack – During its activation, this model can spend 1 focus point to gain Bushwhack this activation. (During its activation, a model with Bushwhack can make its combat action before its normal movement. If it does, it must make a full advance as its normal movement this activation.)

REPULSOR SHIELD

+2 Shield

Repel – When this model hits an enemy model with this weapon during its activation, the model hit is pushed 1" directly away from this model. When this model is hit with a melee attack made by a model in its front arc, after the attack is resolved the attacking model is pushed 1" directly away from this model. This model loses Repel while this weapon system is crippled or locked.

HALBERD

Reach

Powerful Charge – This model gains +2 to charge attack rolls with this weapon.

HEIGHT/WEIGHT: 9′8″ / 4.7 TONS
ARMAMENT: HALBERD (RIGHT ARM), HEAVY REPULSOR SHIELD (LEFT ARM)
FUEL LOAD/BURN USAGE: 445 LBS / 5.5 HRS GENERAL, 75 MINS COMBAT
INITIAL SERVICE DATE: 574 AR
CORTEX MANUFACTURER: GREYLORDS COVENANT (SMUGGLED, MODIFIED)
ORIG. CHASSIS DESIGN: SUL-MENITE ARTIFICERS (INCLUDING COMPONENTS DESIGNED BY ENGINES EAST AND THE KHADORAN MECHANIKS ASSEMBLY)

Blessing of Vengeance has served for three long decades as a direct conduit for the divine. It has channeled prayers of destruction onto the heads of the faithful's enemies and blessed and bolstered the resolve of countless thousands of devoted soldiers. No wonder, then, that the benedictions of Hierarch Severius fly with particular potency when directed through this warjack. Its eyes glow with fervor when it beholds enemies blasted to ash or lit afire by the holy power of Severius or others authorized to pass judgment through it in the name of Menoth. Zealots whisper that Blessing of Vengeance can see straight into men's souls and stands ready to smite the impious.

Hierarch Severius has maintained this Revenger for almost thirty years, though none in the Protectorate would accuse him of sentimentality. Instead, the decision is purely practical: the 'jack contributes significantly to battle, has learned to gauge threats to its master accurately, and has become well tuned to channeling Severius' prayers. The Vassals of Menoth have spent much time and many precious resources rebuilding the warjack, as the hierarch sees the machine as an investment. Severius greets each dawn as a reminder of the countless unbelievers awaiting punishment, and he orders Blessing of Vengeance made ready for him every day when he takes up his staff to conduct battle.

Blessing of Vengeance seems aware that its function as intermediary for holy power requires it to stand unmolested on the field of battle. It perceives the approach of the enemy with a palpable hostility and enthusiastically batters away intruders with its shield or obliterates them with unerring swings of its halberd. It will go to any lengths to avoid distraction in order to answer its master's needs, ready to channel a final reckoning deep into the heart of the enemy.

Since Severius' ascension to hierarch, keeping Blessing of Vengeance pristine and ready for battle has become an even higher priority. An entire choir and a dedicated Vassal of Menoth attend the 'jack at all times, forgoing food and rest if necessary to prepare it for the next day's battles. It stands as the final line of defense against those who would harm the leader of their nation and faith, both a dauntless bodyguard and an intimidating weapon.

CASTIGATOR
PROTECTORATE HEAVY WARJACK

The True Law tells us there is no pain unbearable in the cause of Menoth. The Castigator will engulf any who have refused the True Law with a cleansing shroud of fire.

—Visgoth Ark Razek, overseeing the Sul-Menite artificers

CASTIGATOR						
SPD	STR	MAT	RAT	DEF	ARM	CMD
5	11	6	5	10	19	—

FLAME FIST		
L	POW	P+S
	5	16

FLAME FIST		
R	POW	P+S
	5	16

DAMAGE

1	2	3	4	5	6
	L			R	
L	L	M	C	R	R
	M	M	C	C	

FIELD ALLOWANCE	U
POINT COST	8
LARGE BASE	

CASTIGATOR

⬤ **Immunity: Fire**

Combustion (★Attack) – Models within 2″ of this model suffer a POW 12 fire damage roll ⬤ and the Fire continuous effect ⬤. This model can make additional melee attacks after making this special attack.

FLAME FIST

⬤ **Continuous Effect: Fire**

⬤ **Open Fist**

HEIGHT/WEIGHT:	12′ / 8.4 TONS
ARMAMENT:	FLAME FISTS (BOTH)
FUEL LOAD/BURN USAGE:	665 LBS / 5.5 HRS GENERAL, 1 HR COMBAT
INITIAL SERVICE DATE:	606 AR
CORTEX MANUFACTURER:	VASSALS OF MENOTH
ORIG. CHASSIS DESIGN:	SUL-MENITE ARTIFICERS

TACTICAL TIPS

COMBUSTION – This model cannot use Combustion if it charges because Combustion is not a melee attack.

The fires in the foundries of Imer never dim, for the Protectorate must match the production pace of larger nations and demands tireless devotion from his armories. The Castigator is a product of this expanding wartime industry. The impressive warjack is based on the same chassis as the Reckoner, which is renowned as the first warjack entirely of Menite design. Few outside the Vassals of Menoth know the Castigator was actually conceived before the Reckoner, but problems with its weapon system delayed its unveiling. The displeasure of Visgoth Ark Razek at this failure was so great that he had every mechanik on the project wracked within a breath of death before being restored and put back to work with renewed and terrified determination. Miraculously, the problems were resolved almost immediately.

The Castigator's fists blaze continuously in combat, the intense heat sending rippling waves of distortion through the air as the warjack charges into the enemy. Each fist is equipped with a sophisticated delivery system for Menoth's Fury, which is compressed and piped into direct contact with the ignition temperature of the warjack's powerful furnace. If beset by multiple foes, the Castigator ignites the air around itself in a powerful explosion of incinerating heat that instantly melts iron and cremates living flesh.

One major advantage of the Castigator is the ease with which it is refueled on distant fields of battle. Unlike the Reckoner's Condemner cannon, which requires specially machined shells, the Castigator's fists need only a fresh supply of Menoth's Fury to be ready again for battle. Thus freed from reliance on support from Imer, it has been dispatched to join the Northern Crusade on the front lines to bring the justice of an inferno to all those who have forsaken the Creator of Man.

CRUSADER
PROTECTORATE HEAVY WARJACK

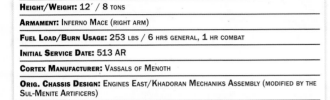

Behold! We have sanctified this weapon, made by the hands of man, to march and fight at our side. By our combined strength we will wrest a nation loyal to the Creator from these forsaken sands!
—Hierarch Gerard Luctine, at the unveiling of the Crusader

HEIGHT/WEIGHT:	12′ / 8 TONS
ARMAMENT:	INFERNO MACE (RIGHT ARM)
FUEL LOAD/BURN USAGE:	253 LBS / 6 HRS GENERAL, 1 HR COMBAT
INITIAL SERVICE DATE:	513 AR
CORTEX MANUFACTURER:	VASSALS OF MENOTH
ORIG. CHASSIS DESIGN:	ENGINES EAST/KHADORAN MECHANIKS ASSEMBLY (MODIFIED BY THE SUL-MENITE ARTIFICERS)

In its peace terms after the Civil War, Cygnar decreed the Protectorate could not keep a standing army. Visgoth Ozeall acquiesced but secretly commanded engineers to build warjacks using cortexes smuggled from Khador down the Black River and Cygnaran parts salvaged from fields of battle. Those early 'jacks were designed with open hands to pass as laborjacks in casual inspection. Meanwhile, artificers worked to forge weapons for these warjacks to wield as Menoth willed.

The greatest of the new Protectorate designs was the Crusader, a massive warjack boasting heavy armor and capable of crushing attacks. The chassis originated during the reign of Hierarch Luctine, who devoted himself to subjugating outlying Idrian tribes. Even when most converted after the earthquake of 504 AR, many tribes resisted and continued to harass the young nation. The Crusader was unleashed to provide an unstoppable force in the battles to come. It also proved its strength against Cygnar when friction between the two nations prompted clashes along the Black River.

OPEN FIST
👊 Open Fist

INFERNO MACE
🔥 Critical Fire

Already possessed of an immensely durable armored frame and powerful laborjack arms, after the development of Menoth's Fury the Crusader was enhanced by the inferno mace. This weapon, inspired by the flaming maces of the Reclaimers, can easily rend most armor into flaming scrap. When the call to arms sounds, Crusaders assemble at the front line ready to hammer and burn the foes of Menoth to dust and ash.

CRUSADER

SPD	STR	MAT	RAT	DEF	ARM	CMD
4	11	6	5	10	19	—

OPEN FIST		
L	POW	P+S
	3	14

INFERNO MACE		
R	POW	P+S
	7	18

DAMAGE

1	2	3	4	5	6
		L		R	
L	L	M	C	R	R
	M	M	C	C	

FIELD ALLOWANCE	U
POINT COST	6
LARGE BASE	

GUARDIAN
PROTECTORATE HEAVY WARJACK

... and those who seek to defile His places of worship shall be struck down with righteous fire, for that which was created can be unmade by His most sacred wrath.

—*The Canon of the True Law*

GUARDIAN						
SPD	STR	MAT	RAT	DEF	ARM	CMD
4	11	6	5	10	19	—

OPEN FIST		
L	POW	P+S
	3	14

FLAME PIKE		
R	POW	P+S
	6	17

DAMAGE

1	2	3	4	5	6
	L	A	A	R	
L	L	M	C	R	R
	M	M	C	C	

FIELD ALLOWANCE	U
POINT COST	9
LARGE BASE	

GUARDIAN

(symbol) **Arc Node**

OPEN FIST

(symbol) **Open Fist**

FLAME PIKE

(symbol) **Reach**

Critical Pitch – On a critical hit, instead of rolling damage normally you can choose to have this model throw the model hit. Treat the throw as if this model had hit with and passed the STR check of a throw power attack. The thrown model suffers a damage roll with POW equal to this model's STR plus the POW of this weapon. The POW of collateral damage is equal to this model's STR.

Powerful Charge – This model gains +2 to charge attack rolls with this weapon.

HEIGHT/WEIGHT: 12′ (NOT INCLUDING BANNER) / 8.4 TONS
ARMAMENT: FLAME PIKE (RIGHT ARM), MARK II DIVINITY ARC NODE
FUEL LOAD/BURN USAGE: 827 LBS / 6 HRS GENERAL, 1 HR COMBAT
INITIAL SERVICE DATE: 588 AR
CORTEX MANUFACTURER: VASSALS OF MENOTH
ORIG. CHASSIS DESIGN: ENGINES EAST/STEAMWERKS UNION (REFITTED BY SUL-MENITE ARTIFICERS)

TACTICAL TIPS

CRITICAL PITCH – A model cannot throw a model whose base is larger than its own.

Each Guardian is a finely crafted instrument of war painstakingly engraved with ornate liturgical verses and illuminations. These warjacks are so infused with holiness that some warpriests use them as battle altars when far from their home temples.

Covered in holy script and able to channel the divine power of Menoth's clergy, the Guardian is a walking icon of the Creator's might. Originally constructed to help defend Menoth's most sacred sites, the Guardian has since become one of the most versatile weapons in the Protectorate's arsenal. At the forefront of crusading forces, the Guardian and its battle banners rise over the Menite army, inspiring the faithful to righteous fury.

Although only a small number of Guardians were initially constructed, the utility of a Divinity arc node augmenting the resilience of a heavy warjack could not be ignored, and Protectorate warcasters soon requested an increase in production. Even so, the tremendous cost of arc nodes is prohibitive to producing them in great numbers.

Inspired by the traditional weapons carried by the guardians of Menite holy sites, the 'jack's primary weapon is a great pike superheated to penetrate even the heaviest armor. With this smoldering implement of destruction in hand, the Guardian wades through battle incinerating any who stand in its way.

Beneath a veil of flame and a shroud of ash, He will walk amongst them. Their flesh will be as dust on the winds.
—The Canon of the True Law

Its name derived from scripture, the Reckoner is heralded in the annals of Protectorate history as the nation's first purely purposed Menite warjack—a symbol of the holy crusade and an icon of the Lawgiver.

The Codex states, "He who is the Grand Reclaimant is, too, the reckoner of Man, burning away the sins of the faithful with but the merest glance." Designed with this image in mind—and said to be an agent of Menoth in the End Times—the Reckoner is a titan of steam and steel. Partially obscured in the haze of incense that issues from its brutal mace, the Reckoner lights the way for the faithful with the blinding fury of its Condemner cannon as it charges across the battlefield, smashing through anything that stands in its way.

The Reckoner was once constructed in secret, a triumph of Menite will and dedication. Now it stands at the forefront of the Protectorate's crusading armies, spreading Menoth's word to the heathen masses in sermons of fire and smoke.

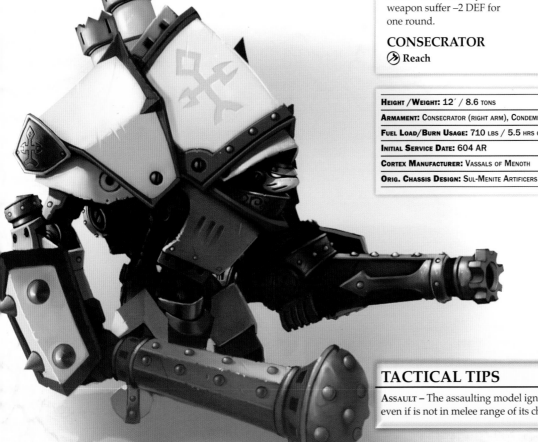

RECKONER

Ashen Veil – This model has concealment. Living enemy models suffer –2 to attack rolls while within 2" of this model.

Assault – As part of a charge, after moving but before making its charge attack, this model can make one ranged attack targeting the model charged unless they were in melee with each other at the start of this model's activation. When resolving an Assault ranged attack, the attacking model does not suffer the target in melee penalty. If the target is not in melee range after moving, this model can make the Assault ranged attack before its activation ends.

CONDEMNER

🔥 **Critical Fire**

🔥 **Damage Type: Fire**

Flare – Models hit by this weapon suffer –2 DEF for one round.

CONSECRATOR

⚔ **Reach**

RECKONER						
SPD	STR	MAT	RAT	DEF	ARM	CMD
5	11	6	5	10	19	—

CONDEMNER			
RNG	ROF	AOE	POW
12	1	—	13

CONSECRATOR	
POW	P+S
6	17

DAMAGE
1	2	3	4	5	6
		L		R	
L	L	M	C	R	R
	M	M	C	C	

FIELD ALLOWANCE	U
POINT COST	8
LARGE BASE	

HEIGHT/WEIGHT: 12´ / 8.6 TONS

ARMAMENT: CONSECRATOR (RIGHT ARM), CONDEMNER CANNON (LEFT ARM)

FUEL LOAD/BURN USAGE: 710 LBS / 5.5 HRS GENERAL, 1 HR COMBAT

INITIAL SERVICE DATE: 604 AR

CORTEX MANUFACTURER: VASSALS OF MENOTH

ORIG. CHASSIS DESIGN: SUL-MENITE ARTIFICERS

TACTICAL TIPS

ASSAULT – The assaulting model ignores the target in melee penalty even if is not in melee range of its charge target after moving.

TEMPLAR
PROTECTORATE HEAVY WARJACK

Like the Wall with which Menoth blessed us, so is the Templar unassailable. With the judgment of the righteous the Templar strikes down our enemies. These are essential virtues of war.

—Hierarch Caltor Turgis

TEMPLAR						
SPD	STR	MAT	RAT	DEF	ARM	CMD
4	11	6	5	10	19	—

SHIELD		
L	POW	P+S
	1	12

FLAIL		
R	POW	P+S
	6	17

DAMAGE					
1	2	3	4	5	6
	L			R	
L	L	M	C	R	R
	M	M	C	C	

FIELD ALLOWANCE	U
POINT COST	8
LARGE BASE	

SHIELD

⊕2 Shield

FLAIL

↻ Reach

Beat Back – Immediately after a normal attack with this weapon is resolved during this model's combat action, the enemy model hit can be pushed 1″ directly away from the attacking model. After the enemy model is pushed, the attacking model can advance up to 1″.

Chain Weapon – This attack ignores the Buckler and Shield weapon qualities and Shield Wall.

HEIGHT/WEIGHT:	12′2″ / 8.4 TONS
ARMAMENT:	SHIELD (LEFT ARM), FLAIL (RIGHT ARM)
FUEL LOAD/BURN USAGE:	253 LBS / 4 HRS GENERAL, 50 MIN COMBAT
INITIAL SERVICE DATE:	539 AR
CORTEX MANUFACTURER:	VASSALS OF MENOTH (CURRENTLY)
ORIG. CHASSIS DESIGN:	ENGINES EAST/KHADORAN MECHANIKS ASSEMBLY (MODIFIED BY THE SUL-MENITE ARTIFICERS)

TACTICAL TIPS

BEAT BACK – The attacking model can advance even if the enemy model is destroyed by the attack.

The Templar embodies the Protectorate's simple philosophy of war: smash enemies with overwhelming force from an unassailable position. The strength with which this warjack wields its iron flail is such that its adversaries are hurled back, their shields smashed from their hands and their armor crushed. Even as the Templar beats down enemies of the Faith, it advances farther into their midst with unstoppable wrath. Those lucky few who survive its initial onslaught are doomed to fall beneath its inexorable enforcement of the Lawgiver's will.

When former Hierarch Caltor Turgis reunited the Temple in 535 AR, he broadened the Protectorate's borders and ordered the construction of Tower Judgment, with the first Templars created to guard this edifice. The isolation of the Tower was such that the Temple dispensed with the usual practice of convincing the Cygnaran authorities the warjacks were actually laborjacks. Freed from this pretense, the Protectorate's artificers armed the Templars with simple but impressive weaponry—forever associating the warjack with defending the Protectorate's most important fortifications. Now Templars are a common sight marching among the crusading ranks of the faithful.

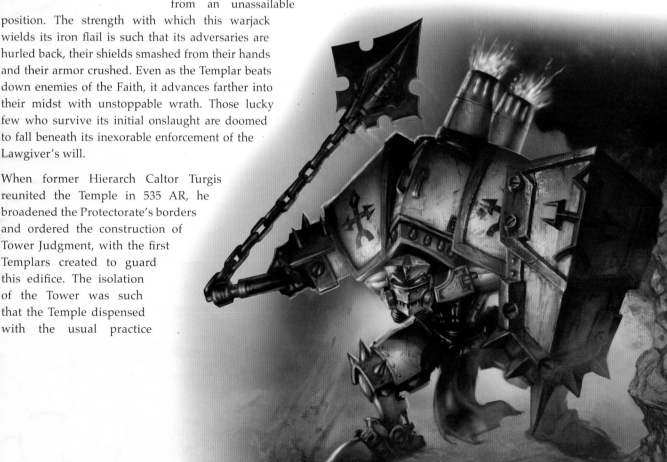

VANQUISHER
PROTECTORATE HEAVY WARJACK

The Canon of the True Law states that his children will walk as giants among men. Perhaps this Vanquisher is the means to a Great Truth.

—High Exemplar Mikael Kreoss

Height/Weight:	12´ / 9.75 tons
Armament:	Flame Belcher (left arm), Blazing Star Flail (right arm)
Fuel Load/Burn Usage:	275 lbs / 5 hrs general, 1 hr combat
Initial Service Date:	598 AR
Cortex Manufacturer:	Vassals of Menoth
Orig. Chassis Design:	Engines East/Khadoran Mechaniks Assembly (modified by the Sul-Menite Artificers)

The Vanquisher is one of the more recently designed warjacks in the Protectorate's arsenal. Originally assembled in secret in the late 590s from imported parts and armed with distinctive Menite weaponry, this heavy warjack is as subtle as the faith it serves—in other words, not at all. Some say the Vanquisher was the first sign of the full crusade that would later come.

The Vanquisher is a towering behemoth, its great flail a whirling harbinger of death. One arm wields a length of chain nearly as long as a man is tall, its end capped with the "blazing star"—a viciously spiked sphere. It visits swift justice upon infidels, crunching limbs, heads, and torsos in one devastating movement.

FLAME BELCHER

🜂 **Continuous Effect:** Fire

🜂 **Damage Type:** Fire

BLAZING STAR

Chain Weapon – This attack ignores the Buckler and Shield weapon qualities and Shield Wall.

Thresher (★Attack) – This model makes one melee attack with this weapon against each model in its LOS and this weapon's melee range.

In addition to the perilous blazing star, the Vanquisher also wields a flame belcher to send destruction from afar. The flame belcher uses a more recently refined form of Menoth's Fury that requires only exposure to air to ignite. Compressed into a heavy cannonball, these shells burst on impact, spreading an oily blaze hot enough to melt metal before consuming itself.

VANQUISHER						
SPD	STR	MAT	RAT	DEF	ARM	CMD
4	11	6	5	10	19	—

FLAME BELCHER			
RNG	ROF	AOE	POW
10	1	4	14

BLAZING STAR	
POW	P+S
5	16

DAMAGE

	1	2	3	4	5	6
			L		R	
	L	L	M	C	R	R
		M	M	C	C	

FIELD ALLOWANCE	U
POINT COST	8
LARGE BASE	

TACTICAL TIPS

Thresher – The melee attacks are all simultaneous.

AVATAR OF MENOTH
PROTECTORATE CHARACTER HEAVY WARJACK

And lo, the mightiest of heathens will bow before His holy light or be set ablaze by His wrathful touch.
—The Canon of the True Law

AVATAR						
SPD	STR	MAT	RAT	DEF	ARM	CMD
5	12	8	6	10	19	—

DIVINE SHIELD		
L	POW	P+S
	1	13

BURNING WRATH		
R	POW	P+S
	7	19

DAMAGE

1	2	3	4	5	6
L	L	M		R	R
	L	M	M	R	

FIELD ALLOWANCE	C
POINT COST	11
LARGE BASE	

AVATAR

⊗ **Terror**

Holy Vessel – This model cannot be part of a battlegroup, does not have a functional cortex, and cannot be allocated focus. During the focus allocation step of your Control Phase, this model receives d3+1 focus points.

Menoth's Gaze – During its activation, this model can spend 1 focus point to use Menoth's Gaze. For one round, enemy models that begin their activation within 8" of this model and in its LOS can advance only toward this model.

Sacred Ward – This model cannot be targeted by enemy spells.

DIVINE SHIELD

⊗ **Magical Weapon**

⊕2 **Shield**

BURNING WRATH

⊗ **Magical Weapon**

⊘ **Reach**

Flame Burst – When this model boxes an enemy model with this weapon, enemy models within 1" of the boxed model suffer the Fire continuous effect 🔥.

HEIGHT/WEIGHT:	13' / 9.75 TONS
ARMAMENT:	DIVINE SHIELD (LEFT ARM), BURNING WRATH (RIGHT ARM)
FUEL LOAD/BURN USAGE:	883 LBS / 5.5 HRS GENERAL, 75 MINS COMBAT
INITIAL SERVICE DATE:	606 AR
CORTEX MANUFACTURER:	NONE
ORIG. CHASSIS DESIGN:	VASSALS OF MENOTH UNDER THE GUIDANCE OF THE HARBINGER OF MENOTH

At the end of their labors, the Harbinger placed her hands on either side of the warjack's helm and whispered the Creator's final imperative to his newest creation. The massive construct filled with soulfire and roared to life, growling like a beast awakened from the depths of ancient slumber. The Avatar lumbered through the portals of the foundry into the night of the Sulese desert, an inferno of divine light in the darkness. The Harbinger and a legion of aspirants and acolytes proudly followed in its smoldering footsteps, their prayers resounding with the words of the Canon of the True Law.

In its right hand the Avatar wields a massive Sulese blade whose name translates from the ancient Icthier tongue as "Burning Wrath." It is inscribed with the words of prayers that have not been spoken aloud in millennia. With each strike, it sunders those who would oppose Menoth's will, casting the impure down in fire and ruin. To fall beneath this weapon is to suffer the unmediated judgment of the Creator.

In its left hand the Avatar bears the Divine Shield. This aegis carries the words of the Lawgiver spoken to the first Menites as he raised the first wall. Indeed, those who observe the Divine Shield liken it to that very wall. Unconquerable and insurmountable, the shield is Menoth's own protection.

A lesser warjack is animated by a mechanikal cortex and guided by the mind of a mortal—but not the Avatar. So far as the faithful is aware, its name is no mere hyperbole; it is believed to be the walking incarnation of Menoth's wrath on Caen. Even the Harbinger cannot guide this supreme manifestation of Menoth.

Where the Avatar treads, the faithless fall.

A sanctified instrument of divine wrath, the Avatar of Menoth is a warjack guided by the Creator's hand alone. It walks unfettered through the carnage of battle heedless of mortal will or interest.

The Harbinger of Menoth personally supervised the construction of this holy engine of war. The vassals who built the Avatar are said to have been driven by some unseen force that completely dominated their wills. They labored endlessly amid wafting fumes from sanctified censers, enraptured by the prayers spilling from the Harbinger's lips, even though they were unable to fully fathom the mechanism they assembled. Menoth's will guided their hands as they painstakingly crafted each part to divinely inspired specifications before offering it to be anointed by holy blessings. The schematics of the Avatar's design were stricken from their minds as sections were completed, leaving nothing but a sense of awe and foreboding.

FIRE OF SALVATION
PROTECTORATE CHARACTER HEAVY WARJACK

The fire of salvation can manifest as a blaze within the soul of the faithful or as a flame turned on the heretic.

—Hierarch Luctine on the importance of crusade

FIRE OF SALVATION						
SPD	STR	MAT	RAT	DEF	ARM	CMD
5	11	7	5	10	19	—

OPEN FIST (L)

POW	P+S
3	14

ABSOLVER (R)

POW	P+S
7	18

DAMAGE

1	2	3	4	5	6
		L		R	
L	L	M	C	R	R
	M	M	C	C	

FIELD ALLOWANCE	C
POINT COST	9
LARGE BASE	

FIRE OF SALVATION

Affinity [Kreoss] – While this model is in Kreoss' control area, its weapons gain Dispel. (When a weapon with Dispel hits a model/unit, upkeep spells on that model/unit immediately expire.)

Imprint: Holy Fervor – During its activation, this model can spend 1 focus point to use Holy Fervor. This activation, this model's melee attack rolls are boosted. When it destroys one or more enemy models with an attack with one of its melee weapons this activation, immediately after the attack is resolved this model can make one additional melee attack.

Righteous Vengeance – If one or more friendly Faction warrior models were destroyed or removed from play by enemy attacks while within 5" of this model during your opponent's last turn, after resolving continuous effects during your Maintenance Phase, this model can make a full advance followed by one normal melee attack.

OPEN FIST
⬤ Open Fist

ABSOLVER
⬤ Continuous Effect: Fire

HEIGHT/WEIGHT: 12' / 8.3 TONS
ARMAMENT: ABSOLVER (RIGHT ARM)
FUEL LOAD/BURN USAGE: 675 LBS / 5 HRS GENERAL, 55 MINS COMBAT
INITIAL SERVICE DATE: 590 AR
CORTEX MANUFACTURER: VASSALS OF MENOTH (LIBERATED, WIPED, AND RECONDITIONED)
ORIG. CHASSIS DESIGN: MODIFIED VARIANT BY THE VASSALS OF MENOTH

TACTICAL TIPS

AFFINITY [KREOSS] – Because they expire immediately, upkeep spells that had an effect when the model was hit or damaged will have no effect.

Those who have joined Grand Exemplar Mikael Kreoss in battle and fought alongside this peerless machine describe its dedication and loyalty as if speaking of another soldier of the faith rather than a creation of iron and steel. Indeed, the eyes of this aureate Crusader carry a weight of presence more akin to a zealot's than to that of a soulless construct. Its fervent wrath strikes terror in unbelievers and kindles rapture in followers of the True Law as they witness its fiery mace Absolver incinerate entire ranks of heathens.

Driven to vengeance by the dying of the faithful around it, Fire of Salvation swings its flame-wreathed weapon until every foe lies shattered and burned. Menites of other nations who have witnessed its righteous fury have been known to fall to their knees, lay down their weapons, and forsake old loyalties. Groveling before the grand exemplar, they beg him to restrain this relentless warjack from executing its just punishment.

The choir priests attending Fire of Salvation know every detail of its chassis. Each rod, piston, and steel plate stands as part of a proud legacy, and the warjack's densely inscribed surface reveals the long and storied history of its participation in the wars of the Protectorate. After every battle, armorers etch new lines into the layers of plated steel to describe its mighty deeds.

Kreoss and Fire of Salvation fought in some of the most dangerous actions in the early days of the siege of Sul, often alongside just a handful of exemplars. Few knights survived these desperate rearguard actions, and Kreoss himself would surely have died had it not been for his favored warjack. Time and again, Fire of Salvation stood between the retreating Menites and the crush of Cygnaran trenchers and storm knights.

Its hull already a memoir of the Caspia-Sul conflict, Fire of Salvation's armor was further ornamented in the days after Hierarch Voyle's death. Its armor plates tell of the countless battles through which it persevered alongside Kreoss as the Protectorate pushed back the invading Cygnarans and laid siege to Caspia. The vaunted Crusader and its master fought their way through the press of heretics again and again, inspiring the other exemplars to follow.

Though its cortex and weaponry are of more recent design, several of the 'jack's armored plates once protected machines that fought in the original Protectorate crusades, those bloody battles that brought conversion or death to the savage Idrians who foolishly opposed Menoth's will. Many of those warjacks were left to the southern sands after their destruction in battles north of Icthier, including the desperate last stand where Hierarch Luctine fell in 521 AR. Laying for decades in blessed proximity to Luctine, these artifacts were imbued with a sanctity whose strength is almost palpable.

The priests of Sul considered it only proper that such relics should gird a warjack that has fought faithfully alongside Grand Exemplar Kreoss since his earliest days of service to the Protectorate. During the ceremony where Kreoss was promoted to grand exemplar in 605 AR, priests affixed these plates along with blessed parchments illuminated with passages from the Canon of the True Law onto its chassis. These formalized and recognized the sanctity Fire of Salvation has earned by righteous conflict while fighting alongside its master.

Fire of Salvation has learned much from fighting alongside Kreoss for almost two decades, and it echoes his footsteps in battle. Its presence inspires his Knights Exemplar, who welcome it to their engagements. It fights as fiercely as a brother knight, seeming to become enraged at the sight of allies laid low and moving to intercept enemies and deliver blazing retribution.

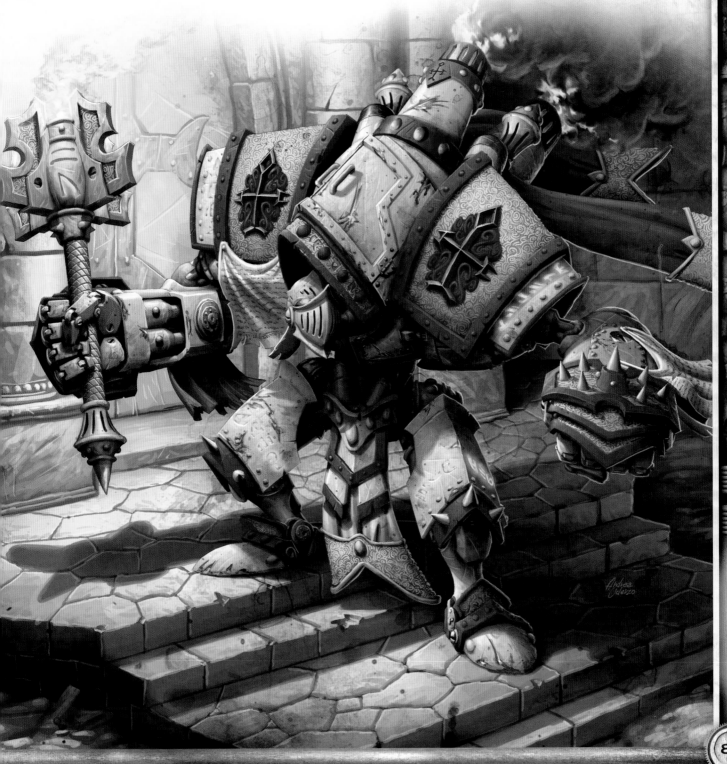

SOLDIERS OF THE PROTECTORATE

That the Protectorate of Menoth has been able to establish itself as one of the great military powers in western Immoren is no miracle but rather, the result of almost a century of effort and dedication. Lacking the larger populations of their neighbors, the Sul-Menites compensate with fanatical resolve. Nowhere else in the Iron Kingdoms are so many citizens willing to fight and die for their nation and beliefs.

The crusades to which the Protectorate military is dedicated create a constant need for greater numbers of combatants. Its dedicated fighting forces come from diverse orders, each with its own role, traditions, and hierarchy. Coordinating these various forces is a monumental undertaking, and different leaders favor different individual orders. These varied orders make for unpredictable fighting forces when the Protectorate takes to the field.

The backbone of its small military is composed of elite Exemplar knights and is supported by expanded ranks of the Temple Flameguard and militias raised from the civilian population. The Knights Exemplar are the pinnacle of the Protectorate's warriors. They are tasked with carrying out Menoth's will on Caen at any cost. To this end they specialize in all facets of warfare and are prepared to enforce the word of the Lawgiver as interpreted by the scrutators without hesitation.

The Knights Exemplar order utilizes a punishing training routine consisting of grueling physical tests accompanied by immersion in radical Menite philosophy. Those who complete the training are irrevocably changed; the commitment to the Exemplar order is for life.

The Temple Flameguard has undergone a substantial transition from defending the Protectorate's temples

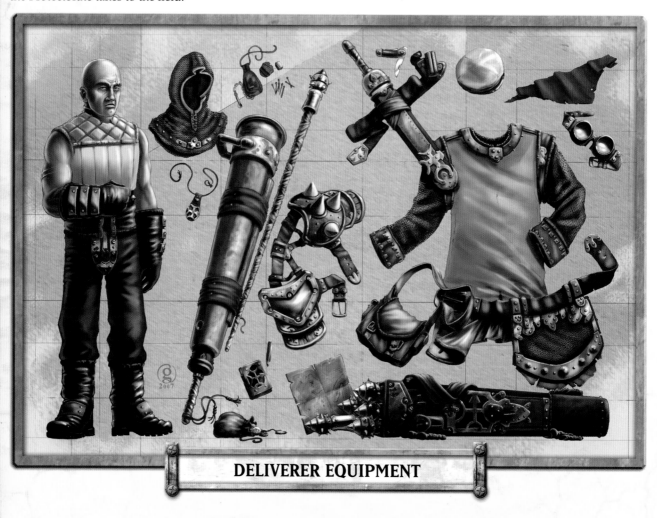

DELIVERER EQUIPMENT

and holy sites to being the largest formal division of its standing army. These citizen soldiers are being trained in unprecedented numbers as they regularly march to war for the first time in the Protectorate's history. The role of the Flameguard began to change during the rule of Hierarch Ravonal, but the process was greatly accelerated under Hierarch Garrick Voyle. At the center of the effort to militarize the Flameguard is Feora, Protector of the Flame. It was Feora upon whom Voyle relied to expand the Flameguard and prepare them for open war in the name of the Protectorate's ongoing crusades.

Any citizen of the Protectorate may apply for induction into the ranks of the Flameguard, but not all pass the rigorous training regimen. Life for the members of the Flameguard is much like that of most professional soldiers in the Iron Kingdoms, except they must continue to serve until the Flameguard priests of the Incendium give them dispensation to return to their normal lives. While this term of service might be as short as five years, in times of war a Flameguard may be required to serve for a decade or longer. Particularly valued soldiers may be retained until they reach an age where they can no longer perform their duties—or, more likely, are killed or severely wounded in battle.

Each soldier earns a modest wage, typically enough to support a family. In the event of a Flameguard's death, his family receives a reasonable stipend. Orphaned children become wards of the state. However, a number of families have become closely associated with the Temple over the years, and service is expected of their children. Often, these individuals are groomed from childhood to become preceptors or members of the Incendium.

The Flameguard supports two specialist arms: the Flameguard Cleansers and the Daughters of the Flame. These specialist branches are open only to recruits of the highest physical and spiritual caliber, and both have earned reputations for ruthlessness and devotion. Cleansers will not hesitate to burn entire villages to the ground if ordered to do so. Whether their targets are enemies met on the battlefield or heretics marked for elimination by the priests of Menoth, the Cleansers care not.

The Daughters of the Flame began as a small group chosen from among those who volunteered for service to the Flameguard with particular motivation: they were daughters or widows of fallen soldiers. These individuals hoped to honor the sacrifices of their loved ones as well as to play a part in avenging them. Due to the losses they had endured, these women proved willing to commit to the most perilous missions, with no regard for their own safety. The successes of this group prompted Feora to expand its operations, and it has become a significant weapon in the

CEREMONIAL ORNAMENTATION

Rather than awarding medals to its brave soldiers, the Protectorate of Menoth has instead adopted the practice of ornamenting both armor and robes worn in battle. Each of the major military orders has its own ornamentation traditions, some specific to certain temples or garrisons. Weaving abstract patterns of red, black, silver, or gold into robes is a common practice; whatever the order, the complexity of the design is commensurate with the soldier's rank and accomplishment. In some cases a soldier will receive pristine ornamented robes during the ceremonies recognizing his elevation in rank. Armored martial orders such as the Order of the Wall and the Knights Exemplar may also affix gemstones prominently to armor, weapons, and shields to denote accomplishment in battle.

Flameguard's arsenal, a surgical strike force employed to assassinate the enemies of the Protectorate wherever they hide. Recruitment and training has broadened to include other zealous members of the faithful who prove they possess the requisite capabilities and combat potential.

It is not only the larger orders that take to the battlefied; in this sanctified state, every priest, monk, and acolyte carries the weight of the True Law on his shoulders and its righteousness in his heart. Each of the several smaller orders serving the Protectorate—among them the Order of the Fist, the Order of Reclaimers, and the Order of the Wall—possesses distinct initiation, training, and advancement traditions that inform their prowess at war. When a member of one of these holy orders applies his spiritual practices to the battlefield, he inspires the faithful with the manifest power of Menoth.

More than any other power in the Iron Kingdoms, the Protectorate is able to call upon its citizenry to bolster the ranks of its armies. In times of need, the Protectorate can expect virtually every able-bodied man and woman to take up arms in the service of their holy nation. These militias and citizen soldiery are organized into lesser orders, such as the Deliverers whose rockets provide crucial ranged support, and are led in battle by the very Menite priests who raise these levies from among their local communities. Despite their limited training and discipline, these irregular fighting forces have proven to be incredibly effective as a result of their fanaticism and sheer numbers.

CHOIR OF MENOTH
PROTECTORATE UNIT

Let the True Law be delivered by word as well as deed. Speak Menoth's holy mandates as a shield against those who oppose us. Voiced by the faithful in our righteous cause, these words will become miracles made manifest.

—Hierarch Sulon during the Cygnaran Civil War

LEADER & GRUNTS

LEADER & GRUNTS						
SPD	STR	MAT	RAT	DEF	ARM	CMD
6	4	4	4	12	12	8

BATTLE STAFF		
	POW	P+S
	2	6

FIELD ALLOWANCE	3
LEADER & 3 GRUNTS	2
LEADER & 5 GRUNTS	3
SMALL BASE	

Hymn – RNG 3. Target friendly Faction warjack. When a model in this unit performs a Hymn special action, choose a hymn. Each activation, all models in this unit performing a hymn must perform the same one. If the target warjack is in range, it is affected by the hymn. While affected by a hymn, a warjack cannot be affected by another hymn.

- **Battle (★Action)** – The warjack gains +2 to attack and damage rolls for one turn.

- **Passage (★Action)** – The warjack cannot be targeted by non-magical ranged attacks. Passage lasts for one round.

- **Shielding (★Action)** – The warjack cannot be targeted by enemy spells. Shielding lasts for one round.

BATTLE STAFF

⊘ Reach

Sacred scrolls in hand, devout warpriests lead the choirs onto the field of battle. These valiant faithful are chosen from among those deemed most likely to demonstrate the rare gift of connecting to and controlling warjacks in battle. The warpriest directs a powerful, ancient canticle reinforcing the existing bonds between warjacks and their warcaster masters. The choir's prayers turn aside incoming projectiles, unravel enemy spells before they can reach their targets, and divinely guide warjack weapons to smite unbelievers. Requiring unassailable concentration and great effort to achieve, these perfect, meditative chants are the choir's sole purpose on the battlefield.

The Protectorate has long had an uncomfortable relationship with the mechanikal tools upon which its military relies. Since shortly after the Cygnaran Civil War, the Menites have seen the need to use the laborjacks and warjacks they had collected and cobbled together, armored, and modified for battle. By the strict interpretation of the tenets of their faith, however, such fabrications are inherently blasphemous.

Hierarch Luctine first derived the means to sanctify the use of these arcane machines of war, purifying profane artifices with fervent prayer and blessings. Successive accomplishments in battle are taken as a sign of Menoth's favor, for it seems the Creator smiles on their efforts. Often choirs of Menoth march alongside the iron-and-steel giants to further empower them with holy chants and prayers.

DAUGHTERS OF THE FLAME
PROTECTORATE FLAMEGUARD UNIT

The Daughters of the Flame are feared even within the Protectorate, as much for their origin as for their well-earned reputation for being silent killers. The order was founded in secret by the Priestess of the Flame with the consent of Hierarch Voyle and was originally charged with the security of Menite sacred places. Over time, this secret order evolved into a precision tool adept at removing both internal and external threats to the Protectorate. Organized into small strike forces called "hands," the Daughters stalk enemies of the faithful with single-minded devotion, emerging from the shadows only to spill the blood of heretics.

The Daughters are chosen from among fresh Flameguard recruits based on their raw potential and total dedication. Nearly all count husbands among the thousands of Menite soldiers who have died defending their faith; others grieve fallen parents, siblings, or betrothed. Though considered part of the Flameguard, those who are accepted into the ranks of this order are trained separately in an exhaustive regimen of physical and mental conditioning.

LEADER & GRUNTS

▶ **Advance Deployment**

✦ **Combined Melee Attack**

Acrobatics – This model can advance through other models if it has enough movement to move completely past their bases. This model cannot be targeted by free strikes. This model ignores intervening models when declaring its charge target.

Anatomical Precision – When this model's melee damage roll fails to exceed the ARM of the living model hit, that model suffers 1 damage point.

LEADER & GRUNTS						
SPD	STR	MAT	RAT	DEF	ARM	CMD
7	5	6	4	15	12	8

SWORD		
x2	POW	P+S
	4	9

FIELD ALLOWANCE	2
LEADER & 5 GRUNTS	**5**
SMALL BASE	

Possessing peerless grace and proficiency in the art of obfuscation, Daughters of the Flame are difficult to follow on the battlefield. They dart from obstacle to obstacle at blinding speed, bending and contorting to maximize available protection and avoid the eyes of the enemy. They are rumored to have been schooled in martial techniques by the Order of the Fist, and in battle they are a blur of fluid motion. Weaving through the enemy, Daughters engage in synchronized strikes, their blades cutting through flesh and penetrating narrow spaces between plates of armor.

Though some claim Feora overreached her authority by expanding the role of the order, none would claim it has been a boon to the Protectorate's war effort. Since the start of the crusade and the subsequent Cygnaran invasion of Sul, the Daughters have served on the battlefield alongside the Temple Flameguard and Flameguard Cleansers. In addition to conducting precision strikes against the enemy, Daughters also provide Protectorate field commanders with vital reconnaissance.

DELIVERERS
PROTECTORATE UNIT

I choose to stand with the faithful and deliver Menoth's judgment upon the faithless as long as I am able.

—Arms Master Krill Mayven

LEADER & GRUNTS						
SPD	STR	MAT	RAT	DEF	ARM	CMD
5	4	4	5	12	11	7

SKYHAMMER			
RNG	ROF	AOE	POW
16	1	3	12

SWORD	
POW	P+S
3	7

FIELD ALLOWANCE	1
LEADER & 5 GRUNTS	5
LEADER & 9 GRUNTS	8
SMALL BASE	

LEADER & GRUNTS

Rocket Volley – Instead of making ranged attacks separately, two or more models in this unit can make a combined ranged attack. Do not add a damage bonus for the number of models participating in the combined ranged attack. If 3–5 models participate in the attack, it has base AOE 4″ and base POW 14. If 6 or more models participate in the attack, it has base AOE 5″ and base POW 16.

SKYHAMMER

Inaccurate – This model suffers –4 to attack rolls with this weapon.

Early deliverers launched the dangerous, self-propelled explosives by hand, holding a length of wood aloft until the fuse burned down and the rocket spiraled into the air. Most of the time the rockets landed within the enemy lines before exploding in a shower of fiery shrapnel. Sometimes, however, they detonated immediately or fell to the ground woefully short of the foe. Ranking arms masters developed reinforced cylindrical tubes that could be aimed at the enemy and provided more control. Even with these improvements, only the most devoted become deliverers: walking into battle loaded down with explosives requires deep and abiding faith and courage.

Whistling through the air in long and deadly arcs, the Skyhammer rockets of deliverers rain down across the battlefield to bring the wrath of the Lawgiver in fiery, thundering explosions. Few enemies are brave or hardy enough to face a withering barrage of Deliverer fire long enough to close, knowing entire formations can be consumed in roaring blossoms of flame.

Expanding the Deliverers from a niche auxiliary unit into a mainstay of the Protectorate was one of several achievements made during Hierarch Garrick Voyle's push to reform the Protectorate military. After assessing the effective Redeemer, Voyle realized the essential role long-range explosives would have on the modern battlefield. Unlike expensive warjacks, the faithful could be easily replaced and thus could be deployed in far greater numbers.

DELIVERER SUNBURST CREW
PROTECTORATE WEAPON CREW UNIT

The heretics think themselves safe across that river. They believe themselves beyond the reach of the Lawbringer. Prove them wrong.
—Arms Master Belthazar Varon

Sunburst crews support the armies of the Lawbringer from afar, hurling flaming death upon their enemies. The annihilating bolts detonate on impact, creating a wide area of devastation that blasts holes in enemy formations and rends warjacks into scrap.

The Sunburst is a product of the disarmament agreement between Cygnar and the Protectorate made centuries before the Menites threw off the yoke of Cygnaran governance. Prohibited from constructing dedicated weapons of war, the Temple's weaponsmiths did not have the luxury of munitions factories to fabricate complex items. Whereas other nations could experiment with cannons and more advanced arms, the Protectorate required artillery that could easily be built from the simple materials found in their resource-poor country. The Sunburst's design thus integrates ancient ingenuity and modern science.

This ballista is one of the oldest siege weapons in western Immoren, dating to before the Thousand Cities era; the vassals of the Protectorate have simply refined it for use on the battlefields of their crusades. Rather than propelling a shell with a charge of blasting powder, the platform mechanically pitches its explosive payload, allowing for the use of a heavier and more destructive charge. The charge itself is contained within a roughly spherical orb containing refined Menoth's Fury surrounded by a lattice of metal designed to splinter into deadly shrapnel upon detonation.

SUNBURST

Light Artillery – This weapon cannot be used to make attacks or special actions during activations this model moves. This model cannot gain the aiming bonus when attacking with this weapon and cannot charge. If this model attacks with this weapon during its activation, it cannot attack with any other weapons that activation.

Range Finder – While B2B with one or more grunts in this unit, this model gains +2 to attack rolls with this weapon.

LEADER						
SPD	STR	MAT	RAT	DEF	ARM	CMD
4	4	4	5	12	11	7

SUNBURST			
RNG	ROF	AOE	POW
16	1	4	16

SWORD	
POW	P+S
3	7

GRUNTS						
SPD	STR	MAT	RAT	DEF	ARM	CMD
4	4	4	5	12	11	7

SWORD	
POW	P+S
3	7

FIELD ALLOWANCE	2
LEADER & 2 GRUNTS	3

LEADER LARGE BASE
GRUNT SMALL BASE

Working in tandem, a Sunburst gunner and his crew can range and attack targets easily as long as they stay in close communication. Deliverer Sunburst crews are proud of the part they play in the Creator's army, knowing their weapons represent the long reach of Menoth's fiery judgment.

EXEMPLAR BASTIONS
PROTECTORATE UNIT

I feel no weight but the eyes of the Creator upon me.

—Exemplar Bastion Warder Joriah Masvan

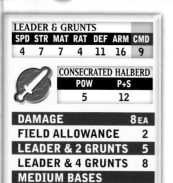

LEADER & GRUNTS						
SPD	STR	MAT	RAT	DEF	ARM	CMD
4	7	7	4	11	16	9

CONSECRATED HALBERD	
POW	P+S
5	12

DAMAGE	8 EA
FIELD ALLOWANCE	2
LEADER & 2 GRUNTS	5
LEADER & 4 GRUNTS	8
MEDIUM BASES	

LEADER & GRUNTS

✠ **Fearless**

Sanguine Bond – When this model would suffer damage from an enemy attack, you can choose one or more models in this unit to suffer any number of those damage points instead, divided as you choose. If you do, this model does not suffer that damage. A model cannot suffer more damage as a result of Sanguine Bond than it has unmarked damage boxes.

CONSECRATED HALBERD

⊘ **Magical Weapon**

⊘ **Reach**

⊘ **Weapon Master**

Blessed – When making an attack with this weapon, ignore spell effects that add to a model's ARM or DEF.

TACTICAL TIPS

SANGUINE BOND – Yes, the model that was originally damaged can be assigned damage points. When taking damage from a simultaneous attack, note that a model in the unit still cannot be assigned more damage than it has unmarked damage boxes.

A select few who take the vows of the Exemplar hear a special calling. During their initial fasting, these knights experience a dream of being interred underground. They feel the weight of the earth, yet they remain calm and unafraid. All exemplars are brothers in arms, yet those destined to follow the path of the bastion are admired for the additional weight that literally rests upon their shoulders.

Initiates stand in the temple courtyard for two days and nights with no food or water, weights loaded upon them. At the end they must find the will to ignore their pain and march across the temple grounds, even though some suffer crippling injuries. Those who succeed prove they have the fortitude to endure the training by which they learn to fight within the bastion armor, which is composed of ancient steel plates borne by past brothers and engraved with holy script taken from the True Law.

The bond each bastion shares with his brothers grants him their collective strength even as injuries threaten to wear him down. Bastion knights are able to ignore the mundane needs of the body and endure days or even weeks without removing their heavy plate. Enemies despair as they watch the bastions take up their glaives and march inexorably forward, eyes filled with fire and stalwart resolve. Their punishing blows grow stronger even as their wounds threaten to overtake them, as if their spirits' looming reunion with the Creator empowers their dying bodies.

They are a self-evident lesson of faith: harm the devout and you only hasten your own judgment before the Lawgiver.

—Grand Exemplar Mikael Kreoss

Armored in the mighty steel plate of fallen exemplars that has been blessed with the words of Menoth, cinerators carry both the fire of the Lawgiver and the sacrifice of their fellows into every battle. If their brother bastions are marching walls of stone, steadily and inexorably advancing in the face of the enemies of Menoth, cinerators are the living fire of the Creator's will, moving ahead of their brothers in arms to breach enemy ranks with flame and steel. Even determined foes quail in the face of their unyielding and fiery advance.

The cinerators' training strengthens them even more than their fellow bastions, preparing them to bear the encumbrance of their massive armor. This punishing regimen takes a significant toll, and some initiates are permanently crippled or even killed. Those who survive have been molded into perfect crusaders.

Years of intense, meditative prayer allow cinerators to internalize wounds that would lay low men of lesser faith. Conduits of Menoth's wrath, the knights redirect and channel their agony into a holy rage, rushing ahead to cut down those who would defy the word of the True Law. Like the first Menite warriors who fought with the ancient priest-kings, cinerators display an almost savage desire to close with their enemies and deliver them unto the Creator.

These cruel warriors are armed with ancient blades and shields, the legacy of knights fallen in righteous battle. Imbued with countless blessings, the blades are warm to the touch and flicker as though with an unquenchable flame that explodes into a white blaze when wielded in battle. When a cinerator strikes down a foe, Menoth shows his approval in a burst of great fire that erupts from the body of the heretic to consume his allies while leaving the righteous unharmed.

LEADER & GRUNTS

✠ **Fearless**

Relentless Advance – When a model in this unit is damaged by an enemy attack, models in this unit gain +2 SPD for one round.

BLAZING SWORD

⊘ **Magic Weapon**

◔ **Weapon Master**

Flame Burst – When this model boxes an enemy model with this weapon, enemy models within 1" of the boxed model suffer the Fire continuous effect 🔥.

LEADER & GRUNTS						
SPD	STR	MAT	RAT	DEF	ARM	CMD
4	7	7	4	11	17	9

BLAZING SWORD	
POW	P+S
5	12

DAMAGE	8 EA
FIELD ALLOWANCE	2
LEADER & 2 GRUNTS	5
LEADER & 4 GRUNTS	8
MEDIUM BASE	

EXEMPLAR VENGERS
PROTECTORATE CAVALRY UNIT

The blood on our lances will water the fields of battle. The crops of our victory will grow tall and strong, ever laden with grain for the stallions that carry us to war.

—Exemplar Seneschal Odan of the Exemplar Vengers

LEADER & GRUNTS						
SPD	STR	MAT	RAT	DEF	ARM	CMD
8	6	7	4	12	17	9

BLESSED LANCE	
POW	P+S
8	14

SWORD	
POW	P+S
3	9

MOUNT	
POW	
10	

DAMAGE	5 EA
FIELD ALLOWANCE	1
LEADER & 2 GRUNTS	7
LEADER & 4 GRUNTS	11
LARGE BASE	

LEADER & GRUNTS

✠ **Fearless**

Battle-Driven – When a model in this unit is damaged by an enemy attack, after the attack is resolved models in this unit gain +2 STR and ARM and Pathfinder ⟳ for one round.

BLESSED LANCE

⟳ **Magical Weapon**

Blessed – When making an attack with this weapon, ignore spell effects that add to a model's ARM or DEF.

Lance – This weapon can be used only to make charge attacks. When this model charges, this weapon gains Reach ⟳ until the charge is resolved.

SWORD

⟳ **Weapon Master**

Close Combat – This model cannot make an initial attack with this weapon during an activation it charged at least 3″.

Nearly two thousand years ago, the horse lords, adherents of the Old Faith, dominated the lands of the north. One by one their barbarian tribes were subjugated and forced to accept the True Law. Since the earliest days of the Exemplar order, there have been mounted knights in service of the Creator—the vengers. These knights are consumed with boundless faith and have long been paragons of ancient tradition and true instruments of Menoth's will.

In the days of antiquity when the Menite priest-kings established their rule, the exemplars served them as unquestioning warriors of faith. The first knights acted as bodyguards and defenders of the first cities, but as time passed the priest-kings wished to extend the laws of Menoth to all Immoren. These knights earned the name "vengers" as they dispensed Menite judgment to the far corners of the Thousand Cities, enforcing the Creator's will and the edicts of the priest-kings with ruthless passion.

Today the vengers are the spearhead of the Protectorate's holy war. Many are direct descendants of the ancient northern horse lords, and their families have retained ties to members of Khador's Old Faith. Hierarch Severius' Northern Crusade continues to advance through Llael supported by the greatest gathering of Exemplar knights in the history of Immoren. The vengers at the fore of the crusade's battles might be more civilized than their ancient predecessors, but they fight with the same resolve. They serve the will of the Creator made manifest through the words of the scrutators without question. Each venger is motivated to be the perfect Menite warrior: faithful, powerful, and relentless.

Exemplar vengers are among the deadliest warriors in the Protectorate's crusading armies. They wield blessed lances and stout blades and ride into battle on war-bred stallions of amazing strength and beauty. The warhorses of those trained in the south are often chosen from the stallion lines preferred by the Idrian tribes. Those vengers of northern descent favor the Pozdyov warhorses ridden by the uhlans of Khador for generations immemorial. This is particularly true among venger knights in Llael. A few of these exemplars are former Khadoran uhlans who converted and are now fully devoted to the southern interpretation of the Lawgiver, gladly laying down their lives in the service of the hierarch. Fueled by their faith, they have no need for advanced mechanika of any kind. Through their Oath of Brotherhood, they feel the pains of their brothers deeply, and they fight harder and more bravely with each drop of venger blood spilled.

A venger charge is a vision out of time, perfect in its terrible beauty. Whole lines of men simply disintegrate beneath precise strikes of blessed lances and a crash of hooves. Should any be left standing, the vengers draw blades to dispatch what could not be trampled.

After each battle exemplar vengers take time to cleanse their weapons, steeds, and armor in sacred rituals. Once wiped away, the tainted blood of the enemy is sacrificed to the Creator in flaming braziers in gratitude for victory. These rites of purification are central to the Venger tradition even in times of constant war. These days the vengers are summoned to battle with ever-greater frequency to crush the enemy under their steeds' thunderous hooves, and it is a duty they tirelessly pursue in the name of the Creator.

EXEMPLAR ERRANTS
PROTECTORATE UNIT

Though our duty might take us from His lands, our hearts will not waver from His flame.

—Oath of the Exemplar Errant

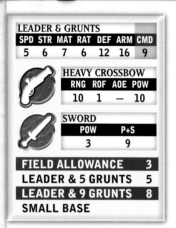

LEADER & GRUNTS						
SPD	STR	MAT	RAT	DEF	ARM	CMD
5	6	7	6	12	16	9

HEAVY CROSSBOW			
RNG	ROF	AOE	POW
10	1	—	10

SWORD	
POW	P+S
3	9

FIELD ALLOWANCE	3
LEADER & 5 GRUNTS	5
LEADER & 9 GRUNTS	8
SMALL BASE	

LEADER & GRUNTS
➤ Advance Deployment

✛ Fearless

Self-Sacrifice – If this model is disabled by an enemy attack, you can choose a non-disabled model in this unit within 3″ of this model to be destroyed. If another model is destroyed as a result of Self-Sacrifice, this model heals 1 damage point.

HEAVY CROSSBOW
⊕ Magical Weapon

Blessed – When making an attack with this weapon, ignore spell effects that add to a model's ARM or DEF.

SWORD
⚔ Weapon Master

The Exemplar order relies on the errants to carry out the Synod's will across Immoren. Traitors and other heretics fleeing the Protectorate might think themselves safely escaped only to be found by a cadre of errants years later. Knights errant also serve the crusading armies of the Protectorate as advance scouts, seeking out and destroying the enemies of the faithful that lie in wait to obstruct their holy mission.

Though all Exemplar knights are required to meet the highest standards of faith and dedication, errants are chosen from among those who embody the spirit of ultimate sacrifice. Driven by the Creator's mandate, these knights allow nothing to deter them from successfully completing their holy tasks. An errant will sacrifice his own life to allow a threatened brother to shrug off wounds and fight on in Menoth's name, particularly if the other's role is more crucial to their cause. With a final prayer, he wills his life to another and passes on to join the Creator's armies in Urcaen, while his brethren continue to do battle in unhallowed lands.

If the Knights Exemplar are the sword of Menoth defending his lands from the unfaithful, the Exemplars Errant are his lance striking deep into the heart of his enemies. Ranging outside the borders of the Protectorate, these crusading knights carry out missions of great importance for the priesthood and the Creator.

As an advance strike force, the Exemplars Errant forego the use of sacred relic blades, lest they fall into the hands of covetous heathens. Instead, they bring lighter and more versatile weapons on their holy missions. The errants are trained every bit as rigorously in the martial arts as any exemplar. Each is armed with a heavy crossbow fortified with blessings and prayers to pierce arcane wards and magical sigils. Each errant likewise bears a shield inscribed with sacred passages taken from the Canon of the True Law to protect him in the execution of his sacred duty. Each knows that should he fall to the enemies of Menoth while bringing the light to foreign lands, his deeds and acts will go unrecorded save in the Annuls of the Faithful in Urcaen, where his brothers who have passed before him wait.

EXEMPLAR ERRANT OFFICER & STANDARD
PROTECTORATE UNIT ATTACHMENT

*Like a fire in the night, so shall we pass through the lands of the faithless,
illuminating the darkness with His radiance.*
—Hierarch Severius

The Exemplars Errant have been involved in every crusade and incursion made by the Protectorate. Ranging far from their homelands, these holy warriors perform critical missions for the priests of Menoth, hunting traitors and heretics and extending their reach into foreign lands. In these glorious times of renewed faith, Exemplars Errant march in greater numbers than at any time in history.

Veterans of countless battles, ranking errants are chosen to lead their brother knights abroad. Pure in heart and thought, they are trusted to carry out their holy missions no matter the bloody price. Their dedication and inspiring example is so great that the knights they lead will make any sacrifice to ensure the success of their sacred tasks.

Exemplar errant phalanxes are always accompanied by an Exemplar standard—a powerful symbol of their faith that can be carried into battle only by a knight of the noblest conviction. Ornamented with the history of the order and touched by the prayers of the visgoths themselves, errants' standards are visible signs of Menoth's favor. The errants consider any deed committed under their standard to be a sacrament and will go to any length to retrieve it should it fall to heathens.

Attachment [Exemplar Errants] – This attachment can be added to an Exemplar Errants unit.

OFFICER

- **Advance Deployment**
- **Fearless**
- **Officer**

Self-Sacrifice – If this model is disabled by an enemy attack, you can choose a non-disabled model in this unit within 3" of this model to be destroyed. If another model is destroyed as a result of Self-Sacrifice, this model heals 1 damage point.

Tactics: Pathfinder – Models in this unit gain Pathfinder.

Tactics: Quick Work – Models in this unit gain Quick Work. (When a model with Quick Work destroys one or more enemy models with a melee attack during its combat action, immediately after the attack is resolved it can make one normal ranged attack. Attacks gained from Quick Work do not count against a weapon's ROF.)

STANDARD BEARER

- **Advance Deployment**
- **Fearless**
- **Standard Bearer**

Purity – While this model is in formation, models in its unit cannot be targeted by enemy spells.

Self-Sacrifice – See above.

HEAVY CROSSBOW

- **Magical Weapon**

Blessed – When making an attack with this weapon, ignore spell effects that add to a model's ARM or DEF.

SWORD

- **Weapon Master**

OFFICER

OFFICER	SPD	STR	MAT	RAT	DEF	ARM	CMD
	5	6	8	7	12	16	9

HEAVY CROSSBOW	RNG	ROF	AOE	POW
	10	1	—	10

SWORD	POW	P+S
	3	9

STANDARD BEARER	SPD	STR	MAT	RAT	DEF	ARM	CMD
	5	6	7	6	12	16	9

OFFICER'S DAMAGE	5
FIELD ALLOWANCE	1
POINT COST	2
SMALL BASE	

TACTICAL TIPS

TACTICS: QUICK WORK – A model can make this ranged attack only if it is no longer engaged after destroying the enemy model.

OFFICER - Because this model is an Officer, when it is destroyed it does not replace a Grunt in its unit. Instead the unit Leader becomes the unit commander.

FLAMEGUARD CLEANSERS
PROTECTORATE UNIT

All the world's execrations must be bathed in the flames of purity.

—Feora, Priestess of the Flame

LEADER & GRUNTS						
SPD	STR	MAT	RAT	DEF	ARM	CMD
5	5	5	5	12	14	8

PURIFIER			
RNG	ROF	AOE	POW
SP 8	1	—	12

PURIFIER BLADE	
POW	P+S
3	8

FIELD ALLOWANCE	2
LEADER & 5 GRUNTS	5
LEADER & 9 GRUNTS	8
SMALL BASE	

LEADER & GRUNTS

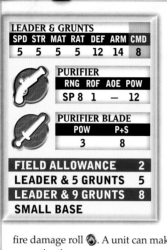

Immunity: Fire

Incinerate (Order) – Models that received this order can participate in a combined range attack. The unit commander must be the primary attacker. This attack has RNG 8, AOE 4″, and POW 12. This attack causes fire damage. The AOE remains in play for one round and is a cloud effect. Models entering or ending their activations in the AOE suffer a POW 12 fire damage roll. A unit can make only one Incinerate attack per activation.

PURIFIER

Continuous Effect: Fire

Damage Type: Fire

Not originally intended for foreign fields of war, the infamous Cleansers were born from the seeds of domestic conflict. They stand as the disciplinary arm of the Flameguard Temple and as such are merciless and unyielding. It is their job to sanctify the land from the touch of heresy, their sacred duty to purify those accused of blasphemy by scouring them in holy fire. The sight of cleansers solemnly marching through a Protectorate settlement is enough to make all but the most pious cringe.

Once called to duty, cleansers sanctify the homes and hiding places of heretics with their flamethrowers, reducing buildings, inhabitants, and the taint of corruption to ash as the scrutators decree. Cleansers stand watch over their blazes, ready to cut down those who might try to escape, though most choose to wound or hobble a burning escapee in order to intercept him and toss him back into the inferno, thus carrying out their holy writs to the letter of the law.

The Purifier, the signature weapon of the Cleansers, is one of the rare mechanikal advances to originate within the Protectorate of Menoth. Designed by vassal mechaniks directed to create a portable weapon that could deliver Menoth's Fury at range, the Purifier is exceedingly deadly. The people of other nations are horrified that this weapon is used against the Protectorate's own people, which reinforces the cruel reputation of the Menite theocracy.

Though they were created to purify the lands of the Creator, the expansion of hostilities has called for the deployment of cleansers against heretics outside the Protectorate's borders. Taking to the field with the same zealotry displayed in the execution of their sacred duties, the cleansers have proved themselves worthy soldiers. Individually, each is capable of clearing a swath through the enemies of Menoth. When they concentrate their purifying flames, they create a conflagration through which only the most foolish or defiant heathen would risk passage. Those who try find they have cast themselves upon their own funeral pyre.

KNIGHTS EXEMPLAR
PROTECTORATE UNIT

May Menoth guide us to strike quickly at the hearts of his foes.
—High Exemplar Kreoss

Many scholars compare the various aspects of the Protectorate to Menoth himself: the faithful serve as the body of Menoth on Caen; the hierarch represents his head; the scrutators his mouth; the masses of the laboring faithful his bones; and the battle-ready zealots his blood. In this analogy, the Knights Exemplar are undoubtedly the weapons in his hands.

Heavily armored in blessed plate engraved with rites and wards of protection, these fanatical warriors stand undaunted as blows glance off their armor with tones akin to a hammer striking an anvil. The mere unsheathing of their relic blades in war is considered a sacrament. Though formidable in their own right, the knights are made nearly unstoppable by the divine gifts they receive from the Creator. They will not be deterred from their cause; even seeing their brethren fall in battle and pass into Menoth's hands makes them stronger, fueling their faith and righteous anger.

The first time exemplars raised arms as a large force was within the City of Walls during the Cygnaran Civil War. At that time only a few hundred of the holy warriors served the clergy. Now their numbers surge with thousands of the faithful who feel the calling to take up the sword.

LEADER & GRUNTS

✠ **Fearless**

Bond of Brotherhood – Models in this unit gain +1 STR and ARM for each model in this unit that has been destroyed or removed from play. The bonuses for a model are lost if it returns to play.

RELIC BLADE

⊘ **Magical Weapon**

⊙ **Weapon Master**

LEADER & GRUNTS						
SPD	STR	MAT	RAT	DEF	ARM	CMD
5	6	7	4	12	15	9

RELIC BLADE	
POW	P+S
5	11

FIELD ALLOWANCE	3
LEADER & 5 GRUNTS	5
SMALL BASE	

TACTICAL TIPS

BOND OF BROTHERHOOD – Do not apply these bonuses until after the attack and its damage resolve. If several Knights are affected by a simultaneous attack, such as Strafe or an AOE attack, the bonus does not increase until after damage has been dealt to all the models.

HOLY ZEALOTS
PROTECTORATE UNIT

Conviction is more lethal than any blade, truth stronger than any shield. No one can withstand the force of so many so eager to die to preserve their faith.

—*Hierarch Sulon to the faithful*

LEADER & GRUNTS						
SPD	STR	MAT	RAT	DEF	ARM	CMD
6	4	4	4	12	12	8

FIRE BOMB			
RNG	ROF	AOE	POW
5	1	3	12

MACE	
POW	P+S
3	7

FIELD ALLOWANCE	3
LEADER & 5 GRUNTS	4
LEADER & 9 GRUNTS	6
SMALL BASE	

FIRE BOMB

⊛ Critical Fire

⬦ Damage Type: Fire

LEADER

Prayers – The Leader of this unit can recite one of the following prayers each turn anytime during its unit's activation. Each model in this unit gains the benefits listed.

- **Fervor** – Affected models gain +2 to attack and damage rolls this activation.
- **Warding** – Affected models cannot be targeted by enemy spells for one round.

To bolster the faith of their people—and remind them of the torments of a coward's death—Menite priests walk among the zealots in combat, sermonizing and leading them in prayer. Should a priest fall in battle, one among the zealots will invariably take up his prayers and lead the faithful.

Although these volunteer forces were at first dismissed as a serious threat, the enemies of the Protectorate soon learned the power of a zealous population. If one fanatic is a dangerous foe, a hundred thousand promise to be cataclysmic.

One of its concessions in the treaties with Cygnar was that the Protectorate was not permitted to retain a standing army. Even as Visgoth Ozeall penned his name to those papers, he knew that should any leader of the Protectorate put forth the call to arms, he would not lack for enthusiastic volunteers. Many regular citizens feel the stirrings of their religion so strongly they would gladly give their lives to confront the enemies of the faith. They are willing to employ any weapon, even bare hands if need be, to serve that cause.

The Menite clergy prepared their citizens, secretly training them for combat and creating massive stockpiles of weapons with which to arm them at a moment's notice. When the zealots heard the call, they knew to rush to one of these weapon caches and prepare to hurl themselves into the chaos of battle. Even after the need for secrecy had passed, this effective system was retained. Protectorate citizens are given the liberty to go about their normal lives, be it farming or other industry, so long as they are ready to fight when called.

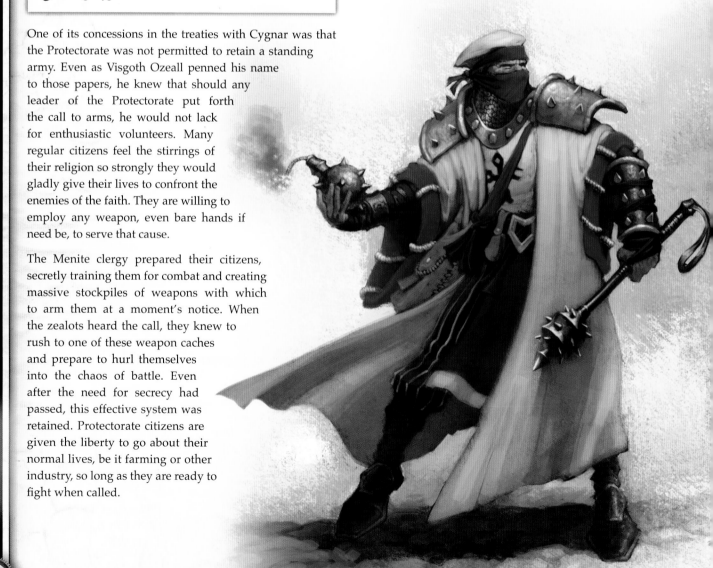

MONOLITH BEARER
PROTECTORATE HOLY ZEALOT UNIT ATTACHMENT

Look upon the power of the Creator and tremble! In his name, all things are made possible!
—Visgoth Juviah Rhoven

The Menofix is a powerful symbol of Menite faith. It embodies generations of past suffering, ancient history, and the certainty of the inevitable. Its very presence on the battlefield can sway the actions of the faithful to greatness. Some feel the call of the Menofix with such zealous piety they are compelled to acts bordering on the miraculous. As a show of their tremendous faith, these zealots bear massive Menofixes of granite or basalt into battle. Despite the great weight of these monoliths, their bearers take to the field praying loudly and singing hymns to the Shaper of Man, driving their fellow Menites into ecstatic frenzy.

Each monolith is a potent Menite icon inspired by the great, ruined Menofixes of antiquity that litter the ground of Ancient Icthier. Often, the stone Menofix was the focus of devotion in a Menite church or monastery until one zealot was divinely compelled to lift it on his back as a sign of the limitless power of his faith.

Attachment [Holy Zealots] – This attachment can be added to a Holy Zealots unit.

BEARER
⚜ Officer

Granted: Fearless – While this model is in play, models in its unit gain Fearless ✠.

Greater Destiny – Once per game during its unit's activation, this model can use Greater Destiny. For one round, models in this unit in formation do not suffer damage except from spells and feats.

Holy Monolith – When one or more models in this unit are destroyed by an enemy attack, after the attack is resolved models in this unit gain +4 ARM for one turn.

BEARER						
SPD	STR	MAT	RAT	DEF	ARM	CMD
6	6	5	5	12	12	9

MACE		
	POW	P+S
	3	9

DAMAGE	5
FIELD ALLOWANCE	1
POINT COST	2
SMALL BASE	

TACTICAL TIPS

OFFICER - Because this model is an Officer, when it is destroyed it does not replace a grunt in its unit. Instead the unit leader becomes the unit commander.

To the teeming masses, a monolith bearer is a powerful reminder of Menoth's awesome power and strength. To the crusading zealots, he is a visible assurance of the righteousness of their cause. In the shadow of the great Menofix the faithful experience ecstatic motivation far beyond that of rational men. Their devotion reaches a fever pitch as the Creator's will is revealed to them, turning aside the blades and bullets of any heathen who would oppose his will.

Such a conspicuous beacon of faith draws the ire of the Protectorate's heretical enemies, and zealots who carry the monoliths rarely survive more than a single battle. Enemy snipers and spellcasters go out of their way to eliminate these living symbols of faith. Should a bearer be struck down, his brethren have been known to tear their assailants limb from limb in holy fury. Knowing this, those who carry a Menofix are prepared to die with a prayer of vengeance on their lips, entreating the Creator to protect the faithful long enough to carry out his work.

IDRIAN SKIRMISHERS
PROTECTORATE IDRIAN ALLY UNIT

Walk alone into the sands where the nomads dwell. Only if you return alive will you earn my respect.
—Amon Ad-Raza to a Sulese priest

LEADER & GRUNTS						
SPD	STR	MAT	RAT	DEF	ARM	CMD
6	6	6	5	13	12	8

MILITARY RIFLE			
RNG	ROF	AOE	POW
10	1	—	11

KOPIS	
POW	P+S
4	10

FIELD ALLOWANCE	2
LEADER & 5 GRUNTS	6
LEADER & 9 GRUNTS	10
SMALL BASE	

LEADER & GRUNTS

➤ Advance Deployment

⌖ Combined Ranged Attack

☾ Pathfinder

Camouflage – This model gains an additional +2 DEF when benefiting from concealment or cover.

TACTICAL TIPS

CAMOUFLAGE – If a model ignores concealment or cover, it also ignores concealment or cover's Camouflage bonus.

Western Immoren has few more dangerous or unpredictable regions than the sweeping barrens east of Cygnar and the Protectorate of Menoth known as the Bloodstone Marches. For centuries, only the Idrian tribes have lived amid these dunes. Their ancient legends speak of a "changing of the earth" that wiped out most of their tribes and scoured their lands. Descendants of the tenacious few who weathered this fabled apocalypse, the Idrian people of today have inherited an immense knowledge of survival. These brave nomads carve out a life they share with the many hostile creatures stalking the sands. Skirmishers, noted for their skill with both rifle and blade, have long guarded their homeland.

Years spent leading ambushes in silence among shifting sands have given the *rhaz* who lead these warriors a deadly coordination and an adaptive cunning. They rise from the sands to intercept enemy forces sent to root them out. They close swiftly with a startling battle cry, often able to slay their enemies before they can react. Though many skirmishers' *kopis* blades have been passed down from generation to generation, these warriors have more recently mastered the rifles picked up in trade at border towns like Ternon Crag.

Though the majority of the varied Idrian peoples converted to the worship of Menoth in 504 AR, not all these men and women joined the Protectorate. Some tribes heeded the word of Menoth but kept to the dunes and oases of their ancestors. A few tribesmen have risen to prominence within the Protectorate, and every year more of the Idrian people take up the Menite faith. In recent years, settled Idrians within the Protectorate have ventured forth to meet with these distant kinsmen in hopes of convincing them of their common cause.

While some skirmishers fight pragmatically for coin, others display true faith. They eagerly strive to end the lives of blasphemers by the explosive report of their rifles or the silent strike of a kopis.

Do not forget that Menoth was the first great hunter, tracking the spawn of the Devourer Wurm across the skies.
—Retek Sabukhari, Idrian guide

Only a man who has won many victories and possesses great force of will can hope to unite Idrian tribes under his leadership. Such a leader can carve a fiefdom from the sands and defend it against his rivals. These great chieftains lead skirmishers in coordinated strikes. In these days, a chieftain proves himself through combat, not birth.

The support of a knowledgeable guide is key to a chieftain's success. These desert guides are peerless trackers with flawless knowledge of the land. The greatest guides can predict the weather a week in advance and possess senses so keen they can translate the slightest trembling of the sands underfoot into a precise count of an approaching army. Pious Menites sometimes feel uncomfortable around these men, as their long hours by themselves amid the dunes give rise to a wildness in their eyes and a predatory skill that borders on the preternatural. They prove their worth, however, by locating the enemy with unerring precision.

Attachment [Idrian Skirmishers] – This attachment can be added to added to an Idrian Skirmishers unit.

CHIEFTAIN

⏩ **Advance Deployment**

🎯 **Combined Ranged Attack**

〰 **Officer**

🌙 **Pathfinder**

Assault & Battery (Order) – Before their normal movement, affected models can make one ranged attack. During their normal movement, affected models must charge or run. The ranged attack is made before declaring a charge target.

Camouflage – This model gains an additional +2 DEF when benefiting from concealment or cover.

Tactics: Combined Melee Attack – Models in this unit gain Combined Melee Attack 🎯.

GUIDE

⏩ **Advance Deployment**

🎯 **Combined Ranged Attack**

🌙 **Pathfinder**

Camouflage – See above.

Go To Ground – Once per game while in formation during its unit's activation, this model can use Go to Ground. For one round or until they move, are placed, or are engaged, models in this unit in formation gain cover, do not suffer blast damage, and do not block LOS.

Huntsman – After deployment but before the first player's turn, choose an enemy model/unit to be this unit's prey. While this model is in play, each model in its unit beginning its activation within 10″ of the prey gains +2″ movement that activation. While this model is in play, models in its unit gain +2 to attack and damage rolls against the prey. When the prey is destroyed or removed from play, choose another model/unit as the prey.

CHIEFTAIN						
SPD	STR	MAT	RAT	DEF	ARM	CMD
6	6	7	6	13	12	9

MILITARY RIFLE			
RNG	ROF	AOE	POW
10	1	—	11

KOPIS	
POW	P+S
4	10

×2

GUIDE						
SPD	STR	MAT	RAT	DEF	ARM	CMD
6	6	6	5	13	12	8

MILITARY RIFLE			
RNG	ROF	AOE	POW
10	1	—	11

KOPIS	
POW	P+S
4	10

DAMAGE	5 EA
FIELD ALLOWANCE	1
POINT COST	3
SMALL BASE	

TACTICAL TIPS

CAMOUFLAGE – If a model ignores concealment or cover, it also ignores concealment or cover's Camouflage bonus.

OFFICER – Because this model is an Officer, when it is destroyed it does not replace a grunt in its unit. Instead the unit leader becomes the unit commander. Remember, only this model can issue the Assault & Battery order.

TEMPLE FLAMEGUARD
PROTECTORATE UNIT

They have proven their dedication watching over our sacred walls and holy temples.
Now let them prove their faith in battle.

—Hierarch Garrick Voyle

LEADER & GRUNTS						
SPD	STR	MAT	RAT	DEF	ARM	CMD
6	5	6	4	13	13	8

FLAME SPEAR		
	POW	P+S
	5	10

FIELD ALLOWANCE	3
LEADER & 5 GRUNTS	4
LEADER & 9 GRUNTS	6
SMALL BASE	

FLAME SPEAR

⊘ Reach

Set Defense – A model in this model's front arc suffers –2 on charge, slam power attack, and impact attack rolls against this model.

LEADER & GRUNTS

⊘ **Combined Melee Attack**

Shield Wall (Order) – For one round, each affected model gains a +4 ARM bonus while B2B with another affected model in its unit. This bonus does not apply to damage originating in the model's back arc. Models in this unit can begin the game affected by Shield Wall.

The Flameguard train ceaselessly with their seven-foot steel spears, the hafts of which are filled with reservoirs of the fiery Menoth's Fury developed under Hierarch Turgis. The liquid is piped to surface vents in the barbed tip and ignited by a mechanism triggered from the base of the spear. In battle, the spears drip oily fire and are capable of inflicting excruciating wounds.

Since the time of Sulon, the stated purpose of the Flameguard has increasingly been a justification for creating a well-trained, well-armed military. Over time, these pious soldiers have become elite infantry prized as both the first and the last line of defense in battle, where they become a living wall protecting the clergy from harm.

Outside the temples of Menoth, the Flameguard stand ever vigilant. The great Hierarch Sulon created the order as it is presently known by conscripting able-bodied Menites in the days leading up to the Cygnaran Civil War. Though the temples had long gathered armed guardians from among the faithful, this Flameguard was something new, unified in instruction and discipline to become true soldiers of the faith.

Garbed in heavy, flowing white tabards and gleaming helms and trained to use spear and shield, the Flameguard protect temples and holy sites and preserve the sacred flame burning in each. In return for making themselves useful to Menoth, they are granted indulgences by order of Sulon and earn favored status and comfort for their families.

TEMPLE FLAMEGUARD OFFICER & STANDARD
PROTECTORATE UNIT ATTACHMENT

I cannot tell the difference between the howl of their weapons and the cries of the vanquished.
They merge to become a symphony of His will. It is music to my ears.
—Grand Scrutator Severius

With the transformation of the Flameguard from a defensive militia to the core of the Protectorate's standing armies complete, Feora, Protector of the Flame has empowered the preceptors to lead the Flameguard into battle. These veteran officers have honed their martial prowess to a razor's edge.

Flameguard preceptors spend their lives mastering the flame spear, and the soldiers under their expert supervision are capable of singular acts of martial prowess. Whirling their weapons in unison to drive fuel to their spear tips, they create an unmistakable keening known as Menoth's Howl. This intimidating attack has become the signature maneuver of the new Temple Flameguard.

Attachment [Temple Flameguard] – This attachment can be added to a Temple Flameguard unit.

OFFICER

 Combined Melee Attack

Officer

Granted: Ranked Attacks – While this model is in play, models in its unit gain Ranked Attacks. (Friendly Faction models can ignore models with Ranked Attacks when determining LOS.)

Iron Zeal – Once per game during its unit's activation, this model can use Iron Zeal. For one round, while in formation models in this unit gain +4 ARM and cannot become stationary or be knocked down.

Tactics: Menoth's Howl – Models in this unit gain Terror 😬 and their melee weapons gain the Fire continuous effect 🔥.

STANDARD BEARER

Standard Bearer

FLAME SPEAR

Reach

Set Defense – A model in this model's front arc suffers –2 on charge, slam power attack, and impact attack rolls against this model.

OFFICER						
SPD	STR	MAT	RAT	DEF	ARM	CMD
6	5	7	4	13	13	9

FLAME SPEAR	
POW	P+S
5	10

STANDARD BEARER						
SPD	STR	MAT	RAT	DEF	ARM	CMD
6	5	6	4	13	13	8

OFFICER'S DAMAGE	5
FIELD ALLOWANCE	1
POINT COST	2
SMALL BASE	

TACTICAL TIPS

OFFICER – Because this model is an Officer, when it is destroyed it does not replace a Grunt in its unit. Instead the unit Leader becomes the unit commander. Remember this model can issue the Shield Wall order to its unit.

The preceptors' standard bearers are chosen from among the ranks for their uncompromising faith. They carry standards engraved with a passage from the Canon of the True Law: *Stand strong as the walls of My cities, and I will protect you always. Push against the tides of chaos, and I will move you. You are My will made flesh.* This message drives the Flameguard forward with faith in their hearts and fire in their veins.

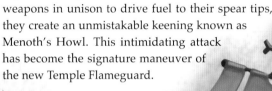

VISGOTH JUVIAH RHOVEN & HONOR GUARD
PROTECTORATE CHARACTER UNIT

Let the wrath I see in your eyes ignite a fire of faith with your blades. Drive the enemy back with our holy righteousness!

—Visgoth Rhoven to the gathered faithful before the assault on Caspia

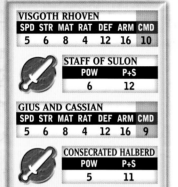

VISGOTH RHOVEN						
SPD	STR	MAT	RAT	DEF	ARM	CMD
5	6	8	4	12	16	10

STAFF OF SULON		
	POW	P+S
	6	12

GIUS AND CASSIAN						
SPD	STR	MAT	RAT	DEF	ARM	CMD
5	6	8	4	12	16	9

CONSECRATED HALBERD		
	POW	P+S
	5	11

DAMAGE	5 EA
FIELD ALLOWANCE	C
RHOVEN, GIUS, & CASSIAN	4
SMALL BASE	

VISGOTH RHOVEN

⬟ **Commander**

✖ **Fearless**

⬙ **Officer**

Battle-Driven – When a model in this unit is damaged by an enemy attack, after the attack is resolved models in this unit gain +2 STR and ARM and Pathfinder 🜂 for one round.

Cleanse (★Action) – Animi and continuous effects on models/units in this model's command range immediately expire.

Menoth's Sight (★Action) – Choose a friendly Faction model. While in this model's command range, for one round the chosen model ignores Stealth and ignores cloud effects when determining LOS.

Negation (★Action) – Remove 1 focus or fury point from enemy models currently in this model's command range.

GIUS AND CASSIAN

✖ **Fearless**

Battle-Driven – See above.

Exemplar – Gius and Cassian are Exemplar models.

STAFF OF SULON

🜂 **Continuous Effect: Fire**

⊘ **Magical Weapon**

⟳ **Reach**

CONSECRATED HALBERD

⊘ **Magical Weapon**

⟳ **Reach**

⬨ **Weapon Master**

Blessed – When making an attack with this weapon, ignore spell effects that add to a model's ARM or DEF.

Set Defense – A model in this model's front arc suffers –2 on charge, slam power attack, and impact attack rolls against this model.

TACTICAL TIPS

RHOVEN – Because this model is an Officer, when it is destroyed it does not replace Gius or Cassian. Instead Gius or Cassian becomes the unit commander.

Ranking priests of the Protectorate, visgoths serve the hierarch directly. Their position affords them almost unparalleled influence and the power of life and death over every citizen. Though such men have traditionally rarely taken to the battlefield, the stakes in the current crusade have simply risen too high. More than ever the fate of the Protectorate's war effort rests on the shoulders of its greatest priests. Visgoth Juviah Rhoven has spent a lifetime upholding the True Law in the walled city of Sul and preparing its garrisons for the crusade. Sul is his domain, and he took its invasion as a personal affront. He now walks into war as a living example to the faithful and as proof that all clergy, no matter their station, should bear arms against the faithless.

In addition to his authority as visgoth, as one of four vice scrutators Juviah Rhoven has access to the inner circle of the faith's dark protectors. He came to this pinnacle of power as the first visgoth to support Garrick Voyle for hierarch, having immediately recognized the divine mandate that had called Voyle to act. Rhoven brought down several key threats in the wake of Voyle's consolidation, and he added scores of names to High Executioner Reznik's death warrants. Though Voyle appreciated Rhoven's ruthless support, it was the visgoth's leadership in the aftermath of these struggles that earned him his place governing Sul. This strategically vital city prospered under Rhoven's uncompromising direction to become a shining example of industry and faith and a pillar of the Protectorate.

Juviah Rhoven has spent most of his tenure more feared than loved—as is expected of a scrutator. The silence in Sul's streets after curfew and the pristine condition of its walls and avenues are signs of the terror Rhoven inspires. Most who live there know of friends or family who were suddenly taken for violating even the most benign of laws or for being suspected of impiety, to suffer brutal penance in dungeons below the visgoth's palace. After Cygnaran soldiers shattered the city walls and marched through the rubble-strewn streets, Rhoven's merciless nature became his most lauded quality, and fear transformed to adoration.

Visgoth Rhoven's tireless honor guard accompanies him wherever he marches. These veteran exemplars bear consecrated halberds anointed with holy oil drawn from the same reservoir that feeds the sacred flame in the Great Temple of Sul. Two decorated senior Sulese knights, Darvik Gius and Martus Cassian, lead the honor guard. Never far from Rhoven's side, these men stand ready to intercept any harm to the visgoth. Both possess a quiet sternness and are widely admired. Many know the story of how Cassian nearly lost his eye to the blow of a Caspian battle blade during an engagement near the Marchfells. Cassian has refused to repair the damage to his helmet in memory of the event, to ensure he remains vigilant.

Rhoven has fought tirelessly since Cygnaran forces first besieged and then invaded his sacred city. He has appeared at most major engagements and raised the Staff of Sulon to inspire the faithful with memories of the martyred hierarch. During the siege of Sul he orchestrated a fervent defense of the city's holy sites, in particular Sulon's Remembrance and the seat of his authority at the ancient Great Temple of the Creator. To the faithful Rhoven embodies grim and unyielding resolve, the unwavering fire of Sul.

ALLEGIANT OF THE ORDER OF THE FIST
PROTECTORATE SOLO

If I do not allow you to strike me, you cannot. Will is stronger than flesh.

—Garrick Voyle, to the first allegiants

ALLEGIANT						
SPD	STR	MAT	RAT	DEF	ARM	CMD
7	7	7	4	15	12	9

PUNCHING GAUNTLET		
	POW	P+S
×2	2	9

DAMAGE	5
FIELD ALLOWANCE	2
POINT COST	2
SMALL BASE	

ALLEGIANT

✪ Tough

Groundwork – While knocked down, this model is not automatically hit by melee attacks and its DEF is not reduced.

Perfect Balance – This model cannot be targeted by combined melee attacks, combined ranged attacks, or free strikes. Models do not gain back strike bonuses against this model. When knocked down, this model can stand up during its activation without forfeiting its movement or action if it is able to forfeit its movement or action to stand up.

Shifting Sands Stance – During its activation, this model can forfeit its movement or action to gain +2 DEF. If an enemy attack misses this model anytime except while it is advancing, after the attack is resolved it can immediately make a full advance. Shifting Sands Stance lasts for one round.

PUNCHING GAUNTLET

Ⓟ Weapon Master

TACTICAL TIPS

PERFECT BALANCE – If the model forfeits both its movement and action for other effects, either voluntarily or as required, it cannot use Perfect Balance to stand up for free.

No warrior looks more unassuming at rest or more devastating in motion than a monk of the Order of the Fist. Disdaining weapons and wearing little armor, these expert pugilists effortlessly evade rifle fire, deflect enemy blades, and counterattack with rapid kicks and punches. An allegiant monk has fused his faith with unwavering discipline and absolute self-control to become one of the most dangerous weapons in the Protectorate's arsenal.

The order was founded by Garrick Voyle a decade before he seized rule of the Protectorate. Voyle deciphered the lost secrets of the ancient priest-kings and their guardians and melded them with the martial skills of the Idrian people to create techniques that unite a mortal body with the eternal will of Menoth. Allegiants study the strength of stone and the fluidity of sand until the application of deadly force becomes as natural to them as breathing.

The Order of the Fist proved its unique strength to the other martial orders when it provided Voyle's inner guard in the bloody months he consolidated his power. Its monks prowled the streets continually, listening for treason and rooting out insurrection before it could begin. Men and women dragged away by monks in the the night simply vanished.

Though lesser members of the order still serve the Temple by blending into the populace, allegiants have joined the active war against the faithless. Monks fought alongside Voyle in the streets of Sul and Caspia, and in the aftermath of those battles many refused to return to their monasteries. They now assist the Protectorate's crusading armies in the destruction of their enemies.

THE COVENANT OF MENOTH
PROTECTORATE CHARACTER SOLO

Menoth's Covenant with the people seems impenetrable and obscure. In truth, it is quite simple: obey the True Law or be washed from the face of Caen.
—The Harbinger of Menoth

Ancient Icthier had long been the site of battles between Menite pilgrims and barbaric Idrian tribes. One of the largest of the ancient conflicts occurred around 2200 BR when the Idrians broke through the city's defenses and fell upon the Menites like desert predators. The slaughter was fast and brutal. The few paladins present were quickly overrun. As they fell, their blood washed away the sand of ages to reveal an ancient scripture. Like the Canon of the True Law, so too was Menoth's holy Covenant inscribed on the walls of Icthier and revealed only by the blood of martyrs.

As the last living Menites were surrounded by the Idrians, a lowly acolyte named Pontithius began to read the newly revealed Covenant loudly and without fear or hesitation. His words were like fire in the ears of his fellows. The Creator promised them victory, and they acted upon his word. Picking up stones and the weapons of the fallen, ten Menite pilgrims fought off a hundred Idrian warriors. After the battle Pontithius personally transcribed the Covenant

COVENANT
✠ Fearless

Ancient Shroud – When a damage roll against this model exceeds its ARM, it suffers 1 damage point instead of the total rolled.

Flames of Wrath (★Action) – Choose a friendly Faction model/unit. For one round, while affected models are in this model's command range, enemy models directly hit by their melee or ranged attacks suffer the Fire continuous effect 🔥.

Lawgiver's Creed (★Action) – For one round, enemy models cannot cast spells while in this model's command range.

Man-Sized – This model is treated as a model with a small base and occupies the space from the bottom of its base to a height of 1.75˝.

Power of Faith (★Action) – For one round, friendly Faction models cannot be knocked down or made stationary while in this model's command range.

Spell Ward – This model cannot be targeted by spells.

COVENANT						
SPD	STR	MAT	RAT	DEF	ARM	CMD
5	5	4	4	12	12	10

DAMAGE	5
FIELD ALLOWANCE	C
POINT COST	2
LARGE BASE	

TACTICAL TIPS

SPELL WARD – This model is shielded from friendly and enemy spells alike.

into in a single massive tome that he chained to his back and carried many weeks to the feet of Priest King Golivant in Calacia before collapsing. It is said that with the Covenant in hand, Golivant was unstoppable. Soon the last of the Molgur were driven from the Wyrmwall.

After Golivant's death, the Covenant was returned to Icthier in secret. Hidden for more than two millennia, the Covenant was studied only by select priests. Now that the flames of the crusade are spreading, however, its passages are being spoken across Immoren.

Whereas the Canon of the True Law is the guide by which all Menites live, the Covenant of Menoth is a call to war. Its holy scriptures summon powerful miracles when read aloud in the heat of battle. The Covenant was discovered by blood, and only by blood will its holy promise be fulfilled.

EXEMPLAR ERRANT SENESCHAL
PROTECTORATE SOLO

No distance, obstacle, or heretic can prevent us from executing our duty to the Creator.

—Errant Seneschal Heremon Ellenos

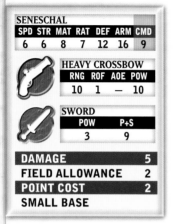

SENESCHAL						
SPD	STR	MAT	RAT	DEF	ARM	CMD
6	6	8	7	12	16	9

HEAVY CROSSBOW			
RNG	ROF	AOE	POW
10	1	—	10

SWORD	
POW	P+S
3	9

DAMAGE	5
FIELD ALLOWANCE	2
POINT COST	2
SMALL BASE	

SENESCHAL

▶ **Advance Deployment**

✪ **Commander**

✠ **Fearless**

☾ **Pathfinder**

Assault – As part of a charge, after moving but before making its charge attack, this model can make one ranged attack targeting the model charged unless they were in melee with each other at the start of this model's activation. When resolving an Assault ranged attack, the attacking model does not suffer the target in melee penalty. If the target is not in melee range after moving, this model can make the Assault ranged attack before its activation ends.

Call to Sacrifice [Exemplar Errants] – If this model is disabled by an enemy attack, you can choose a non-disabled trooper model of the type indicated in its command range to be destroyed. If another model is destroyed as a result of Call to Sacrifice, this model heals 1 damage point.

Hunter – This model ignores forests, concealment, and cover when determining LOS or making a ranged attack.

Leadership [Exemplar Errants] – While in this model's command range, friendly Exemplar Errant models gain Hunter.

HEAVY CROSSBOW

⊘ **Magical Weapon**

Blessed – When making an attack with this weapon, ignore spell effects that add to a model's ARM or DEF.

SWORD

⚔ **Weapon Master**

TACTICAL TIPS

Assault – The assaulting model ignores the target in melee penalty even if is not in melee range of its charge target after moving.

first entering foreign soil they take pains to learn the lay of the land, gathering what information they can to aid those who will follow in their footsteps. They are the trailblazers of the crusade, each a skilled combatant capable of rooting out foes no matter the terrain.

Despite his peerless weapons skill, a seneschal's most formidable asset may well be his understanding of Menoth's purpose for him on Caen. Where lesser exemplars simply follow orders, the seneschal has the experience and wisdom to interpret the needs of his superiors while still adhering to absolute obedience. Any brother errant would volunteer to take his seneschal's place in Urcaen, so clearly do they see his special duty and so unwavering are they in their beliefs.

Attaining the rank of seneschal among the Exemplars Errant is a recognition of a knight's particular skills and qualities. As one of the superlative few chosen to command the knights, a seneschal must be a veteran of numerous missions on foreign soil who has demonstrated a tireless devotion to judging the enemies of the Protectorate.

These commanders possess a zeal to carry their faith to the far corners of the world. Success requires more than simple faith, and each seneschal must prove himself an expert in wilderness survival. On

Let the sound of prayer and the litany of the True Law be the only music your ears apprehend.
—Hierarch Severius

From among the senior warpriests leading the choirs of Menoth arise dedicated and fervent spiritual leaders who for decades have bolstered warjacks with pious hymns. As these individuals reach an advanced age, some demonstrate a powerful affinity with the warcasters whom they have long served. Such respected priests learn through exposure and practice to harmonize their prayers with those of the warcasters and to use faith to protect these battle leaders. Such warpriests, called hierophants, form a small but revered company who remain near a warcaster to chant prayers or offer counsel.

Each hierophant carries scrolls of selected excerpts from the Canon of the True Law with the greatest bearing on war. As the warcaster fights, the hierophant adeptly finds the hymn or passage most applicable to the situation and elevates his warcaster's mindset and power through the inspiration

HIEROPHANT

Attached – Before the start of the game, attach this model to a friendly Faction warcaster for the rest of the game. Each warcaster can have only one model attached to it.

Harmonious Exaltation (★Action) – RNG 5. Target this model's warcaster. If it is in range, once this turn when the warcaster casts a spell, reduce its COST by 1.

Heal (★Action) – Choose a friendly living model B2B with this model. That model heals d3 damage points.

Spiritual Conduit – While its warcaster is in this model's command range, when the warcaster casts a spell and is the point of origin for the spell, the spell gains +2 RNG.

STAFF
⊘ Reach

HIEROPHANT						
SPD	STR	MAT	RAT	DEF	ARM	CMD
5	5	5	4	13	13	7

STAFF		
	POW	P+S
	3	8

DAMAGE	5
FIELD ALLOWANCE	1
POINT COST	2
SMALL BASE	

TACTICAL TIPS

Attached – This model cannot be reassigned if its warcaster is destroyed or removed from play.

Spiritual Conduit – Channeled spells and spells with a RNG of SELF, SP, or CTRL cannot gain this bonus.

of faith. Hierophants also serve their warcasters as clerks and attendants. Great deeds are noted and written into future hymns glorifying valor in the name of Menoth. They also take note of other acts of valor—and cowardice—by lesser soldiers for later commendation or punishment.

The verses chosen by the hierophant speak eloquently to the necessities of battle. The words of the True Law spoken aloud by the devout resonate with the Creator's design. At the hierophant's direction, the righteous can be healed of the most terrible wounds so that they can continue to fight in Menoth's name. The warcaster's divine spells are carried farther by the songs of the Canon, manifesting the Creator's plans on Caen. The faithful are blessed, the faithless destroyed—thus is Menoth's will conveyed by the hierophant and executed by the warcaster.

KNIGHTS EXEMPLAR SENESCHAL
PROTECTORATE SOLO

In the Synod's judgments shall we know our duty.

—Devotional oath of the Exemplar

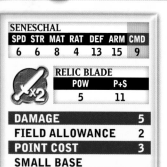

SENESCHAL						
SPD	STR	MAT	RAT	DEF	ARM	CMD
6	6	8	4	13	15	9

RELIC BLADE ×2		
	POW	P+S
	5	11

DAMAGE	5
FIELD ALLOWANCE	2
POINT COST	3
SMALL BASE	

SENESCHAL

✪ **Commander**

✠ **Fearless**

Aegis – This model is immune to continuous effects.

Restoration – When a living friendly Faction model in this model's command range is destroyed by an enemy attack, after the attack is resolved this model heals 1 damage point. When this model is disabled, it is knocked down instead of becoming boxed and its activation immediately ends. While this model is disabled, it cannot activate. If this model is disabled at the beginning of your Maintenance Phase, it is destroyed.

Righteous Fury – When one or more friendly Faction warrior models are destroyed by an enemy attack while in this model's command range, this model gains +2 STR and ARM for one round.

RELIC BLADE

⚡ **Magical Weapon**

🗡 **Weapon Master**

Chain Attack: Smite – If this model hits the same model with both its initial attacks with this weapon, after resolving the attacks it can immediately make one additional melee attack against that model. If the additional attack hits, the target is slammed d6″ directly away from this model. The POW of the slam damage roll is equal to the STR of this model + the POW of this weapon. The POW of collateral damage is equal to the STR of this model.

TACTICAL TIPS

RESTORATION – This model is never boxed. A disabled model that heals damage is no longer disabled.

CHAIN ATTACK: SMITE – The slammed model is moved only half the distance rolled if its base is larger than this model's.

A seneschal is nothing less than a force of nature on the battlefield. With his twin blades he relentlessly wades through the enemy, reaping death with every step. Those unfortunate enough to be caught within the onslaught of the blades are smote by the sheer power of Menoth's righteous mandate. A seneschal's holy fury cuts through the ranks of his foes like a thresher in a field of wheat.

Most notable is a seneschal's inherent bond with his fellow Menites. Like the exemplar knight who rages at the sight of a fallen battle-brother, a seneschal feels the demise of the faithful like the cutting of his own flesh. Such is the conviction of a seneschal that he will never relent from his holy duty until his broken body can carry him no farther.

The seneschals of the Knights Exemplar are living pillars of faith, and where they go the will of Menoth follows. Field commanders of the Exemplar order, they are among the Creator's most diligent servants. Their duty sends them to wherever the scrutators command, bearing orders to be carried out with the highest priority.

PALADIN OF THE ORDER OF THE WALL
PROTECTORATE SOLO

Among Menoth's first gifts to man was the Wall, by which we protect our people.
Atop the first wall at civilization's dawn, a paladin stood vigil.
—High Paladin Dartan Vilmon

With members who embody ideals at odds with the harsh dictates of the ruling scrutators, the Order of the Wall has experienced a turbulent past. Its enrollment has periodically dwindled to near extinction, only to surge back again in periods of turmoil to reassure the population that Menoth offers protection and not only wrath. Paladins of this order have served mankind since the first words of the Canon of the True Law, acting as bastions of stability when the wilderness threatened to overthrow civilization. The wall of their namesake stands for every barrier erected to shelter a community from external threats.

Paladins prioritize mercy and protection of the innocent, which can force them to disobey orders given by the scrutators. Priests take this as a sign that paladins lack the

PALADIN OF THE ORDER OF THE WALL

✠ **Fearless**

Stone-and-Mortar Stance – During its activation, this model can forfeit its normal movement or action to gain +5 ARM. The affected model cannot be knocked down. Stone-and-Mortar Stance lasts for one round.

FIREBRAND

⚜ **Critical Fire**

⚙ **Magical Weapon**

⚔ **Weapon Master**

PALADIN						
SPD	STR	MAT	RAT	DEF	ARM	CMD
6	7	8	4	13	16	9

FIREBRAND		
	POW	P+S
	7	14

DAMAGE	5
FIELD ALLOWANCE	2
POINT COST	2
SMALL BASE	

obedience that is the hallmark of the Knights Exemplar. Paladins prefer to protect the members of Menoth's flock rather than drown them in rivers of blood, and they believe even the wayward can be guided back to the path of the Creator—a philosophy for which they are beloved by the people.

Encased in the protection of tempered steel and trained to hold against any enemy, each paladin is akin to an unbreakable fortress. When a paladin strikes with his Firebrand sword, it erupts in holy fire like a sliver of the sun. Those who witness a paladin in combat cannot doubt Menoth's power flows through him.

For every soul saved by a paladin's actions, two are lost to the wracks and thumbscrews of the scrutators. Paladins cannot be deterred in their sacred obligation to protect the faithful, believing that each martial order has its function in Menoth's temple. If theirs is to be one of endless sacrifice, so be it.

RECLAIMER
PROTECTORATE SOLO

The Testament has loosed the first of the bindings from the Reclaimant's Altar, and so his order is freed to move unfettered. So it was written, and so it comes to pass.

—Hierarch Garrick Voyle

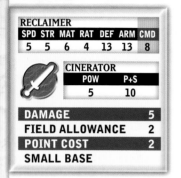

RECLAIMER						
SPD	STR	MAT	RAT	DEF	ARM	CMD
5	5	6	4	13	13	8

CINERATOR		
	POW	P+S
	5	10

DAMAGE	5
FIELD ALLOWANCE	2
POINT COST	2
SMALL BASE	

RECLAIMER

Communion (★Action) – RNG 5. Target friendly Faction warjack. If the warjack is in range, spend up to three soul tokens to allocate it 1 focus point for each soul token spent.

Gatekeeper – This model gains one soul token for each friendly living Faction warrior model destroyed in its command range by a continuous effect, an enemy attack, or collateral damage of an enemy attack. This model can have up to five soul tokens at a time. During its activation, this model can spend soul tokens to gain additional attacks or to boost attack or damage rolls at one token per attack or boost.

Soulstorm – While this model has one or more soul tokens, enemy models entering or ending their activations within 2″ of it immediately suffer 1 damage point.

CINERATOR

Continuous Effect: Fire

Reach

Each reclaimer carries with him dozens of simple iron Menofixes. Wherever he releases a soul to the Creator the reclaimer marks the place with one of these icons. In the wake of the huge battles of the recent crusades, survivors can gaze upon a plain covered with bodies and the small Menofixes that signify reclamation. Many welcome the sight, but there are those who fear that the increased wartime appearance of these silent ferrymen heralds darker changes to come and that the souls of the dead are becoming a commodity to be used on this plane to fulfill some forgotten prophecy.

From the moment a reclaimer dons the iron mask that will forever be the tomb of his thoughts, he knows the sound of Menoth's Voice. The last words he speaks are a promise to send chosen souls to the Lawgiver in Urcaen on wings of flame and ash. He knows neither pain nor emotion, and he is driven only by the will to serve. No man nor machine can stand in his way once the Voice has whispered a name in his heart—no explanation, no refusal, no hesitation.

Since the dawn of the Protectorate, reclaimers have followed the hierarch's armies to ease the transition of death for the chosen, sending the souls of the fallen to the afterlife. The soul energy that courses through a reclaimer during this service cloaks him in a conflagration of spiritual energy, searing the flesh of any who dare approach his sacrosanct presence. Bearing some mystical connection to their mechanikal iron brethren, reclaimers are even able to fuel the divine cortexes of warjacks with the souls of the faithful.

Prayer alone cannot maintain the warjacks of the Protectorate. Menoth does not bless each of his tools equally, and even Choir battle hymns can fall silent under an onslaught of heathen aggression. At these times the faithful rely on the mechaniks of the Vassals of Menoth to do the dangerous field repair work required in the heat of battle.

The Sul-Menites have never had an entirely comfortable relationship with mechanika, but the realities of war in western Immoren require that they maintain and expand their warjack capabilities. Though the Protectorate has increased its warjack production, it still lags behind other nations—making maintenance and repair even more crucial. The mechaniks who learn their trade from the vassals view their duties as a holy necessity.

MECHANIK

Iron Sentinel – While B2B with a friendly Faction warjack, this model gains +2 DEF and ARM and cannot be knocked down.

Repair [8] (★Action) – This model can attempt repairs on any damaged friendly Faction warjack. To attempt repairs, this model must be B2B with the damaged warjack and make a skill check. If successful, remove d6 damage points from the warjack's damage grid.

MECHANIK						
SPD	STR	MAT	RAT	DEF	ARM	CMD
5	5	5	4	13	13	8

MULTI TOOL		
	POW	P+S
	3	8

DAMAGE	5
FIELD ALLOWANCE	3
POINT COST	1
SMALL BASE	

TACTICAL TIPS

Repair – A wreck marker cannot be repaired.

The vassals themselves, many being kidnapped heretics, are too few in number and their skills of cortex fabrication too valued to be given the task of repairing the Protectorate's warjacks. During the reign of Hierarch Voyle, the organization was directed to instruct promising Menites in the repair and maintenance of warjacks and military mechanika in order to provide this vital support.

These volunteers are courageous not only for their resolve in performing battlefield repairs but also for their willingness to tamper with the impure forces of arcane mechanika. To keep their faith strong in the face of such dangerous work, apprentice mechaniks continue to devote a significant portion of their training time to studying Menite scripture even as they learn their practical art. By the time a mechanik completes his training with the vassals he is as expert in the psalms and passages of the Canon of the True Law as he is with his spanner wrench.

A mechanik's greatest weapon is his aptitude for keeping Protectorate warjacks running no matter how severely they are damaged. Armed only with their tools and their faith, vassal mechaniks follow warjacks into the thick of battle, using the 'jacks themselves as moving fortresses. More than one battle has been turned in the Creator's favor by a determined mechanik with a spanner in hand and a prayer on his lips.

VASSAL OF MENOTH
PROTECTORATE SOLO

Chain my arms, but you cannot shackle my mind. I loan you my power, but I refuse to pray to your god.

—Vassal Dominigo Marshall, former member of the Ordic Fraternal Order

VASSAL						
SPD	STR	MAT	RAT	DEF	ARM	CMD
5	5	5	4	13	13	6

DAMAGE	5
FIELD ALLOWANCE	2
POINT COST	2
SMALL BASE	

VASSAL

Iron Sentinel – While B2B with a friendly Faction warjack, this model gains +2 DEF and ARM and cannot be knocked down.

Magic Ability [7]

- **Ancillary Attack (★Action)** – RNG 5. Target friendly Faction warjack. If the warjack is in range, it immediately makes one normal melee or ranged attack. A warjack can make an Ancillary Attack special action only once per turn.

- **Arcane Bolt (★Attack)** – Arcane Bolt is a RNG 12, POW 11 magic attack.

- **Enliven (★Action)** – RNG 5. Target friendly Faction warjack. If the warjack is in range, the next time it suffers damage from an enemy attack while it is not advancing, immediately after the attack is resolved the warjack can make a full advance, then Enliven expires. The warjack cannot be targeted by free strikes during this movement. Enliven lasts for one round.

TACTICAL TIPS

MAGIC ABILITY – Performing a Magic Ability special action or special attack counts as casting a spell.

Establishing the Vassals of Menoth was one of the most significant measures Hierarch Garrick Voyle initiated to modernize the Protectorate's military. The Synod granted these wizards and arcane mechaniks sanction to pollute their souls in order to create and maintain the machines of modern war. Menite clergy, however, do not entirely trust them.

The most talented vassals are foreign-born wizards "liberated" to serve the Creator, construct warjack cortexes, and lend them power in battle. Specially tasked cadres of Knights Errant and initiates of the Order of the Fist have abducted some of the most brilliant arcanists in Cygnar; even members of the Fraternal Order of Wizardry have been taken. These pampered prisoners receive certain luxuries but remain guarded. Even native-born vassals suffer these restraints, though they daily prove themselves fervent believers.

Menites have always harbored hostility toward arcane magic because its use violates the will of the Lawgiver, but during the Cygnaran Civil War many leaders recognized the necessity of warjacks. Allocating resources for the capture and conditioning of individuals capable of building and attending these weapons has proven a wise decision. Vassals demonstrate their worth in battle with spells that can annihilate the enemy directly or bolster a warjack's power.

The demands of the crusades have forced the Protectorate to increase its efforts to discover native-born talent. It seems strange to outsiders that any man would volunteer for slavery, yet Sul-Menites born with arcane talents are so ashamed of their ungodly power that they welcome their chains as penance. They enter the House of Truth in Imer to learn how to master their powers and to pray daily for forgiveness for their innate corruption.

. . . and thine ears will not close to the hymns of man. May their throats grow dry and crack with their praises. Finer gifts dare not be given than the prayers of offered flesh.
—The Canon of the True Law

The scrutators of the Protectorate offer the screams of heretics as sacrifice, and the wrack is one of their favored tools for obtaining this fuel for their holy work. The construct was once a common sight across western Immoren; when the priest-kings battled the hordes of Molgur, they celebrated victories with row upon row of penitent barbarians affixed to symbols of their Menite faith.

Today the wrack is once more a common sight, an instrument much valued by the scrutators for the awe it inspires in the faithful and heathen alike. The recent crusades have reintroduced the wrack to the enemies of the faith as Menite armies carry the means to both punish and terrify the unjust.

Those sentenced to the wrack spend days or weeks hanging from chains and shrouded in a fog of incense. The suffering are forced to reflect upon their sins as they cry out through unbearable pain. Even the strongest wills quickly erode.

WRACK
⏵ Advance Deployment

Death Blast – When this model is disabled, center a 5″ AOE on it, then remove this model from play. Models in the AOE suffer a POW 14 blast damage roll.

Immobile – This model has no movement or action and cannot be knocked down or moved. Its front arc extends to 360°. It has no melee range, cannot engage, and is automatically hit by melee attacks.

Suffering's Prayer – This model begins the game with 1 focus point. During your Control Phase during the focus allocation step, it receives 1 focus point if it does not have any. This model cannot have more than 1 focus point at a time. While this model has a focus point, ranged attacks targeting it automatically miss. During a friendly Faction warcaster's activation, it can remove 1 focus point from this model in its control area and add that focus point to its own total. Each warcaster can do this only once per turn. When a focus point is removed from this model, roll a d6. On a 1, 2, or 3, this model explodes with the same effect as Death Blast and is removed from play.

WRACK						
SPD	STR	MAT	RAT	DEF	ARM	CMD
—	1	0	0	5	10	10

FIELD ALLOWANCE	**1**
3 WRACKS FOR 1 POINT	
MEDIUM BASE	

TACTICAL TIPS

IMMOBILE – This model can be placed.

SUFFERING'S PRAYER – This allows the warcaster's focus points to exceed his FOCUS.

While most are wracked as punishment, some few seek out this suffering willingly, hoping for absolution from the burden of their heavy souls. The sight of wracked martyrs, glowing with divine radiance in suffering, has sometimes been sufficient to end battles before they even begin.

Prior to the release of death, the wracked individual's soul is redeemed whether his contrition is forced or voluntary, and his body glows white-hot under the scrutiny of Menoth's gaze. The Lawgiver's redemption cleanses the penitent, whose soul becomes a radiant source of power for the Protectorate's warcasters. When the sufferer relinquishes his soul, the release of energy is consumed in an eruption of fiery essence—yet another tangible reminder of the righteousness of Menite faith and glory.

HIGH EXEMPLAR GRAVUS
PROTECTORATE DRAGOON CHARACTER SOLO

The death of flesh is meaningless. All that matters is earning your place in Urcaen to fight on in Menoth's name.

—High Exemplar Gravus

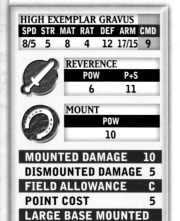

HIGH EXEMPLAR GRAVUS						
SPD	STR	MAT	RAT	DEF	ARM	CMD
8/5	5	8	4	12	17/15	9

REVERENCE		
	POW	P+S
	6	11

MOUNT	
	POW
	10

MOUNTED DAMAGE	10
DISMOUNTED DAMAGE	5
FIELD ALLOWANCE	C
POINT COST	5
LARGE BASE MOUNTED	
SMALL BASE DISMOUNTED	

HIGH EXEMPLAR GRAVUS

✪ **Commander**

✤ **Fearless**

Brother's Keeper – While in this model's command range, friendly Exemplar models cannot be knocked down or made stationary.

Crusader's Requiem – This model gains one soul token for each friendly living Exemplar model destroyed in its command range by a continuous effect, an enemy attack, or collateral damage of an enemy attack. This model can have up to three soul tokens at a time. During its activation, this model can spend soul tokens to gain additional attacks or to boost attack or damage rolls at one token per attack or boost.

Dragoon – While mounted, this model has base SPD 8 and base ARM 17. While dismounted, it has base SPD 5, base ARM 15.

REVERENCE

⊘ **Magical Weapon**

⊘ **Reach**

⊙ **Weapon Master**

Chain Weapon – This attack ignores the Buckler and Shield weapon qualities and Shield Wall.

Dispel – When this weapon hits a model/unit, upkeep spells on that model/unit immediately expire.

TACTICAL TIPS

BROTHER'S KEEPER – This includes Gravus.

DISPEL – Because they expire immediately, upkeep spells that had an effect when the model was hit or damaged will have no effect.

Members of his order describe High Exemplar Sarvan Gravus as the unbreakable weapon of their faith. He shrinks from no task, no matter how bloody or terrible. He has rent the weak flesh of both Devourer worshipers and Cygnaran soldiers and sent their souls screaming to Urcaen. He leads the Exemplar Vengers into battle shouting resounding prayers to the Creator of Man that rise above the thundering of hooves.

When Grand Exemplar Hurst died defending the Harbinger from Cryxian horrors, many among the Synod supported High Exemplar Gravus to succeed him. Though Mikael Kreoss eventually took command of the order, Gravus was the only other knight who could have risen to the esteemed post. The people admire Kreoss for his dignity and defense of the faithful, but they respect Sarvan Gravus for his merciless pragmatism and his unwavering adherence to the Exemplar code. Gravus hopes to die in battle and fears only that he might outlive his usefulness as a warrior. Any who have witnessed him riding into the throng of the enemy

while his blessed flail crushes one skull after another know that time has not yet arrived.

The high exemplar will admit age has taken its toll—riding into battle every day strains a man of his years—but his will to fight remains undiminished. A cavalry knight first and foremost, Gravus claims to take strength from his faithful mount Fidelitus, which descends from a distinguished lineage that has served the Vengers for centuries.

It was during the reign of Hierarch Ravonal, when the Knights Exemplar transformed into a true force of war, that Gravus rose to prominence. Cygnaran soldiers on the other side of the Black River learned his name well and recognized him as the Protectorate's premier cavalry commander for his bold strikes. On several occasions he led small forces of Knights Exemplar against far greater numbers, inflicted tremendous casualties, and returned victorious.

Gravus has a similarly strong reputation among the northerners who once inhabited the lazy town of Fisherbrook, though for very different reasons. When Grand Scrutator Severius gave the order to sweep through the eastern portion of town and raze its structures to the ground, thereby stirring up the garrison defenders who might have otherwise retreated to Stonebridge Castle, Gravus at once took his men to the outskirts of town and killed every man, woman, and child he could reach before sending his vengers to ride down those who fled.

In his lifetime of service, Gravus has never questioned the clergy. He believes it their role to interpret the will of the Creator and his role to obey. The only time he has ever evidenced even the slightest displeasure with his superiors occurred upon hearing word of the Protectorate's withdrawal from Caspia after the death of Hierarch Voyle. Even regarding this he has not spoken against the visgoths, though his eyes burn with anger and a desire to avenge his fallen leader.

As ever seeking to stand amid the most intense battles of his order, Gravus has marched north past the desert sands to renew his oaths of service to the new hierarch. He has promised his strength to the Northern Crusade, even knowing he will likely not live to return to his ancestral home. He feels his good death approaching with a sound like hooves on stone, and he will not shy away from it.

HIGH PALADIN DARTAN VILMON
PROTECTORATE CHARACTER SOLO

With a few more men like Dartan Vilmon, the walls of Sul would never have been breached. It was foolish of us to allow their order to languish.

—Grand Exemplar Mikael Kreoss

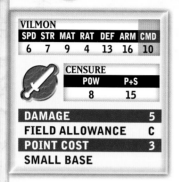

VILMON						
SPD	STR	MAT	RAT	DEF	ARM	CMD
6	7	9	4	13	16	10

CENSURE		
	POW	P+S
	8	15

DAMAGE	5
FIELD ALLOWANCE	C
POINT COST	3
SMALL BASE	

VILMON

⭐ **Commander**

✠ **Fearless**

Elite Cadre [Paladins of the Order of the Wall] – Friendly Paladin of the Order of the Wall models gain Impervious Wall.

Impervious Wall – During its activation, this model can forfeit its normal movement or action to gain Impervious Wall for one round. A model with Impervious Wall is immune to continuous effects, does not suffer damage or effects from non-magical ranged or melee attacks, and cannot be knocked down.

Stone-and-Mortar Stance – During its activation, this model can forfeit its movement or action to gain +5 ARM. The affected model cannot be knocked down. Stone-and-Mortar Stance lasts for one round.

CENSURE

🗘 **Magical Weapon**

➷ **Reach**

🛡 **Weapon Master**

A devotee of one of the Protectorate's most ancient orders, the Order of the Wall, Dartan Vilmon embodies the noblest aspects of his faith and serves as a defender of his people in their time of greatest need.

Dartan found his calling as a child growing up in the looming shadow of Sul's western wall. He fasted unmoving on the doorstep of the order, where he prostrated himself for days before finally losing consciousness from heat exhaustion. Relenting, the paladins took him into their halls, where his rebirth and training began. He devoted himself to their strict codes and training for years, until he was remade in living stone.

Dartan proved singularly gifted in battle; even early in his training, his blade moved in his hands with a speed and precision most could not attain after a lifetime of work. His ability continued to refine itself over the years as he gave himself over to the sublime grace of his blade's edge in motion. To Dartan, the stances and meditations of his order are prayers, and the perfect execution of his movements brings him closer to the divine. Even former Grand Exemplar Baine Hurst spoke his praises, calling him the finest swordsman ever to serve the Creator.

As with others of his order, Vilmon has had to walk a tightrope of duty and responsibility, obeying the clergy while retaining an awareness of mercy, compassion, honor, and valor. He has attempted to soften the harsh dictates of the scrutators and is compassionate toward the Protectorate's poor. He gives relief to those forced into hard labor, and sometimes he delivers a merciful death to those enduring unavoidable agony.

The Harbinger of Menoth chose him to protect her during her pilgrimages to prepare for the her march to war. Vilmon was present, alongside Grand Exemplar Baine Hurst, when the eldritch Goreshade ambushed her. The grand exemplar ordered him to take the Harbinger to safety while Hurst sacrificed his life to buy them time.

Vilmon was chosen again when the Harbinger made her journey north to intercept a great evil in the Thornwood, and he witnessed her sacrifice to liberate Menite souls trapped in the Orgoth Temple of Garrodh. Vilmon and the Testament fought side-by-side, along with the Avatar of Menoth, to preserve the Harbinger's body and soul and journeyed back to Imer to deliver her to Hierarch Voyle.

In recognition of those tireless deeds, Vilmon was promoted to high paladin. He returned to Sul and joined the fight alongside other paladins who had flocked to that ancient city to reclaim the shattered city wall. He put aside his shield in favor of his holy blade Censure, counting on his brothers in arms to be his aegis. When Sul was reclaimed and the armies of the faithful marched into Caspia, Vilmon was once again at the fore marching alongside the Harbinger and the hierarch. It was Vilmon alone who defied Voyle's command to kill hundreds of unarmed Protectorate civilians. True to his primary duty to the Creator and not the hierarch, he was prepared to give his life to protect the innocent—and surely would have if not for the intervention of the Harbinger herself.

In the aftermath of that battle, Vilmon's courage inspired not only his order but also the Protectorate as a whole. At one time in decline, the Order of the Wall has undergone a resurgence in both respect and initiates. It is the dawning of a new day for the order, brought about by its greatest champion: High Paladin Vilmon.

At first glance the paint scheme for the Protectorate of Menoth may appear to use a simple red and white palette reminiscent of historical Knights Templar. Upon closer consideration it becomes clear that the sanguine edging creates a subtle color contrast with the Protectorate's white areas. As red and white do not contrast with each other, how is this achieved? There's a trick: choose a white with a strong yellow bias and a red that is very strongly on the purple side of the spectrum to create a yellow/purple contrast. The eye picks up on the contrast but translates it into the red/white context, giving you a result that is pleasing to the eye.

Another trick we use on the studio models is painting the white armor plates in a style similar to the non-metallic metal technique, which makes the armor appear to be polished and reflective. The bifacial nature of the Protectorate armor plates lends itself well to this style of painting and helps create the most contrast on a model without it appearing busy.

PAINTING TERMINOLOGY

BASECOAT

The initial coat of paint on which everything else will be built. It is important that the basecoat is very clean and every color is where it should be. Your shades and highlights will coordinate with the basecoat and main color choices.

GLAZE

A mixture of water and a small amount of ink that is applied in successive layers to subtly tint an area.

HIGHLIGHTING

A lighter color applied to the basecoat in the raised areas of a miniature to create the look of light hitting the surface. When highlighting in multiple steps, keep a little bit of the underlying color showing, overlapping them like shingles on a roof.

SHADING

A darker color applied to the basecoat in the recessed areas of a miniature to create shadows. Exaggerating the shade and highlight colors will add to the visual appeal of a model.

WASH

A combination of mixing medium, water, paint and/or ink that is liberally applied to the basecoat to create detailed shading. The wash will run into the smallest crevasses on a model and dry as a shadow, so it needs to be a darker color than the basecoat. The wash mix works well as 4 parts mixing medium, 1 part paint/ink, and 3 parts water.

SANGUINE

Step 1) Layer Sanguine Base onto the area until you have a solid basecoat.

Step 2) Add a bit of Exile Blue to Sanguine Base and apply this mixture for the first layer of shading.

Step 3) Add a few small dabs of Coal Black to the previous mixture to create a nice, colorful black. Use this for the final shading.

Step 4) Apply highlights of Sanguine Highlight.

Step 5) Using the edging technique, apply a final highlight of Sanguine Highlight mixed with Menoth White Base.

- ■ Sanguine Base
- ■ Exile Blue
- ■ Coal Black
- ■ Sanguine Highlight
- ☐ Menoth White Base

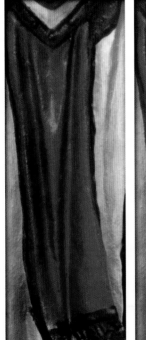

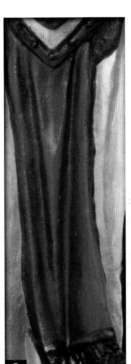

1   2   3   4   5

When two sanguine surfaces are set side by side, it can be useful to have a trick for maintaining contrast. Giving one of the sections a couple of thin glazes of red ink will shift it into the warm side of the spectrum and separate it from the other section.

MENOTH WHITE

Step 1) Basecoat the area in Menoth White Base. Use a couple of thin layers of paint to ensure a smooth, solid basecoat with absolutely no patchiness.

Step 2) Thinly shade the area with Cryx Bane Highlight.

Step 3) Apply additional shading using Bastion Grey.

Step 4) Add some Thornwood Green sparingly to the deepest recesses as final shading.

Step 5) Apply a strong highlight of Menoth White Highlight, blending it for a smooth transition. Some painters may prefer to apply this highlight in multiple layers, mixing it with Menoth White Base to achieve the blending.

1

2

3

4

5

- ☐ Menoth White Base
- ◼ Bastion Grey
- ◼ Thornwood Green
- ◼ Cryx Bane Highlight
- ☐ Menoth White Highlight

MENOTH WHITE BROCADE

Adding freehand brocade to Menoth White areas is relatively easy and can give your characters that extra flair they need to stand out in the crowd.

Step 1) Basecoat the area with Menoth White Base.

Step 2) Shade the area with Cryx Bane Highlight.

Step 3) Using Thornwood Green, freehand your brocade design. If you're new to freehand, keep the design simple—but if you've got some experience, go for it!

Step 4) Mix Menoth White Highlight with a drop of Mixing Medium and use this for highlighting. You may need to apply a few layers to achieve the desired opacity.

▢ Menoth White Base	▢ Cryx Bane Highlight	▢ Thornwood Green	▢ Menoth White Highlight

1

2

3

4

Don't feel obligated to apply the brocade treatment over the entire area. It can also make a nice border, as on High Paladin Dartan Vilmon's cloak.

BLACK

Step 1) For a good-looking black, start with a solid basecoat of Thamar Black. This basecoat is essential to the overall look of the area.

Step 2) Mix a dot of Thamar Black into Coal Black and use that for the top half of each black area.

Step 3) Add Menoth White Base to the previous mixture and apply the resulting color as a highlight to the Coal Black areas. Blend the layer as you go.

Step 4) Add Menoth White Highlight to the previous mixture and use this to apply final, subtle highlights.

■ **Thamar Black**   ■ **Coal Black**

□ **Menoth White Base**   □ **Menoth White Highlight**

1   2   3   4

FREEHAND MENOFIX

1

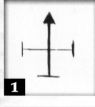

2

3

Any time you paint freehand, try to break the task into a few simple steps to ease the painting of your design and create a more satisfying result. The Menofix is basically a cross with a simple shape attached to each arm.

Step 1) Start your Menofix by painting a symmetrical cross. The top of the cross should end in an arrowhead. Add a line to the ends of the other three branches; they should look like the letter "T" with the line at the bottom a bit wider than the left and right.

Step 2) Enlarge the lines of the cross so they appear thick and bold. Draw an arc across the three "T" shapes and fill them in to make half circles. Draw two lines down from the arrowhead to create a diamond shape.

Step 3) Using the background color, subtract a diamond shape from the head of the Menofix. Then subtract a half-circle from the bottom of the Menofix to create its bent feet. Lastly, subtract round shapes from the right and left arms to complete the half-moon shapes.

STEEL

Step 1) Apply a solid basecoat of Pig Iron to the steel areas.

Step 2) Use a mixture of Greatcoat Grey, Battlefield Brown, and Pig Iron to shade the model.

Step 3) Add a dot of Thamar Black to a mixture of Brown Ink and Blue Ink for the final shading.

Step 4) Highlight the figure with Cold Steel, then coat the model with matte sealant.

Step 5) Add final, shining highlights with Quick Silver.

Pig Iron	Brown Ink
Greatcoat Grey	Blue Ink
Battlefield Brown	Cold Steel
Thamar Black	Quick Silver

    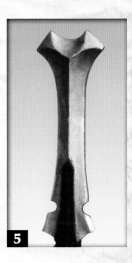

GOLD

Step 1) Create a solid basecoat with multiple layers of Rhulic Gold.

Step 2) Mix Brown Ink and Yellow Ink together with some Rhulic Gold and apply the resulting color to the model as shading.

Step 3) Add a final layer of shading with a mixture of Umbral Umber, Sanguine Base, and Brown Ink.

Step 4) Use Solid Gold for highlighting, then coat the model with matte sealant.

Step 5) Mix Solid Gold and Cold Steel together for the final, shining highlights.

Rhulic Gold	Sanguine Base
Brown Ink	Solid Gold
Yellow Ink	Cold Steel
Umbral Umber	

  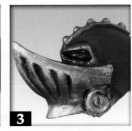  

PARCHMENT

Step 1) Basecoat the parchment area with a solid coat of 'Jack Bone.

Step 2) Paint any freehand script and designs you want to include using a mixture of Umbral Umber and Thamar Black.

Step 3) Apply shading with a mixture of Mixing Medium, Ember Orange, and Cryx Bane Highlight.

Step 4) For the deep shading, mix Gun Corps Brown and Ironhull Grey with a lot of Mixing Medium.

Step 5) Mix Menoth White Highlight, 'Jack Bone, and Mixing Medium and carefully use this mixture to apply some highlighting.

Step 6) Finally, touch up the script in any place it was overly covered by the layers.

- 'Jack Bone
- Umbral Umber
- Thamar Black
- Cryx Bane Highlight
- Gun Corps Brown
- Ember Orange
- Ironhull Grey
- Menoth White Highlight

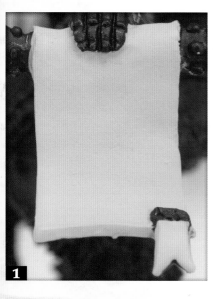

1

2

3

4

5

6

FIRE

Step 1) Apply a basecoat of Menoth White Base to the flames. This should ensure that the flames are the brightest area on the model—a good rule to follow when painting objects that are casting light.

Step 2) Give the whole area a wash of Heartfire.

Step 3) Hotter flames appear as lighter colors, so have the colors darken from base to tip. With this in mind, paint the upper part of the flames with a mix of Ember Orange and Khador Red Highlight.

Step 4) Apply a mixture of Umbral Umber and Sanguine Base to the tips of the flames in thin, diluted layers.

Step 5) Add Thamar Black to the previous mixture and apply the resulting color to the extreme tips of the flame as a final layer.

- Menoth White Base
- Heartfire
- Ember Orange
- Thamar Black
- Khador Red Highlight
- Umbral Umber
- Sanguine Base

1 2 3 4 5

To show fire burning hotter than normal, keep the colors light throughout the flames, as shown here on Feora, Protector of the Flame.

**HIGH EXEMPLAR
KREOSS**
Warcaster

**HIGH EXEMPLAR
KREOSS VARIANT**
Warcaster

GRAND EXEMPLAR KREOSS
Epic Warcaster

THE HIGH RECLAIMER
Warcaster

TESTAMENT OF MENOTH
Epic Warcaster

GRAND SCRUTATOR SEVERIUS
Warcaster

HIERARCH SEVERIUS
Epic Warcaster

FEORA, PRIESTESS OF THE FLAME
Warcaster

FEORA, PROTECTOR OF THE FLAME
Epic Warcaster

**HIGH EXECUTIONER
SERVATH REZNIK**
Warcaster

**VICE SCRUTATOR
VINDICTUS**
Warcaster

**HIGH ALLEGIANT
AMON AD-RAZA**
Warcaster

THE HARBINGER OF MENOTH
Warcaster

FIRE OF SALVATION
Heavy Warjack

TEMPLAR
Heavy Warjack

DAUGHTERS OF THE FLAME
Unit

BLESSING OF VENGEANCE
Light Warjack

THE COVENANT OF MENOTH
Solo

EXEMPLAR BASTIONS
Unit

EXEMPLAR CINERATORS
Unit

CHOIR OF MENOTH
Unit

VANQUISHER
Heavy Warjack

CRUSADER
Heavy Warjack

**PALADIN OF THE ORDER
OF THE WALL**
Solo

**PALADIN OF THE ORDER
OF THE WALL VARIANT**
Solo

REPENTER
Light Warjack

REVENGER
Light Warjack

RECLAIMER
Solo

**VISGOTH JUVIAH RHOVEN
& HONOR GUARD**
Unit

KNIGHTS EXEMPLAR
Unit

EXEMPLAR ERRANTS
Unit

KNIGHTS EXEMPLAR SENESCHAL
Solo

HIGH PALADIN DARTAN VILMON
Solo

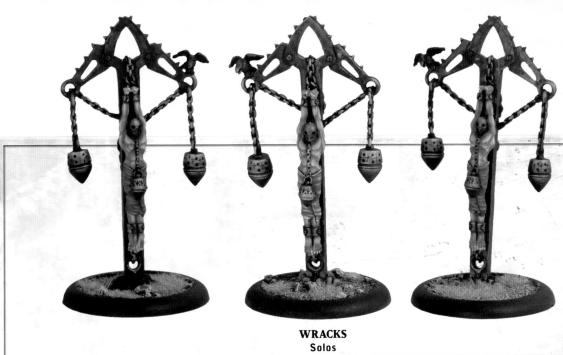

WRACKS
Solos

RECKONER
Heavy Warjack

CASTIGATOR
Heavy Warjack

DERVISH
Light Warjack

DEVOUT
Light Warjack

EXEMPLAR VENGERS
Unit

HIGH EXEMPLAR GRAVUS
Dragoon Solo

TEMPLE FLAMEGUARD
Unit

TEMPLE FLAMEGUARD OFFICER & STANDARD
Unit Attachment

AVATAR OF MENOTH
Heavy Warjack

FLAMEGUARD CLEANSERS
Unit

HIEROPHANT
Solo

**ALLEGIANT OF THE
ORDER OF THE FIST**
Solo

VASSAL MECHANIK
Solo

GUARDIAN
Heavy Warjack

VASSAL OF MENOTH
Solo

IDRIAN SKIRMISHERS
Unit

IDRIAN CHIEFTAIN & GUIDE
Unit Attachment

MONOLITH BEARER
Unit Attachment

HOLY ZEALOTS
Unit